THE STOR
AND THE WAR ON BLOOD

MW00875686

WES PENRE

PREVIOUS BOOKS BY WES PENRE:

NON-FICTION

Spiritual Handbook for the Twenty-First Century *(2013)*
Synthetic Super Intelligence and the Transmutation of Humankind:
A Roadmap to the Singularity and Beyond *(2016)*

THE ORION BOOK DUOLOGY:
The ORION Book Volume 1 *(2023)*
The ORION Book Volume 2 *(2023)*

FICTION
THE ISMARIL'S JOURNEY TRILOGY:
The Book of Secrets *(2021)*
The Underworld *(2022)*
Ismaril's Sword *(2023)*

Acknowledgement

I want to dedicate this book to all my wonderful friends, patrons, and forum members who have supported me through the entire writing process. Your support has been a massive inspiration for me.

A special dedication to the Lady of Fire, who personally encouraged and aided me with such enthusiasm. You also know who you are. Your commitment is very much appreciated and has greatly helped me through the process of writing this book.

CONTENTS

Introduction to the Isis Mystery

Once upon a time, there were gods roaming the Earth. They were not true gods; only in the eyes of the humans they interacted with. Perceived as such, they seemed to carry wisdom and magic we humans lacked.

And they came here to rule.

These "gods" have been called many things, depending on which culture, but in today's world they are probably best known as the *Anunnaki* from the Mesopotamian/Sumerian, Akkadian, Assyrian, Egyptian, and Babylonian ancient texts[1]. A few other names for them are *the Archons* (The Nag Hammadi Gnostic texts), *the ASA gods* (Norse mythology), and *the Elohim* (the Bible). Christian and Jewish scholars believe Elohim is another name for the One God, but the suffix *-im* clearly denotes plural. This is how it's often explained away,

> Though Elohim is plural in form, it is understood in the singular sense. Thus, in Genesis the words, "In the beginning God (Elohim) created the heavens and the earth," Elohim is monotheistic in connotation, though its grammatical structure seems polytheistic. The Israelites probably borrowed the Canaanite plural noun Elohim and made it singular in meaning in their cultic practices and theological reflections.[2]

There is little doubt that the word Elohim is the equivalent of

---

[1] Wikipedia: *The Anunnaki*
[2] Britannica: *Elohim*

the Anunnaki, and their Chief Imposter, also known under the title En.ki, fancies himself as *God the Creator*. In my Wes Penre Papers (WPP), I call these beings *the Alien Invader Force* (AIF), *the Overlords*, or *the Khan Kings*; the latter referring to the intruder faction from Sirius, who title themselves *Khans* or *Khan Kings*.

These gods are often the central focus of ancient texts from virtually all cultures across the world. Only their names, or rather titles, differ from civilization to civilization. In the western parts of the modern world, we know some of them as En.ki, En.lil (Ninurta), Marduk, Ereškigal, and Isis. *All these supposed names are not names but titles*. Their real extraterrestrial names are not known to historians. That they are titles and not names is important to understand. We could compare this concept to human trade. Take a carpenter, for example. If that is your trade, you could say you are a carpenter. But if you change trades and instead become a baker, you are not a carpenter anymore but a baker. However, someone else might take your place as a carpenter, and thus, this other person would inherit your title and become a carpenter. The same thing applies to En.ki, for instance. His title translates as the *God of Earth*, or more specifically, *[he or she who came] from Heaven (the Orion Empire) to Earth*. *En* or *An* are interchangeable and mean *Heaven (the Orion Empire),* and *Ki* means Earth. Consequently, ANU (or AN-U) means *Heaven* in singular in Orion language, where the U denotes *one*. We know AN-U as the Chief God in the old Middle Eastern texts, and it refers to the *one God* in Orion, which is Khan En.lil, the Queen's consort. We tend to call a specific deity En.ki, referring to just one being across time, which is fine for the sake of simplicity. Still, if we hard draw it, the En.ki is the person or deity who occupies the traits and is associated with the obligations related to that title. In modern times, we could argue that the title En.ki, the God or Lord of Earth, is occupied by Satan, in the Babylonian texts called Marduk. Again, for the sake of simplicity, I will still refer to Marduk as Marduk, and the Archangel Uriel, brother of Prince En.lil/Ninurta, as En.ki (also called Yaldabaoth or the Demiurge in the Nag Hammadi Gnostic texts). Otherwise, it gets too confusing.

I will not go into details about these gods with a small "g" in this book, since I cover the topic in detail elsewhere, such as in *the Wes*

Penre Papers (WPP), free online[3], and *The ORION Books*, Volume 1, and Volume 2[4]. A few of these Overlords are the creators of the Matrix, and their Chief Architect and Genetic Engineer is En.ki. He also tinkered with the original human DNA and created *homo sapiens*. However, he is not the creator of the spiritual part of us, which is our true selves. We, the primordial humankind, were created by the Mother Goddess, also called *Sophia*, the *Orion Queen*, or the *Queen of the Stars*. This is also covered in the above references. This book will primarily focus on one goddess, Isis. She has had a significant impact on our history, as we will discover.

Disclaimer

Before we start, I want to put a disclaimer here. The spiritual journey is an ever-ongoing journey for us all, and I discover new things as I continue my path. I stumble on information; I do research, and I develop ideas that I explore to find a greater understanding of the Universe we live in and my place in it. We must not forget that we all have the answers within us; we just need to discover them; therefore, it's important to go inside ourselves to find the deeper meaning of existence, or we'll never find the correct answers. We can read books and explore other people's research, which is fine up to a certain point, but at the end of the day, we are alone with ourselves and must attend to our own inner journey because earthly knowledge only brings us so far.

Therefore, I consider philosophy, where we use our imagination and creative abilities as spirited beings, senior to anything we can learn in this Matrix, regardless of how hard we study. As the Gnostics put it, we must connect to our Spirit to reach *gnosis*, i.e., Knowledge through Spirit/wisdom. No gnosis (spiritual knowledge), no wisdom.

Keep in mind I am human, and I sometimes take a wrong turn and must go back and rethink certain things. The reader of my work must understand that I share my journey with you in the direction it takes me, and as it came to me, linearly. I rarely go back and revise or erase older material that I have later expanded on or after I have changed direction. It's all a part of my journey—sometimes I'm

---

[3] Wespenre.com.
[4] Amazon.com.

correct and sometimes I'm not. That's how it must be, and that's how it is for everybody, but when I realize I am incorrect about something, I readdress the issue in later work.

I have never met Isis, so I have not interviewed her. Therefore, I know nothing about what is going on inside her mind. All I must go on is existing sources, use my intuition and imagination, and put the dots together to create a better understanding. Eventually, when the dots connect, I have a hypothesis, but no stone-solid truth. I do have a likelihood of truth, however, which can change in the future if or when new information becomes available. Meanwhile, I have, in this book created a working hypothesis that I think is close to the truth—certainly as an overall comprehensive story, albeit not in every single detail. Therefore, if the reader feels uncertain about some information in here, I strongly encourage you to do research on it to make up your own mind.

I hope the reader of my material takes in the information and meditates on it and ponders it. What does it mean to you? Does it ring true? Do you disagree? It's crucial that we do our *own* thinking and research—not the least when we dwell in someone else's work.

On another note: In this book, I have done my best to follow Isis' path through the Matrix, her whereabouts, and her participation in the overall earthly drama. However, I have mainly concentrated on the Western monarchies, which play a monumental role in world history for the early in the Matrix to the present and into the future.

I barely touch on the Eastern part of the world in this book, save for the life of Jesus/Yeshua. It would be too massive to fit into one volume. Still, it is most likely redundant because the same story repeats itself everywhere, but with other players. Therefore, the research in this book is more than sufficient to show the true agenda of the Overlords and how they have worked in secret behind the scenes to fulfill a very scary plan in which humankind is the center of interest. Not a good thing, I should add.

Last, I strongly advise not to skim or skip through sections or chapters because you might think you already know the ball part of it. It's crucial to read the book from cover to cover to get a full understanding—significant information is often embedded in subjects covered in previous works. The sequence of this work is thoroughly thought through to give the fullest picture I can possibly give in one volume.

I can't stress enough how important it is to know this information.

It's a life changer in Knowledge, and a lifesaver for our immediate lives; but more importantly, our eternal lives. It's a matter of life and death for us humans on a cosmic scale.
    --Wes Penre, January 2024.

Isis — The Backstory

1 **There have been various** controversies about Isis in history and in mythology. In the WPP, she had a significant role in the human history—even before the creation of Earth. After being quite present until way into the Third Construct (the Matrix), she suddenly disappeared from history, only briefly heard from again from time to time. But that is only because people don't know where to look. She lives and dies just like us, and she incarnates in new bodies with new names. If we can track her that way, we can get a clue on her whereabouts over time. Since I wrote the WPP, I have received lots of concerned emails and messages from readers, wondering if Isis is okay and where she is today. Although I have no information about her immediate whereabouts, I think I have traced her at least to the 20th Century England. Furthermore, I believe I can shed some light on certain details about her groundbreaking actions after she created her unique bloodline at Lake Baikal some thousands of years ago[5]. But first, let's give some backstory to explain who she is and her major involvement with us humans.

Isis was born in the Sirius star system to her Sirian mother, Gula, and her Aryan (from Orion) father, Ninurta, also called Prince En.lil in the ancient texts. Wikipedia tells us, "Passages in the Pyramid Texts connect Isis closely with Sopdet, the goddess representing

---

[5] See *The Wes Penre Papers* and *The ORION Book, Volume 2.*

the star Sirius..."[6] Sopdet being another title for the same semi-god-dess—Isis.

And this is what Wikipedia tells us about Gula (or Ba), Isis' mother from Sirius, the Dog Star, as astronomers sometimes call it (my emphasis):

> Gula (Sumerian: "the great") was a Mesopotamian goddess of med-icine, portrayed as a divine physician and midwife. Over the course of the second and first millennia BCE, she became one of the main deities of the Mesopotamian pantheon, and eventually started to be viewed as the second highest ranked goddess after Ishtar. **She was associated with dogs**, and could be depicted alongside these ani-mals, for example on kudurru (inscribed boundary stones), and receive figurines representing them as votive offerings.
>
> While Gula was initially regarded as unmarried, in the Kassite pe-riod she came to be associated with Ninurta[7].

As we can see here, Gula is associated with dogs. In the WPP, I described the Sirians as a dog species (from the dog star, Sirius), a wolfen-reptilian race. I portrayed Ninurta as an Aryan (which means he is from Orion); however, Orion is not just a star constel-lation but also the name of the Greater Universe—the Universe in which the Earth Matrix is encapsulated. Therefore, Sirius, as well as Earth, is part of Orion. It is mostly a confusion of terms, but I will try to be as clear and distinct as possible. Also, the context will usu-ally determine what is what.

So, Gula is a being from Sirius, present on Earth with Ninurta during the Second Construct, also called the Atlantis Era. When Noah's Flood happened at the end of that construct, all these dei-ties, save a few, left Earth and returned to the Greater Universe—Orion. Left on the physical Earth were En.ki, Marduk, Ereškigal, and Isis, and except for En.ki, the other three are supposedly still within this immediate matrix system. More about En.ki's fate later.

Before we move on, we need to understand that extraterrestri-als in the Greater Universe, at least mostly, don't procreate through sex as we know it in our human form. There might be species in the developing worlds (in the material/physical universe) who procre-ate akin to us, but during my five-six years of researching and

---

[6] Wikipedia: *Isis.*
[7] Wikipedia: *Gula.*

writing the WPP (2010-2015), collaborating with particularly one source from Orion, I learned that most species in the developing worlds reproduce through cloning, and others are androgynous and hermaphrodites, just like we humans once were, while living on our original planet, Tiamat, existing a higher dimension[8]. Here on Earth, there are still certain species, such as snails and slugs that are hermaphrodites.

Fig. 1:1. Gula with her Sirian dog (Mesopotamia).

Most species evolve in their home worlds up to the point when they are ready to leave their environment and their physical bodies behind and become non-physical. Then they leave their planet or star and move into the Greater (Spiritual) Universe, also called the KHAA in the WPP. There they have no solid physical bodies anymore, traveling and communicating with thoughts; and they can move from one part of the Universe to another in an instant, just by thinking themselves to that location. Even though these more evolved beings don't have dense bodies as we do, they can shapeshift into any shape and form they wish by reorganizing their Avatar (their collective soul or spirit fires), and from their perspective, the environment is perceived to be just as physical as ours, but much less dense. If we could see those realities, they would look nebulous and transparent to us.

---

[8] See the WPP and the two ORION books.

Ninurta and Gula did not have sex like we do when they produced Isis' body in Sirius a very long time ago. In Orion, when new beings are made, the couple (Ninurta and Gula in this case) can decide which gender they want the child to be by how they treat the egg. If the male does not fertilize the egg, the offspring becomes a male, without having a father, but if the male fertilizes the egg, the offspring becomes a female; it's the exact same principles used by bees on our planet (bees are of Orion). An egg can be fertilized through genetic tinkering, when two beings mix their DNA, or the female creates a female without involving a male's DNA in a natural way. In Isis' case, Ninurta fertilized the egg, so his DNA was added to the mix of DNA that made up Isis' body on Sirius. Into this body, the 3-UC of Isis descended. She was considered Queen Sophia's daughter on a spiritual level, while on a physical level, she was half Sirian and half Orion, and her parents were Ninurta and Gula. The 3-UC being of the Mother Goddess, she was Royal, meaning she had the Royal Spirit in her DNA. *Her Royal status is important to remember for the rest of this book.*

From the gods' viewpoint, blood and DNA are synonymous. Thus, we have the term *bloodlines*. When a spirited being enters a physical body, the DNA of the body and that of the 3-UC mix with each other, so in that sense, both body and 3-UC share and combine their DNA. The same thing applies to us humans in our homos sapiens sapiens bodies. More on this in a moment. This also means that Isis, when her Sirian body died, she inherited Sirian DNA from that body, carrying it with her in her 3-UC. Her task as Isis in Sirius was to overview the Sirian star system to make sure there was no uproar of rebellion against Orion after the Peace Agreement between Sirius and Orion.

Some species, who are androgynous and hermaphrodites, can take care of the entire fertilizing process themselves, since the same being comprises both genders, and usually don't need an external male to fertilize the egg.

The next thing we know about Isis is that she was present when Queen Sophia (The Queen of the Stars, i.e., the Spirit Sophia manifesting herself in the Universe as a separate player and Creatrix) created humankind as the only species in the Universe born as soul-minds with *spirit bodies* attached as a part of a sacred experiment. Other star races are born with only a soul and mind, making up an Avatar, with which they travel through the Universe. They

9

can, however, gain *access* to Spirit as they evolve, and can thus become *creator gods* in their own right and create in their imagination and manifest that inner construction in the external universe at will. We humans have the innate power to do so and don't need to gain anything—we already have it. However, when we were entering the Matrix, we got amnesia, and most humans no longer know who they are and what they are capable of—we have been dumbed down. However, these soul-minds never achieve a spirit body, which is what makes us humans truly immortal and creator gods from birth. The soul-minds are thus not genuinely perpetual but can exist so long as the Greater Universe exists. We humans will outlive even the destruction of the entire Universe because we are eternal. From here on, when I am addressing humans, I will refer to us as *3-UCs*, which stands for soul/mind/spirit body—we are three units in one. Those who lack spirit body (those of soul-minds only), I will call *2-UCs* since they comprise two units in one, lacking spirit bodies. UC denotes *Unit Composite*. Almost all extraterrestrials are either 2-UCs, or 2-UCs who somewhere in their development got access to Spirit and could become creator gods.

Marduk's Genocide

As conveyed in my previous work, there was a war in Heaven, in Greek mythology called *The Titanomachy*[9]. It was a war between the greater or elder gods (the Titans) and the lesser or younger gods (the Olympians), a war the latter group won. The Titans were the group of creator gods, led by Queen Sophia, who created humankind on the planet Tiamat in our solar system between Mars and Jupiter, but in a higher spiritual dimension. We see 3-D remnants of it today as the asteroid belt. The lesser gods, from Sirius, led by Marduk, won the war and destroyed Tiamat and all life on the planet with nuclear weapons. A few surviving humans fled together with Ninurta, who was part of the creator god team, away from our solar system, but many of us humans fell into a coma from the shock and later became part of the Earth experiment, which started with the Atlantis Era. More correctly, it should be called the Second Atlantis. The First Atlantis was Tiamat, which I

---

[9] Wikipedia: *Titanomachy*.

learned was a "water planet." This doesn't mean it was all covered with water, however. Our human scientists call the universe "space," and say it's a vacuum when it would be more accurate to call it "cosmic water," where water denotes ether or Spirit, the cosmic "ocean" from where all creation stems. Tiamat existed in the cosmic water—it was a spiritual world, not a physical one.

Isis, who helped Sophia with the Tiamat Project, educated by her, also fled the solar system together with the Queen, Ninurta, and En.ki, but later returned when En.ki helped Orion create the Second Construct, Atlantis.

Isis and the Bloodlines of Cain, Abel, and Seth

After the Tiamat disaster, En.ki returned to the solar system. He asked his mother, the Queen, if he could terraform a chunk of the remnants from Tiamat and continue the Human Experiment on what was to become Earth.

It should be noted that En.ki had nothing to do with the Sirian Invasion, contrary to previous hypotheses. He was part of Sophia's team, although he was not happy with the tasks handed to him. En.ki was the Queen's firstborn, and thus also the Crown Prince of Orion, the Heir. Therefore, he saw it as his birth-given right to oversee the Tiamat Experiment, cooperating directly with his mother as the Chief Geneticist. However, because of his pride and grandiose manner, En.ki had earlier been demoted by the Queen and her consort, Khan En.lil. Initially, he was appointed to be the Chief Geneticist when creating humankind, and thus contribute with his DNA, but he lost his position in favor of his younger brother, Prince Ninurta, aka Prince En.lil, who instead inserted *his* DNA in the primordial human. When Tiamat and the human soul group were created, the Queen gave his second-born son, Ninurta, the solar system as a gift to oversee, be responsible for, and to protect against intruders, having his MIKH-MAKH defense force to assist him if needed. Ninurta was also promoted to the Crown Prince and Heir of Orion instead of En.ki. This hurt En.ki's pride, and as the arch-narcissist he is, he planned on showing his mother and the rest of the Universe that he was worthy of the titles Chief Geneticist and Heir of Orion.

After the Tiamat disaster, En.ki saw his opportunity, hoping to regain his position as the Heir, replacing Khan En.lil as the King of

11

Orion should something happen to him. In certain terms, I think En.ki was pleased with the Tiamat incident because the outcome made his brother, Ninurta, look incompetent, having failed to protect the solar system and the newborn human race alike, forced to flee the situation. En.ki now wanted to prove that he could do a much better job than his brother if Orion gave him a chance. Before En.ki came forth with his idea, the Orion Council had decided to discontinue the Human Experiment altogether because, from their perspective, it failed when Tiamat was destroyed.

However, the Queen had invested a lot in the Human Experiment. She had contributed with her own 3-UC (making us mini-copies of herself, i.e., she gave spiritual birth to us, making us Royal, too).We literally became her children. She wanted to create a soul group that was spirited from birth, and thus born as creator gods. But before she let us free in the Greater Universe to create, she wanted to put us in a harsh environment, so we could grow up to mature beings, ready to take on the Universe. Her hope for us was that we would graduate from the Tiamat Experiment with more compassion and empathy than before we started, i.e., we would grow up and gain Wisdom. The Queen wanted to breed more compassionate and responsible creator gods to stop the warlike behavior that sometimes disturbed the order of the Universe. Therefore, En.ki's idea probably did not seem so bad, and the Queen was eager to give it a try.

Hence, Orion gave En.ki a chance. He got the green light to set up and continue the Experiment on Earth. This he did, and after much experimentation with different body types, he came up with homo sapiens, which was at that point a semi-ethereal species of a lower density than the original Tiamat humans, i.e., us when we lived on Tiamat. In the WPP, I called the original human species the *Namlú'u*[10]. I will continue using that term in this book, interchangeably with other terms, such as the *Primordial Human*, the *3-UC,* etc.

Because of En.ki's innate character flaws, Orion must have not completely trusted En.ki with the task, aware of his grandiose and sometimes tricky and manipulative behavior, although they apparently thought he'd made some progress since he was demoted. They wanted to give him a chance to continue where his brother

---

[10] A term I borrowed from the French researcher, Anton Parks.

had failed and to prove himself. Therefore, he was now allowed to add *his* DNA to the new human bodies, which means we got a part of his personality inserted. To supervise and oversee the new experiment, Orion put their own people on Earth, and Prince Ninurta was in command of the Orion team to En.ki's dismay. I presume that must have annoyed En.ki. He did not like his brother because he had been unjustly favored from En.ki's perspective, and now he had to deal with Ninurta a second time as his "supervisor" and "overseer."

Time passed, and we humans evolved on Earth. Successively, Sirians also arrived on Earth. This was allowed, because the reason for the Titan War was a Sirians conflict with Orion over the ownership of the solar system, leading to the Invasion and Destruction of Tiamat. The argument about who owns what was not resolved, so the Sirians, per Orion's laws, still was allowed access to Earth and the solar system until the argument was settled and the ownership established. Isis returned to Earth before Ninurta and his Orion team, from what I understand together with En.ki to be his helper if necessary. En.ki and Isis are both master geneticists. The Orion overseers came into the picture later.

At one point, En.ki and Isis chose to have a human child together to strengthen En.ki's bloodline, keeping it as pure as possible, and they had a baby boy. In Egypt, En.ki was known as Osiris, and Isis, in her human form, gave birth to Horus. The 2-UC inhabiting Horus was the dreadful Marduk, who had led the Olympians to destroy Tiamat. Marduk has reincarnated into the Elite bloodlines ever since, and he is still on Earth today, taking on the role of the biblical Satan[11]. Whether the two knew that Marduk was going to take the Horus body is up for debate, but it stands to reason they did not. Marduk saw an opportunity to incarnate into the pure En.ki-Isis bloodline and take part in the human experiment. It is my conclusion that he had plans for humankind already then, and the plans were and are indeed demonic, as we shall see further into this book. Marduk is known as the son of En.ki, which is true on a physical level, since he is the biological offspring of En.ki (Osiris) and Isis; but on a soul level, there is no *fundamental* relationship between the two, aside from that Marduk, through this incarnation as Horus,

---

[11] As a side note, remarkably, *Santa*, as in *Santa Claus*, is an anagram of *Satan*.

also inherited both Isis' and En.ki's DNA. Marduk is initially a full-blooded Sirian and had no kinship with En.ki or Isis until the Horus incarnation.

At the end of the Atlantis Era, En.ki started tinkering with genetics again, and he and his Sirian cohorts copulated with human females, which is a high crime in Orion. Gods can copulate with each other in human bodies to strengthen bloodlines, but they are not allowed to have sex with human directly. Beings from outside the construct of a developing species are not allowed to mix their DNA with the inhabitants of that world, having no relationship to that place. It completely messes up the entire purpose and destiny of that species. This intervention, in which En.ki and some Sirians had sex with human females, resulted in strange mutations called the *Nephilim*, who were the *giants of renown*, as mentioned in the Bible. However, En.ki didn't stop there. He also created many other abominations, and therefore, he completely contaminated the Human Experiment, which was now rendered useless. Orion decided to call the human soul group home to Orion again and thus finish the disastrous experiment for the second time. Therefore, the gods orchestrated Noah's Flood. Orion initiated it, so the human 3-UCs could leave the nightmare that had emerged on Earth and return home, and En.ki was commanded to execute it. The plan was to wipe out all life on the planet, but En.ki tricked Orion by kidnapping a certain number of humans, including Noah and his family, to create his own experiment after the Flood without Orion's supervision. All humans 3-UCs existing on Earth today were in the group of hijacked 3-UCs, including you and me.

Isis as the Mother Goddess (The Creation of Atlantis)

Before we move on to discuss what happened at the time of, and after, Noah's Flood about 9,600 years ago, let's rewind to the beginning of the Earth Experiment, following the destruction of Tiamat.

En.ki had just terraformed a piece of the exploded planet, floating around in the asteroid belt in the 3rd Dimension, and he was ready to continue the Human Experiment, eager to start, as being told in the Nag Hammadi Gnostic texts, the Sumerian cuneiform, and in the Enûma Eliš, the Babylonian creation story.

In the beginning, while looking for "gold," En.ki started out with creating clones of different humanoid species, letting Sirian 2-UCs inhabit them and do some physical work on Earth to help with the terraforming. It should be noted they were not really looking for gold, as in the *metal* gold—it is a metaphor for creating us humans—we are the "gold." En.ki was trying to create the perfect human body that could house a human spirited 3-UC (gold). The Sirians, however, were very uncomfortable with these early bodies that En.ki cloned. So, they rebelled, and En.ki stopped using those prototypes and let the Sirians off the hook.

Eventually, he thought he had created great prototypes to house human 3-UCs; he had created the first Adam in the "Garden of Edin," which is the name of a restricted area, where his genetic experiments could take place. En.ki created an artificial soul in the astral dimension, specifically made to work in our density, and he attached it from the astral onto the physical body via the so-called *silver cord*. The homo sapiens body would act as a physical version of the human spirit body, to which the 3-UC could attach. However, the bodies could not house human composites, so we "bounced off," and Adam was unable to move around. En.ki worked in sweat and tears trying to make this work, eager to show himself off to his mother. He must not fail now, or he would not be given another chance.

Then Isis, who was spirited, came to En.ki's assistance. Being of a lower manifestation of Queen Sophia, but with her unique personality, she moved to Earth from Sirius, where she had been an Orion Overseer of that System, following the old peace agreement between Orion and Sirius in the past.[12] In the Nag Hammadi texts Isis was called Zoë Sophia. *Zoë* means *life* in Greek,[13] and Isis was giving life to homo sapiens in the Second Construct, thus becoming *Eve*, which in Hebrew means *to live, to give life, or to breathe*.[14] She told En.ki that the human bodies needed a "breath" of Spirit into them for our 3-UCs to attach. This is thoroughly described in the Nag Hammadi texts. So, En.ki and Isis, the two geneticists, now worked together, and Isis blew her creative "dragon breath" into the cells of the lifeless Adam, who then started coming to life. Then,

---

[12] See my both *The ORION Books, volumes 1 and 2*.
[13] Dictionary.com: *Zoe*.
[14] Firmisrael.org: *Eve in Hebrew and the Word for Life in the Bible*.

Isis incarnated with her 3-UC into the body of Adam. Now the 3-UC could connect because Isis' Spirit life force was breathed into Adam, mixing with the body's DNA. Therefore, to be accurate, the first working homo sapiens was not male but female—it was Isis who made the body come alive. Adam, at that stage, was genderless, and the spirited Adam, created by female energy, was Eve, akin to Isis. Thus, the female came before the male. It is Spirit that creates, and Spirit is feminine.

This was the point when En.ki created two genders. He had little choice because he could no longer clone human bodies without Isis constantly blowing her breath into each separate cloned body. Creating two genders was a better solution, he mused. Then humans could procreate on their own, and their offspring automatically inherit Spirit through the parents' DNA, and new 3-UCs could attach to the offspring.

But he needed to also create something that made humans *want* to procreate, so he invented sex as a very pleasurable thing that humans would love. He was right. Adding sex made human 3-UCs very curious and eager to incarnate, and En.ki therefore had no problems inserting 3-UCs into the Adam bodies—we attached willingly. Thus, En.ki and Isis created man and woman.

The two geneticists both incarnated in human bodies, and En.ki, who is not spirited, but a 2-UC (soul-mind), got a feel for how it is to be attached to Spirit via the physical body, and he gained some *creative abilities*. The demi-god and the demi-goddess then had sex in human bodies and created Abel, and then Cain. Thus, En.ki had added his own DNA into the blood of Adam and Eve. Abel was the firstborn, so En.ki preferred him over Cain, and we know the rest: Cain got jealous and killed his elder brother to get the sole attention from his "father." In the meantime, Isis, as Eve, had sex with a human rather than with En.ki, and the Seth bloodline saw the light of day, jumpstarting a new bloodline. The Seth bloodline thus had lesser En.ki blood/DNA than the Cain bloodline, which was created with En.ki's DNA, directly mixed with Isis'. Therefore, the Cain bloodline, having En.ki's, Isis', and Ninurta's DNA (because Isis was Ninurta's daughter), turned out to be more intelligent than the Seth bloodline. Thus, En.ki chose humans from the Cain bloodline to supervise the Sethians. They eventually became today's "Global Elite," while the Seth lineage comprised most human 3-UCs.

However, there was another "problem." In the beginning, when humans were few, there was a lot of incest, and that had devastating consequences; it deteriorated the physical bodies after a few generations, and people most likely became retarded. Therefore, En.ki and Isis must create more bodies together that were not directly connected to the main bloodline, so they continued tinkering with DNA, without diluting the DNA they themselves had contributed with earlier. The new bodies were still of the same semi-god/semi-goddess DNA-mix but created separately from the original ancestor lineages to avoid the negative effects from incest. Consequently, they let the existing humans copulate with these new bodies, wherewith the ancestral lines became more alienated from each other over time. I would suggest this is when En.ki created different blood types, different eye colors, and people with diverse skin color, separate from the original humans, who were black. This made it easier to distinguish between different upgrades, and he could comfortably decide who would be allowed to procreate with whom in the beginning. However, En.ki was very careful to keep a string of Cain's bloodline as pure as possible, making sure it was minimally diluted. Proving himself worthy to Orion, he needed his own DNA to be as dominant as possible in humans, and he needed Ninurta's DNA to be there, too, to strengthen the connection to Orion in favor of Sirius. But Ninurta's blood must be secondary. If En.ki's DNA was more dominant in humans than that of Ninurta, he could claim the human soul group as his own, rather than Ninurta's, whose DNA now was less. In Orion, to claim ownership of a star race, the creator god must prove the soul group comprises his or her dominant DNA. It's all about DNA and bloodlines. Without his dominant DNA, En.ki can't claim ownership to the human species.

It is my impression that the early homo sapiens were held in captivity in Edin for a long time, and En.ki decided which humans could have sex with whom for the experiment to work properly. When there were enough of us in the contained Edin, he let us loose in the world, and he said, "Go out and procreate."

Before that happened, something else occurred, which bothered En.ki and the Sirian Khan Kings. Very soon, En.ki noticed how intelligent Adam was when he/she was spirited. He consulted with the Sirian Overlords (the Khan Kings), and they all became frightened because Adam was smarter than they were, which was not acceptable, or the Overlords could not control the human soul group.

Therefore, as the Gnostic texts say, En.ki threw Adam further down into the Abyss, which means he lowered the frequency of Earth, making Adam forget who he primarily was. After that, the Overlords felt more comfortable.

In the WPP and the ORION books, I discussed how En.ki lost his creative abilities after he was castrated by Ninurta in the Rigel star system and thrown into the ABZU, which likely is the lowest density of the astral, where he is contained since then. What does *losing creative abilities* truly mean? It was kind of a mystery to me until recently when I realized what it must be: En.ki, the Sirians (including Marduk), and other Invaders, who are all 2-UCs, gain creative abilities as soon as they enter a human body, which is spirited, credit to Isis. Thus, the Sirians have creative abilities when they inhabit human bodies, albeit not to our extent because we have Spirit innately and in abundance through our original spirit bodies. En.ki, locked up in the ABZU, can thus not attach to human bodies anymore, and therefore, he's lost his "creativity."

The Importance of our Physical Body

In the "spiritual" community and in parts of the New Age movement, we are told to neglect our homo sapiens bodies as much as possible because they are of the Matrix and not important. However, after having done deeper research and come to new conclusions, I see this as false. After everything we've discussed so far in this chapter, we can see that the body itself contains Orion DNA and Isis' Spirit, and it is very psychic. As much as we need to connect to the Spirit Realm, we also need to attend to our body, communicate with it, nurture it, and listen to it—it's a living being and there to assist us in the 3-D realm. It gives us signals and cues, but people often ignore them. It warns us of danger, and it tells us what to do in certain critical situations. The body even has its own spiritual emotions. If we neglect it, it will get sick, deteriorate, and possibly die prematurely, "thinking" that it fills little purpose. Our sapiens body is our connection to Spirit in the physical world. Thus, Spirit and the physical body become interconnected and are just two sides of the same thing. Therefore, it was needed for Isis to breathe her life force into Adam so our Divine Spirit could anchor into a body functioning as a spirit attachment and connection to the physical realm.

18

Cain's Bloodline and En.ki's Mutiny

When Orion decided to terminate the Human Experiment about 10,000 years ago when Noah's Flood happened, En.ki ferociously protested, claiming homo sapiens to be his "children." However, eventually he must give in, but told Noah, in secret, to "build an ark"(which was basically an airborne ship, not a boat), to survive the Flood. It says in the Bible that Noah's family was the last of the Cain bloodline, which En.ki wanted to preserve, since it contained his dominant DNA. Thus, Noah and his family survived, and En.ki also hijacked many human 3-UCs to continue the experiment in secret after the Flood, as mentioned earlier. They are us, the 3-UCs who were not allowed to leave the Earth Construct and go home to Orion during the Flood. Noah's three sons then became the three branches of the En.ki-Isis-Ninurta bloodline surviving the Deluge. En.ki did some additional tampering, making Ham's offspring black, as briefly mentioned in *The ORION Book, volume 2.*

We have learned from the Bible that it was the Cain bloodline that was terminated in the Flood, which is not true. The Cain bloodline is what *survived* the Flood, although it didn't wipe out all people on Earth. It was the Seth bloodline that succumbed—the dominant human bloodline before the Flood. There were those who survived, e.g., the Native Americans and the Aborigines in Australia, both survivors from Lemuria; Aborigine meaning "original inhabitant" in Latin.

It was at point in time Lucifer's Rebellion took place, and En.ki disobeyed orders and created his own experiment, which became the Matrix we are current contained in.

Isis and Mother Goddess (in the Matrix)

After the Flood, En.ki, in secret, terraformed the Earth once more, and he created a physical Dome around the planet[15], so no physical being could enter or leave this realm. Eventually, when he had created new bodies for the 3-UCs to inhabit (homo sapiens sapiens, the modern man), he also created a frequency fence, a Grid, around the planet, so no non-physical beings could enter or leave without En.ki's permission. Many Sirians, calling themselves the

---

[15] See The Holy Bible, *Genesis 1.*

19

Khan Kings, and a few other rebelling star beings from different star systems, followed En.ki to the new Earth and are still here today. The Grid comprises our human soul energy that is captured in a revolving energy grid surrounding the planet. This keeps humans together as a mass consciousness, making us all connected on an energetic soul level. This has trapped us all within the grid system. Moreover, En.ki "tilted" the planet, which had consequences; one being that it created amnesia for us humans because it put us within a denser, more solid frequency range. This also made our planet difficult to find for those of the Greater Universe. Thus, the rebels cloaked not only us humans from the outside universe, but these Overlords could also hide within this system behind all the barriers and layers they created. Orion discovered too late what En.ki had done, and he and his cohorts now had what they considered the "perfect system," where they could have privacy to hijack the original experiment and create their own by tricking us humans into inhabiting this new, denser homo sapiens. As usual, we were tricked by sex.

In previous work, I have argued that we reincarnate into our own immediate bloodline each time we return here. We have no choice in the matter. This exact procedure is important to the Overlords, so they can keep track of us; but also, so they feel they have given us a chance to evolve, all per the contract they have "signed" with Orion, promising to let us evolve and graduate to return to Orion. Every time we die, most souls go through the Tunnel of Light and end up in the Overlords' recycling center. The astral workers, whose job it is to recycle us into new bodies, wipe our memories clean, destroy the astral body that contains the memories of our immediate past life, and give us a new astral body, free from any memories, with a clean slate, and shoot us down into a new body of our own previous bloodline (e.g., into our own grand- or great grandchild's body). We are born without memories, with full soul amnesia, but we inherit some memories, skills, and experiences that we retrieve in new lifetimes, all running through our DNA from our direct ancestral lineage. Therefore, certain talents or traits are inherited. We create a new personality each lifetime, based on our upbringing and our environment, forming experiences that influence our choices in life. This is very cruel, and even though we might make minimal progress from life to life, it is, at best, two steps forward and one step backward, or one step forward and two step backward, depending on the individual's responses to the environment and choices in life. Sometimes, it's just backward, depending on how we live our lives, where each lifetime becomes the foundation for our next incarnation. Thus, we bring our actions with us into our next life through our genetics. This alone determines our evolution or devolution, respectively—not our direct soul memories, which are destroyed together with the astral body. If we are to believe in karma, we create it with our actions in each lifetime by leaving our thoughts, actions, and intentions embedded in the DNA of our bloodline, so when we incarnate the next time, the choices we made in our previous lives influence us in our new life. If we were serial killers the last time, that would greatly impact our behavior in this life. This is also why the Pleiadians, channeled by Barbara Marciniak, said that what we do in this lifetime also affects our entire ancestral line because our actions always alter our DNA along the lines of time—good or bad. It was never supposed to be this way; this is the Overlords' solution to keep us here in the Matrix as long as they deem necessary, but still keeping their word, letting us evolve.

Non-Player Characters (NPCs)

I would suggest that here in the Matrix, all homo sapiens bodies have Isis' Dragon breath in them as a part of the blueprint. Yet we often hear people talk about *NPCs* (Non-Player-Characters), who are allegedly spiritless. I believe they exist—non-spirited beings occupy many human bodies, and they are of two kinds, from what I can see: 1) 2-UCs (soul-minds without spirit bodies), using Matrix sapiens bodies. These beings got trapped in this Matrix and caught up in the recycling system, as discussed in my *The ORION Book, Volumes 1 and 2,* and in the WPP. They are not NPCs in the sense the term is normally used in the alternative community, but they are not spirited either, besides the sprinkle added to the human body, nor are they players that count in the bigger scheme of things. The real NPCs, I believe, are, 2) human bodies possessed by an *artificial soul* with an *artificial mind*, created with AI with synthetic consciousness.

What does this imply? I would suggest the Overlords insert an artificial soul and an artificial mind in certain bodies, i.e., an astral body, letting no real 2-UCs or 3-UCs inhabit them. They become truly artificial intelligence (AI), restricted to operating only here in the Matrix. There is no true consciousness in them. They are the real NPCs or the so-called *background people*. These beings cannot evolve—they are 100% Overlord-run programs—biological robots or "inverted cyborgs." By that I mean the body is biological and the soul-mind is AI, contrary to the cyborgs being created these days, where the body will be half machine and half biological, housing our 3-UCs, making us cyborgs. It might be incorrect to say they have no true consciousness at all, though, because the human body, which they are attached to, has Isis' breath of Spirit in them. The NPCs have only one life, and when their human bodies die, these souls (avatars/astral bodies) are destroyed, and new ones are created, shot down, and forced into another human body. Some people who have deep-studied narcissism and psychopathy can notice the similarities between them and AI; they seem to run completely on a program. This idea comes from psychologists and life coaches who are not even alternative researchers. I believe they are correct. True narcissists who can be diagnosed with NPD (narcissistic personality disorder) or psychopathy (malignant narcissism or APD, anti-social personality Disorder) may often be type two NPCs, sent down here to traumatize the spirited humans, such as ourselves. They are copy-cats with no true minds of their own. However, they are brilliant when it comes to mimic human behavior—even emotions—and use those against us to lead us astray and traumatize us. Therefore, we see more and more narcissism in our society today than ever before. This is because more NPCs are incarnated into our realm now than perhaps ever before in history—the ratio in favor of NPC is greater rather than that of spirited humans, I would argue. Narcissists are famous for changing the personality of their targets, and the targets (spirited humans), become more and more like them. They can possibly never become true narcissists because they are spirited with true consciousness, but narcissism runs on a gradient scale from, let's say, 1-10, but only a 10 could be an NPC, if my theory is correct. Even a 9 is still a spirited 3-UC who can recover (albeit unlikely so), and sometimes they may be non-spirited 2-UCs. An NPC has no genuine thoughts and can't genuinely think on their own—they copy their environment so we think they are "real," and they can therefore appear extremely intelligent—even brilliant. Some of them reach lofty positions in society. They lack true emotions, empathy, and compassion because they are not real—there is no genuine consciousness. It's a machine. Therefore, psychologists scratch their heads, wondering where psychopaths come from. Many of them don't seem to have an abusive childhood or any other signs of abuse that could have created such complicated, inverted people—not even in their family history can such traits be traced. I suggest these people are inserted NPCs from birth.

Those who are not narcissists or psychopaths are the so-called NPC-based *background people*. These are not necessarily abusive, but they are still AI, completely grounded in the physical world, and can't conceive of spiritual evolution or true self-healing. They are the ones who ridicule everything that can't be perceived with the five senses, grinning, and shaking their heads when we try to educate them. They are purely physical and can't be anything else. These beings are probably here to discourage us from exploring what is outside the box. We all have encountered them since they are in the majority. They usually do not believe in an afterlife because they don't have one—they are NPCs and artificial. Some of them pretend to be religious or believe in life after death, but there is no depth to it, and just a way to adapt to their environment so they can fit in.

Isis Trapped

En.ki, as the genetic scientist he is, went to great lengths to keep us confined here—he created something we call *the Matrix*. Many people think the Matrix is the Earth with all that exists here, but the essential Matrix is this modern human body. As soon as the 3-UC enters the body with each incarnation, our perceptions of reality become extremely limited to only five senses. During the Atlantis Era and earlier, we had many more perceptions and could experience a wide range of the electromagnetic spectrum. In these bodies, we are restricted to perceiving the tiny spectrum of visible light, which is only 4% of the Universe. With technology, En.ki turned off 96% of our DNA, which is the building block of existence, making it possible for a being to experience the fullness of the Greater Universe. Scientists call the inactivated DNA "junk DNA," which is nonsense. The human body is a biological computer. The human 3-UC is a bio-computer with the brain as the circuit board (a literal circuit board with its blueprint in the astral body). Once we're hooked within these bodies, we live in a simulation, a hologram of sorts, and the brain decodes the electrical impulses from the outside according to how the body is programmed and limited to perceive the outside universe. We live in an illusion, and not until we have an out-of-body experience (OBE) or a near-death-experience (NDE) can we move outside the Matrix and into the astral, which is an intermediary zone between the "physical" and the non-physical Greater Universe outside the Grid—Orion.

Whether Isis voluntarily followed En.ki and Marduk into the Third Construct is uncertain; all we know is that she did, and here she created new bloodlines with both En.ki and Marduk, explained in my previous work, but particularly in the WPP and *The ORION Book, volume 2*. The first bloodline she created was with En.ki, and when her father, Prince En.lil, became aware that Isis had been raped, he got furious, and he "castrated" En.ki and cast him out of Orion. That was the end of the classical story of Lucifer's Rebellion, which started immediately after the Flood. En.lil didn't only castrate his brother literally, from what I understand: the word *castrate* can also mean, "to deprive of vitality, strength, or effectiveness."[16] Although he apparently did castrate his brother physically in the Rigel star system, as discussed in the WPP, the Fourth Level of Learning, that would only have stopped him so long as he was incarnated in that current body, but En.lil made sure it cut deeper than that. I was told he put a "curse" on En.ki, most likely castrating his astral body as well, after he threw him out of Orion and imprisoned him in the ABZU/Hell, where Queen Ereškigal rules. By keeping En.ki in containment in the lowest regions of the Matrix, he was indeed made impotent in its larger sense.[17] Ten years ago, I learned he is still in the ABZU, so I would assume nothing has changed. I suspect this is what my source meant when he talked about taking away En.ki's "creative abilities." He no longer has access to human bodies. Therefore, he is completely dependent on his human minions, who do his bidding here on Earth's surface.

What about the rest of the Invaders, e.g., Marduk, Ereškigal, and the Khan Kings? Do they have their creative abilities intact? Yes, and no. None of them is spirited, except Ereškigal, I would suggest,

---

[16] Merriam-Webster: *Castrate, def. 2b.*
[17] This is told in the "mythological" story about Prometheus.

being the lowest manifestation of Sophia. But if so, she is so far gone that she is mentally and emotionally disconnected from it. Not being spirited, they can't create with their minds, so they are dependent on technology to create. In other words, they take what was already created by spirited beings (such as the Queen, and by us), distort it with technology, and create bad copies of something that already exists in near perfection. However, with En.ki, who is the true engineer, being stuck in the ABZU, the rest of the Invaders were suddenly without the present of their brilliant leader. It is En.ki who has the greatest knowledge in Orion technology; he is the technical expert. However, I have reasons to believe it is *not* En.ki who is giving humankind our technology, as previously believed, and I will explain later why this is. However, Isis is also a genetic scientist, and it seems to me the Khan Kings now use *her* knowledge to build Metaverse and the Singularity. From having learned more about Isis through this research, I believe she does not want the Singularity, but she has been forced by Marduk to give him the technology needed. Through Tesla and other geniuses, he has thus let this information channel through them, so our human scientists can learn Orion technology, such as computer science, and advanced artificial intelligence.

After Prince En.lil castrated En.ki a few thousand years ago, Marduk became the Lord of Earth, so we could say Marduk took on the title as En.ki. He has been in charge here on Earth ever since. This doesn't mean En.ki is *completely* handicapped in the Abyss. It's true he currently can't move into our dimension, but being a souled entity, he can still split his soul fires and send them off into our realm and thus communicate with his minions on Earth—his proxy, whom we often call the Global Elite. The question is, how many of them are still loyal to him? This book will try to answer that question.

Marduk had no second thoughts; he enthusiastically raped Isis and created his own bloodline. As we can see, they used Isis as a breeder for the two Patriarchs, who both wanted to make sure they had their own pure bloodline to incarnate into.

Isis at Lake Baikal

What is tricky about putting these stories together is the timeline. When did what happen? We know that Isis "helped" both En.ki and Marduk to create new bloodlines, and we also know that En.ki gave Isis the MEs (the Tablets of Destiny) when he was drunk, not knowing what he was doing, and when En.ki woke up from his drunkenness, he noticed the MEs were gone, and he desperately wanted them back. So, he searched for Isis everywhere but could not find her. Yet they failed to search for her at Lake Baikal, where she spent her time creating a new bloodline, free from the two rapists' DNA. She wanted to repent and honor her father, Prince En.lil/Ninurta, and create a branch of humans that had a mix of Isis and Ninurta DNA; she wanted nothing more to do with En.ki and Marduk.

Thus, she created the *Isis Bloodline*—the red-haired Ladies of Fire. Although this bloodline was created at Lake Baikal, at some point later, many of these people migrated and ended up in today's Ireland and Scotland, both having an established red-haired populations. There is a reason the bloodline moved to Europe, which we shall discuss later. As we know, "redheads" are often "fiery." Isis' and Ninurta's blood run through their veins, although it has been diluted since then.

It is uncertain when Isis escaped with the MEs because it had to have happened before En.lil threw En.ki into the pit. The only thing that makes sense to me with the limited information I have about that part of the timeline is that Isis ran away with the MEs *before* En.ki went to war in the Rigel star system, where his brother confronted him because En.ki was still on Earth. Hence, it probably happened shortly before 2024 BCE, when En.ki disappeared from Earth and never returned. With the MEs, comprising instruction to Orion technology, she ran off and created her new bloodline. After En.ki was eliminated, Marduk must have found her and kept her under surveillance. After that, the goddess, as Isis, almost completely escaped from history.

But she didn't disappear. She went silent, but she was not inactive; she just hid her identity. My records of Isis, as far as the WPP goes, more or less ended with her creating her bloodline, but there is so much more to the story that has come to light recently, since I have reviewed old information, done more research, and then connected the dots. It ties in with the story of Jesus and Mary Magdalene, which shouldn't come as a surprise to most reader. That story is not new, per se, but I strongly argue that all these stories are somewhat incorrect because a big, crucial piece of information has been missing and been misunderstood. When I connected the dots recently, things made so much more sense, and to me, it shone a light on one of the greatest mysteries in human history; something that has been debated for millennia.

This brings us to Isis, Jesus (Yeshua) and the Knights Templar.

Was There a Real Jesus?

2 **There have been many** speculations about whether a physical Jesus walked the Earth 2,000 years ago, or if the entire story is fabricated and hijacked from earlier historical events. My hypothesis is in favor of the idea that Jesus existed, which was also my main source's perspective from the WPP years. However, Jesus was not Divine, i.e., of the Mother Goddess, and he was not like what the Bible tells us. That narrative is a rebound story, based on earlier, similar stories—Osiris, Isis, and Horus being one of many. I will use an example of how the Overlords warp stories and put their own slant on it. Let us go to the Nag Hammadi Gnostic texts.[18]

In these texts, which were excluded from the canonical gospels, it says that Sabaoth, an Archon, who, according to the texts, was a son of Yaldabaoth (the equivalent to En.ki). Sabaoth descended to Earth and inhabited a human body, born from a "virgin" and became Jesus. Please beware that although there are similarities between the Nag Hammadi and the WPP, they are two separate pieces of work, and therefore, some things will correspond, and others will not. I doubt not for a second that the gods themselves (En.ki and Marduk) dictated the Nag Hammadi to the human scribes, the Gnostics, who wrote the information down. It may, or may not at all be what the actual, physical Jesus preached.

---

[18] The Nag Hammadi Library is free to read online: _http://www.gnosis.org/naghamm/nhlalpha.html_

By the time they were written down on scrolls, a few centuries had usually passed since Jesus supposedly died. And as always is the case when the Overlords dictate something to humans, it is *their* version of history that is being recorded, and it's usually heavily biased. We can clearly see this in the Sumerian texts, the Enûma Eliš (the Babylonian creation story), the Vedas, and many others. Like the WPP, the Nag Hammadi (NH) tell the story of the two brothers, En.ki and En.lil (although they are portrayed as father and son in the Gnostic texts), and how the younger brother, En.lil (Sabaoth in the NH) was preferred by the Queen before Yaldabaoth (En.ki), and he became known as St. Michael in both the WPP and the NH. Saint Michael and Jesus are supposedly synonymous.

Then the Overlords cleverly altered the story in the Gnostic texts.

The NH tells us it was Sabaoth who descended into the body of the biblical Jesus. In the Gnostic description of Sabaoth, he corresponds with Ninurta, aka Prince En.lil. The Overlords wanted the Gnostic followers to believe Sabaoth, as depicted in the NH, was Jesus for later reference. This would serve the Overlords' agenda. They wanted humankind to believe Ninurta was incarnating as Jesus Christ, and not Marduk, who was the "real" Jesus. Why? Because it fits in with later texts that were already in the planning, such as the Book of Revelation; Ninurta being the Archangel Michael from Orion, who will one day defeat the Archons (the Overlords), according to Bible prophecy. And who was dictating the Book of Revelation to John the Divine? The Overlords (the Archons), of course.

The Book of Revelation is an Overlord falsehood. The narrative makes it sound as if the Forces from Heaven (Saint Michael and his MIKH-MAKH army, i.e. Ninurta/Sabaoth) will come and defeat Satan, and Michael, aka Jesus, will reign for 1,000 years here in a new version of Heaven (which also triggers our yearning for the Tiamat "Heaven," our original home). But if the Overlords make us think Jesus was Michael (Ninurta/Sabaoth), the Savior in the End Days must also be Michael/Sabaoth returning. However, Michael, as Jesus, was *not* Ninurta but Marduk/Satan—something they have kept hidden from us. This means that the Jesus/Archangel Michael who will defeat Satan's forces in the End Days, and who will reign openly for 1,000 years, is Marduk. This is how the Overlords take over titles to trick us, and however we look at it, unless we know the truth, we think the returning Jesus is good-natured and has our best interests in mind. The Overlords take the titles of Divine Beings from outside the Matrix and give them to themselves to suit their own purpose to control us and fulfill their goal. If the purpose with a certain title was one thing, the Overlords invert it and make it mean the opposite. Then they can blame any adverse result on Orion when necessary.

So, Sabaoth in the NH turned from being the equivalent to Prince Ninurta to becoming Marduk when he incarnated on Earth. One hypothesis is that En.ki, playing the role of God, funneled the "divine" message through Jesus' (Marduk's) physical body, while Marduk, the soul-mind (2-UC), takes the backseat. The narrative itself was the same rehearsed narrative that had been used so many times before in history, mostly unbeknownst to the population two thousand years ago in the Middle East. This is mostly what the Nag

Fig. 2:1. Isis and Horus (left), and Mary and Jesus (right)

Hammadi says happened, although in those text, Jesus was Sabaoth.

But there are also other options: Marduk had the narrative so well-rehearsed that he needed no channeling from En.ki. If so, he either pretended to channel "God," or he relayed no message at all to humankind. Instead, the message was relayed *after* Jesus' supposed death and completely made up—a pure retell of the same old narrative from eons prior, while the Jesus who walked the Earth had nothing to do with miracles and preaching—he was on a completely different mission, and the canonical story and the NH gospels are misleading distractions and convenient lies En.ki and Marduk needed to get into circulation when their mission was actually to create a completely new bloodline, as we will discuss later. The Jesus story, however, worked perfectly to create a new religion, which was Jesus' main purpose, just like so many times before in history, when the same narrative was used—new religions were created. Note that the birth of Christ also introduced a new astrological era—we went to the Age of Pieces, which has been Marduk's age. It was time to put aside all these pagan gods and create a new monotheistic religion,

Christianity, and they used their human minions a few hundred years after Jesus' death to orchestrate that. There is evidence that St. Paul, the true founder of Christianity, was initiated in a number of secret societies across the world, which was revealed by, among others, "Acharya S," who is a historian and an archaeologist, having done lots of research into the ancient texts, including the Bible.[19]

I feel certain there was a Jesus walking around on Earth two thousand years ago because it was needed for a few reasons: A physical reference point was crucial to build a religion, and it's most likely that Marduk walked around and spread the narrative, although the last option that the whole story was invented afterward may also hold water. Either way, Marduk was here in the flesh as the "divine" being—the son (sun) of "God" (En.ki). I know from my Orion correspondence that Horus and Tammuz indeed were here, too, long before Jesus, with the same narrative. However, I doubt any of them were nailed to the cross. Marduk would hardly want to go through that at the end of his missions, whether he's Jesus, Horus, or Tammuz, respectively. I could of course be wrong, but that's my current stand. Still, crucifixion was a real punishment in the days of Jesus.

Contemporary Mentioning of Jesus Outside the Bible

While doing research, I stumbled upon a Christian man, who had investigated whether there were any mentioning of Jesus outside the scriptures, and he found some quite interesting sources for those who want to be more certain whether he existed or not. It is a little lengthy, but I want to include it here for those who want to look deeper (the bracketed footnote references in the text should be clickable in the Kindle version of this book):

> Let's begin our inquiry with a passage that historian Edwin Yamauchi calls "probably the most important reference to Jesus outside the New Testament." Reporting on Emperor Nero's decision to blame the Christians for the fire that had destroyed Rome in A.D. 64, the Roman historian Tacitus wrote:
>
> Nero fastened the guilt . . . on a class hated for their abominations, called Christians by the populace. Christus, from whom the name

---

[19] YouTube: *Acharya S: Who Is Jesus? - The Christ Conspiracy - Interview with D. M. Murdock - FULL*

had its origin, suffered the extreme penalty during the reign of Tiberius at the hands of . . . Pontius Pilatus, and a most mischievous superstition, thus checked for the moment, again broke out not only in Judaea, the first source of the evil, but even in Rome. . . .

What all can we learn from this ancient (and rather unsympathetic) reference to Jesus and the early Christians? Notice, first, that Tacitus reports Christians derived their name from a historical person called Christus (from the Latin), or Christ. He is said to have "suffered the extreme penalty," obviously alluding to the Roman method of execution known as crucifixion. This is said to have occurred during the reign of Tiberius and by the sentence of Pontius Pilatus. This confirms much of what the Gospels tell us about the death of Jesus.

But what are we to make of Tacitus' rather enigmatic statement that Christ's death briefly checked "a most mischievous superstition," which subsequently arose not only in Judaea, but also in Rome? One historian suggests that Tacitus is here "bearing indirect . . . testimony to the conviction of the early church that the Christ who had been crucified had risen from the grave."{6} While this interpretation is admittedly speculative, it does help explain the otherwise bizarre occurrence of a rapidly growing religion based on the worship of a man who had been crucified as a criminal.{7} How else might one explain that?

Evidence from Pliny the Younger

Another important source of evidence about Jesus and early Christianity can be found in the letters of Pliny the Younger to Emperor Trajan. Pliny was the Roman governor of Bithynia in Asia Minor. In one of his letters, dated around A.D. 112, he asks Trajan's advice about the appropriate way to conduct legal proceedings against those accused of being Christians.{8} Pliny says that he needed to consult the emperor about this issue because a great multitude of every age, class, and sex stood accused of Christianity.{9}

At one point in his letter, Pliny relates some of the information he has learned about these Christians:

They were in the habit of meeting on a certain fixed day before it was light, when they sang in alternate verses a hymn to Christ, as to a god, and bound themselves by a solemn oath, not to any wicked deeds, but never to commit any fraud, theft or adultery, never to falsify their word, nor deny a trust when they should be called upon to deliver it up; after which it was their custom to separate, and then reassemble to partake of food–but food of an ordinary and innocent kind.{10}

This passage provides us with a number of interesting insights into the beliefs and practices of early Christians. First, we see that Christians regularly met on a certain fixed day for worship. Second, their worship was directed to Christ, demonstrating that they firmly believed in His divinity. Furthermore, one scholar interprets Pliny's statement that hymns were sung to Christ, as to a god, as a reference to the rather distinctive fact that, "unlike other gods who were worshipped, Christ was a person who had lived on earth."{11} If this interpretation is correct, Pliny understood that Christians were worshipping an actual historical person as God! Of course, this agrees perfectly with the New Testament doctrine that Jesus was both God and man.

Not only does Pliny's letter help us understand what early Christians believed about Jesus' person, it also reveals the high esteem to which they held His teachings. For instance, Pliny notes that Christians bound themselves by a solemn oath not to violate various moral standards, which find their source in the ethical teachings of Jesus. In addition, Pliny's reference to the Christian custom of sharing a common meal likely alludes to their observance of communion and the "love feast."{12} This interpretation helps explain the Christian claim that the meal was merely food of an ordinary and innocent kind. They were attempting to counter the charge, sometimes made by non-Christians, of practicing "ritual cannibalism."{13} The Christians of that day humbly repudiated such slanderous attacks on Jesus' teachings. We must sometimes do the same today.

Evidence from Josephus

Perhaps the most remarkable reference to Jesus outside the Bible can be found in the writings of Josephus, a first century Jewish historian. On two occasions, in his Jewish Antiquities, he mentions Jesus. The second, less revealing, reference describes the condemnation of one "James" by the Jewish Sanhedrin. This James, says Josephus, was "the brother of Jesus the so-called Christ."{14} F.F. Bruce points out how this agrees with Paul's description of James in Galatians 1:19 as "the Lord's brother."{15} And Edwin Yamauchi informs us that "few scholars have questioned" that Josephus actually penned this passage.{16}

As interesting as this brief reference is, there is an earlier one, which is truly astonishing. Called the "Testimonium Flavianum," the relevant portion declares:

About this time there lived Jesus, a wise man, if indeed one ought to call him a man. For he . . . wrought surprising feats. . . . He was the Christ. When Pilate . . .condemned him to be crucified, those who had . . . come to love him did not give up their affection for him. On the third day he appeared . . . restored to life. . . . And the tribe of Christians . . . has . . . not disappeared.{17}

Did Josephus really write this? Most scholars think the core of the passage originated with Josephus, but that it was later altered by a Christian editor, possibly between the third and fourth century A.D.{18} But why do they think it was altered? Josephus was not a Christian, and it is difficult to believe that anyone but a Christian would have made some of these statements.{19}

For instance, the claim that Jesus was a wise man seems authentic, but the qualifying phrase, "if indeed one ought to call him a man," is suspect. It implies that Jesus was more than human, and it is quite unlikely that Josephus would have said that! It is also difficult to believe he would have flatly asserted that Jesus was the Christ, especially when he later refers to Jesus as "the so-called" Christ. Finally, the claim that on the third day Jesus appeared to His disciples restored to life, inasmuch as it affirms Jesus' resurrection, is quite unlikely to come from a non-Christian!

But even if we disregard the questionable parts of this passage, we are still left with a good deal of corroborating information about the biblical Jesus. We read that he was a wise man who performed surprising feats. And although He was crucified under Pilate, His followers continued their discipleship and became known as Christians. When we combine these statements with Josephus' later reference to Jesus as "the so-called Christ," a rather detailed picture emerges which harmonizes quite well with the biblical record. It increasingly appears that the "biblical Jesus" and the "historical Jesus" are one and the same!

Evidence from the Babylonian Talmud

There are only a few clear references to Jesus in the Babylonian Talmud, a collection of Jewish rabbinical writings compiled between approximately A.D. 70-500. Given this time frame, it is naturally supposed that earlier references to Jesus are more likely to be historically reliable than later ones. In the case of the Talmud, the earliest period of compilation occurred between A.D. 70-200.{20} The most significant reference to Jesus from this period states:

On the eve of the Passover Yeshu was hanged. For forty days before the execution took place, a herald . . . cried, "He is going forth to be stoned because he has practiced sorcery and enticed Israel to apostasy."{21}

Let's examine this passage. You may have noticed that it refers to someone named "Yeshu." So why do we think this is Jesus? Actually, "Yeshu" (or "Yeshua") is how Jesus' name is pronounced in Hebrew. But what does the passage mean by saying that Jesus "was hanged"? Doesn't the New Testament say he was crucified? Indeed it does. But the term "hanged" can function as a synonym for "crucified." For instance, Galatians 3:13 declares that Christ was "hanged", and Luke 23:39 applies this term to the criminals who were crucified with Jesus.{22} So the Talmud declares that Jesus was crucified on the eve of Passover. But what of the cry of the herald that Jesus was to be stoned? This may simply indicate what the Jewish leaders were planning to do.{23} If so, Roman involvement changed their plans!{24}

The passage also tells us why Jesus was crucified. It claims He practiced sorcery and enticed Israel to apostasy! Since this accusation comes from a rather hostile source, we should not be too surprised if Jesus is described somewhat differently than in the New Testament. But if we make allowances for this, what might such charges imply about Jesus?

Interestingly, both accusations have close parallels in the canonical gospels. For instance, the charge of sorcery is similar to the Pharisees' accusation that Jesus cast out demons "by Beelzebul the ruler of the demons."{25} But notice this: such a charge actually tends to confirm the New Testament claim that Jesus performed miraculous feats. Apparently Jesus' miracles were too well attested to deny. The only alternative was to ascribe them to sorcery! Likewise, the charge of enticing Israel to apostasy parallels Luke's account of the Jewish leaders who accused Jesus of misleading the nation with his teaching.{26} Such a charge tends to corroborate the New Testament record of Jesus' powerful teaching ministry. Thus, if read carefully, this passage from the Talmud confirms much of our knowledge about Jesus from the New Testament.

Evidence from Lucian

Lucian of Samosata was a second century Greek satirist. In one of his works, he wrote of the early Christians as follows:

The Christians . . . worship a man to this day–the distinguished personage who introduced their novel rites, and was crucified on that account. . . . [It] was impressed on them by their original lawgiver that they are all brothers, from the moment that they are converted, and deny the gods of Greece, and worship the crucified sage, and live after his laws.{27}

Although Lucian is jesting here at the early Christians, he does make some significant comments about their founder. For instance, he says the Christians worshipped a man, "who introduced their novel rites." And though this man's followers clearly thought quite highly of Him, He so angered many of His contemporaries with His teaching that He "was crucified on that account."

35

Although Lucian does not mention his name, he is clearly referring to Jesus. But what did Jesus teach to arouse such wrath? According to Lucian, he taught that all men are brothers from the moment of their conversion. That's harmless enough. But what did this conversion involve? It involved denying the Greek gods, worshipping Jesus, and living according to His teachings. It's not too difficult to imagine someone being killed for teaching that. Though Lucian doesn't say so explicitly, the Christian denial of other gods combined with their worship of Jesus implies the belief that Jesus was more than human. Since they denied other gods in order to worship Him, they apparently thought Jesus a greater God than any that Greece had to offer!

Let's summarize what we've learned about Jesus from this examination of ancient non-Christian sources. First, both Josephus and Lucian indicate that Jesus was regarded as wise. Second, Pliny, the Talmud, and Lucian imply He was a powerful and revered teacher. Third, both Josephus and the Talmud indicate He performed miraculous feats. Fourth, Tacitus, Josephus, the Talmud, and Lucian all mention that He was crucified. Tacitus and Josephus say this occurred under Pontius Pilate. And the Talmud declares it happened on the eve of Passover. Fifth, there are possible references to the Christian belief in Jesus' resurrection in both Tacitus and Josephus. Sixth, Josephus records that Jesus' followers believed He was the Christ, or Messiah. And finally, both Pliny and Lucian indicate that Christians worshipped Jesus as God!

I hope you see how this small selection of ancient non-Christian sources helps corroborate our knowledge of Jesus from the gospels. Of course, there are many ancient Christian sources of information about Jesus as well.[20]

According to some of these contemporary sources, Jesus was indeed crucified, so we need to leave that open to speculations. In one Nag Hammadi gospel, however, Jesus was replaced by a Simon of Cyrene,[21] and thus, Marduk/Jesus got away scot-free.

But how do I know Jesus wasn't Ninurta after all? I know this for two important reasons: First, Ninurta was not here at all in the Third Construct (the Matrix). How could he (there were no holes in the Grid), and *why* would he? The Overlords were very strict with not letting anyone from the Orion Council into this Construct. That was the last thing they wanted. Second, there is no doubt the Jesus

---

[20] Quora: *Where and who are the present descendants of Jesus Christ?*
[21] Nag Hammadi gospel: *Second Treatise of the Great Seth.*

narrative comes from En.ki and Marduk. Queen Sophia would *never* channel Divine Messages through Marduk or En.ki, and because Jesus can't have been Ninurta or anyone else from the Orion Council, it is self-evident En.ki and Marduk schemed the entire Jesus hoax.

Fundamental Truths in Jesus' Narrative

The readers might ask themselves why En.ki revealed so many truths to humankind, tricking us into thinking they to are truths coming from the Divine? After all, there is wisdom in Jesus' message.

The answer becomes obvious if we understand the Overlords' long term Agenda. If they want to spread propaganda, they know that for something to persist, it must be a mix of truths and lies in the message. Therefore, the most brilliant way to relay a message is to tell as many truths as possible, but not before they are twisted and reversed to fit an underlying, occult purpose. Those who have followed my work know that the true Creatrix of the Universe is feminine. Thus, all the Overlords had to do was relay Sophia's Wisdom and dedicate it to their own masculine God—En.ki. The Divine gems Jesus revealed were hijacked and now in the Overlords' possession, and all worship, sacrifices, prayers, and all the rest of it now landed in their lap, and they could feed from it and swallow up all the energies devoted Christians sent their way through worship and prayers. They fooled a large part of the world and could now more easily brainwash the masses via the Roman Catholic Church and all the sects, cults, and different churches going under the umbrella of Christianity.

But why does the Catholic Church worship Mother Mary, the Madonna? This is something interesting we shall explore, perhaps shocking to some.

Regarding Christ's message, I am often referring to that it originates in much older records, such as the aforementioned Osiris-Isis-Horus story, and that of Semiramis (Isis) and her son, Tammuz (Marduk). According to this story, Tammuz was crucified with a lamb at his feet and then transferred to a cave (just like Jesus). When the rock was removed three days later, his body was gone. We've heard that before.

Jesus was the son of God. In Egypt, and Horus was the son of God—both were sun gods. Jesus was the Light of the World. Horus was the Light of the World. Jesus was the Way, the Truth, and the

Life, and Horus was the Truth and the Life. Jesus was born in Bethlehem, the "house of bread." Horus was born in Annu, the "place of bread." Jesus was the Good Shepherd; Horus was the Good Shepherd. Seven fishers boarded a boat with Jesus. Seven people boarded a boat with Horus. Jesus was the Lamb, and Horus was the lamb. Jesus is related to a cross, and Horus is related to a cross. Jesus was baptized at 30, and so was Horus[22, 23].

And the list goes on...[24]

So, there is no wonder why people think the Jesus story is fabricated. In fact, it is. It seems that when the Overlords need a new religion to be established, they recycle this story with a new character as the protagonist. Does this mean Horus, Krishna, Tammuz, and Jesus, to name a few, never existed in the physical? They did, according to my research, but they were all playing out a narrative, given to them by "God," En.ki. That's the common denominator—it's always En.ki, and then there is a son, which is En.ki's/God's son, i.e., Marduk, who always seems to play the role of the physical Messiah—the Messenger of God. Marduk is the true messenger, not Thoth, Hermes, or Mercury (same deity), who are *supposedly* God's messenger. They are only other titles for Marduk. Thoth is connected to the builder and destroyer of civilizations, and so is Marduk as Shiva. They are all one and the same. The mother is always Isis, except in the Third Construct, the Matrix, where she sometimes is Ereškigal. They compose the Unholy Trinity, where God is En.ki, the son is Marduk, and Isis and Ereškigal, interchangeably, are the (Un)Holy Ghost/Spirit because they possess Spirit. According to my Orion Source, the true Trinity is Khan En.lil, Prince En.lil, and Sophia.

The Overlords need a physical person incarnated here for two major reasons: 1) It becomes more legitimate (religiously and otherwise), and 2) on occasion throughout time, the Overlords have been forced to strengthen their bloodlines. Marduk entered our planet through Osiris and Isis, and the En.ki-Isis-Ninurta bloodline could thus be strengthened—a bloodline that goes all the way back

---

[22] David Icke: *The Biggest secret, p. 80ff.*

[23] Providence College: *The Power of Mothers: A Comparison of the Egyptian Goddess Isis and Virgin Mary During the Roman Empire Through Literature and Art*

[24] Jessica Jewett: *Did Isis Become the Virgin Mary?*

to the "Garden of Edin" and Adam and Eve.

When my Contact told me Jesus was feminine, and the Jesus story was based on a composite of much older stories, I believe he meant that the message the Overlords conveyed was originally that of the Divine Feminine, twisted into Masculine, and the older texts he referred to were most likely the Osiris and the Tammuz stories, and a quite a few more. I don't think he referred to that a physical female "Jesus" walked on the Earth.

Now it's time to introduce the Knights Templar to the story; a Military Order operating under the pope and the Catholic Church, but with a very specific core mission, which was *not* to protect pilgrims on their way to Jerusalem. Their most important task was to protect the Holy Grail with their lives, and they took that task seriously. But what *is* the Holy Grail? This book will put a new slant on this subject, slightly different from earlier alternative research, such as *The Holy Blood and the Holy Grail*.

Ninurta's Cross and the Knights of the Temple

3 **In the WPP, I claimed** that the red cross, which was the emblem of the Knights Templar (the red cross on their chest and banner against a white background) was the Cross of Ninurta. Others have made the same observation (my bold emphases and brackets **[ ]**):

> ... if you compare the description of the cross bearer, the son of God, Ninurta, with the description of God's son Jesus in the Creed; **"the savior god Ninurta/Nabû, who was elevated to his father's right hand [Khan En.lil] and omnipotence after his victory over death and the forces of evil**. It sure sounds familiar. We say about Jesus in the Christian creed; on the third day he rose again from the dead, ascended into heaven, **seated at the right hand of his Father**, God almighty" [En.ki's copy of a semi-real event].

Parpola also writes the following about Ninurta in his article Sons of God:

"The Ninurta myth is known in numerous versions, but in its essence it is a story of the victory of light over the forces of darkness and death. In all its versions, **Ninurta, the son of the divine king** [Khan En.lil], sets out from his celestial home to fight the evil forces that threaten his father's kingdom. He proceeds against the "mountain" or the "foreign land," meets the enemy, defeats it and then returns in triumph to his celestial home, where he is **blessed by his father and mother** [Khan En.lil and the Queen]. Exalted at their side, Ninurta becomes an omnipotent cosmic accountant of men's fates."

The cross was thus the emblem of Ninurta. Even today

Christians signify the cross as the sign of victory, **but there are few linking its significance with Ninurta's victory over the forces of evil.** Not even the Assyrians themselves have been taught this relationship by their scholars. The Christian Assyrian history is full of examples of denial of the pre-Christian era, described as pagan.[25]

This further confirms what I wrote in the WPP. Also, today's "Red Cross," the organization giving blood transfusions to those in need, e.g., in case of war battles, has as its emblem Ninurta's cross.

The above quote implies Christianity took Ninurta's Cross, distorted it, and made it their own (which is true), and that the biblical Jesus story is based on the much earlier story of Ninurta's fight against evil on Earth. This is also true, but with a caveat; it is part of a grander distortion by the Overlords. Those who have followed my work are aware that the Overlords are patriarchs, and they hate the feminine—they even hate human women in general, who we could say are the Divine Feminine representatives on Earth. So, they bluntly skipped the feminine part of the Jesus story.

Fig. 3:1. Knight Templar with Ninurta's Cross (red in original).

Why did the Templars use Ninurta's cross as their emblem?

To answer this question, we must refer to the WPP, where I wrote that the Knights Templar were shocked about what they found under Solomon's Temple in Jerusalem. First, here is what the official version tells us:

> The Templars Knights excavated Solomon's temple for about nine years, from 1119 to 1128. During their excavation, they came across various ancient Christian artifacts. The artifacts found included gold and silver gems, a map to the hidden treasures, the holy grail and cup of Christ, the Ark of the Covenant, scrolls containing early christ's [sic] teachings, and secret scrolls of the early

---

[25] "Christianity rests on Assyrian ground," (AUGINHANINKE.BLOGG.SE): https://auginhaninke.blogg.se/2017/october/christianity-rests-on-assyrian-ground.html

church.[26]

If we forget about the gold and silver, which are irrelevant to our purpose, and instead concentrate on the "cup of Christ" (the Holy Grail), the "Ark of the Covenant," and the "secret scrolls of the early church," it suddenly gets very interesting.

Fig. 3:2. The Red Cross Organization's emblem on a white background.

Here is an excerpt from the Wes Penre Papers (WPP), The Fourth Level of Learning:

> One book that according to Manly P. Hall was lost to the masses is the Book of Thoth. He claims that the book is still in existence, though, and "continues to lead the disciples of this age into the presence of the Immortals." Furthermore, Hall said that "its faithful initiates carried it sealed in a sacred casket into another land." Where have we heard something similar to that before? Wasn't that how the *Ark of the Covenant* was transported in Genesis in the Bible, carefully led and monitored by the biblical imposter, Yahweh, who stole the name and authority from the Mother Goddess herself and changed genders into a masculine God? I'm sure "someone" was overlooking the transportation of the "Book of Thoth" as well, to make sure it remained in "the right hands."
>
> Could it be that this was the book, which told the true secrets of the

---

[26] Homework.study.com: *What did the Templars find under Solomon's Temple?*

Universe—a piece of work that "God" was willing to kill for if a commoner got hold of it?[27]

So, did the Templars find the Ark of the Covenant and the "book" and/or the scrolls, containing the "secrets of the Universe," i.e., the fact that the Universe is feminine in nature, and not masculine, as the Catholic Church insisted? Did they find out that the Church had lied to them and the rest of humankind, when indeed the Catholic Church knew all the time the Universe is feminine, and the Creatrix is a "Queen" and not a "King?"[28]

According to Freemasonry, the Ark of the Covenant indeed was placed under Solomon's Temple,

> Before Solomon, the Hebrew Bible describes the story of Solomon's father, David, who united the Israelites and captured Jerusalem. Solomon's father received messages from God to construct a great Temple that would provide a final resting place for the Ark of the Covenant...[29]

I can imagine this was a tremendous shock for the Templars, who had strictly followed the orders from the Church. They must have felt extremely betrayed, but when the Catholic Church found out about what the Templars found under the Temple, I believe they might have been persuaded by the Church—at least for a while.

According to my Orion source, the Knights found evidence of the Mother Goddess and the Divine Feminine, which must have shaken their religious belief in its foundation, since the Catholic Church taught God is masculine. I may be wrong, but what if they found what we now call the Nag Hammadi Gnostic texts, which are Christian doctrines that were excluded from the Bible, such as *The Secret Gospel of John, The Gospel of Philip, The Gospel of Thomas, and even The Gospel of Mary*. There are many more of those, and they speak of a feminine Creatrix of the Universe called Sophia, who descended into her own creation (our universe) as Queen Sophia, the Mother Goddess. The God the Templars had worshipped was Yaldabaoth,

---

[27] *The Wes Penre Papers, The Fourth Level of Learning*, p. 298, PDF version.

[28] Today, it is claimed the Ark of the Covenant is in Ethiopia, in the town of Aksum, in the St. Mary of Zion cathedral. If this is indeed the genuine Ark, it no longer contains its original content.

[29] (Freemasonry): "The Grand Lodge of Ohio: *King Solomon's Temple and Freemasonry: A Framework for Self-Improvement.*"

Sophia's unwanted son, who was not God at all. If these were the texts the Knights Templar found under Solomon's Temple, the Church must have convinced them there was a reason these gospels were not parts of the canonical bible and might have told them they were forgeries. Regardless, the Church was very keen to safeguard the bloodline of Jesus Christ. There is even some evidence that the Catholic Church, at least once, admitted that it could be true that Jesus had children through Mary Magdalene. The Templars, being devoted Catholics, might have swallowed this explanation in the beginning, although that would change eventually, as we shall see. An alternative is that the Templars did not believe the Pope's explanation but pretended to, so they could accomplish their own Holy Mission, which differed from that of the Church: The Order wanted to preserve the bloodline of Mary Magdalene, the feminine bloodline, caring very little about Christ. Whichever is correct, either of these options leads in a very specific direction, which we will cover later.

If it was the Nag Hammadi texts they found, it raises another interesting question. The Nag Hammadi Gnostic texts were, in modern times, found buried and hidden in urns in Nag Hammadi, Egypt, in 1945, and have since then been translated into many languages. Were these texts hidden in Nag Hammadi by the Templars and not by the early Gnostics, who earlier hid them under Solomon's Temple?

Another thing the Templars allegedly found under the Temple was the full lineage of the Jesus bloodline, back to David,[30] and David, in his own right, was the descendent of Noah (which made Jesus of the En.ki-Isis bloodline from before the Flood—at least, so it seemed).

If these were the only things they found, it must have been stunning enough, but what about the Holy Grail, the so-called "cup" that Jesus drank from during the Last Supper, or alternatively, contained the blood of Jesus after a Roman soldier poked Jesus with a spear (another made-up story)? Instead of a literal cup, did they find the truth about the Holy Grail? Well, according to the Orion source, the Templars, after the findings under Solomon's Temple, started protecting the Divine Feminine rather than serving the Catholic Church, although they might have pretended to follow the

---

[30] Baigent, Leigh, Lincoln (1980): *The Holy Blood and the Holy Grail*

Church to protect themselves. Shortly after they excavated the Temple between 1119 and 1128, they started calling themselves the Knights Templar (*Knights of the Temple*, after the Temple of Solomon), and their mission was to protect the true Holy Grail, not the false Grail the Catholic Church pretended to protect against better knowledge. The Templars changed their mission later, which eventually also led to a devastating destruction of parts of the Order, forcing surviving members to continue their mission under the radar, in obscurity and out of reach from the Church of Rome. We will also discuss later how the Templars split into two major factions, and that may explain a lot why the Catholic Church decided to eventually execute many Knights.

It is obvious to me that the Holy Grail is not a cup. If it's not, what is it?

> Various traditions describe the Holy Grail as a cup, dish, or stone with miraculous healing powers, sometimes providing eternal youth or sustenance in infinite abundance...[31]

The Holy Grail is not an artifact. The above definition mentions "eternal youth," referring to immortality, i.e., the return to our true immortal, spiritual selves. "Drink from the Fountain of Youth, and you will get eternal life," as the saying goes. This is, of course, a metaphor, and refers to the *Hero's Journey*, one could say—the search for the Holy Grail of immortality within each one of us, also told as the *Story of Gilgamesh* in the old Mesopotamian days. The question is what eternal life really refers to in this case. As we know, the Overlords are planning thousands of years ahead. Later, we are going to discuss what eternal life really means in this context.

There are more references to the Knights Templar in the *King Arthur Saga*, where the knights were on a quest to find the Holy Grail—a story that has fascinated us since it was first told. *The Knights of the Round Table* were, of course, Knights Templars, and King Arthur was the Grandmaster of the Order. It is interesting to note that the King Arthur "saga" occurred at the same time as the Merovingian kings sat on the throne of the Franks (today's France). The Merovingian bloodline was obsessively protected by the Priory of Sion, an Order that will be discussed on and off in this book.

Here is another relevant interpretation of what the Holy Grail is:

---

[31] Wikipedia: *Holy Grail*.

> In the 15th century, English writer John Hardyng invented a fanciful new etymology for Old French san-graal (or san-gréal), meaning "Holy Grail", by parsing it as sang réal, meaning "royal blood". This etymology was used by some later medieval British writers such as Thomas Malory, and became prominent in the conspiracy theory developed in the book The Holy Blood and the Holy Grail, in which sang real refers to the Jesus bloodline.[32]

In the above reference, it talks about blood, which is the next clue. But whose blood? Jesus'?

More clues:

> The opposing view dismissed the "Celtic" connections as spurious, and interpreted the legend as essentially Christian in origin. Joseph Goering identified sources for Grail imagery in 12th-century wall paintings from churches in the Catalan Pyrenees (now mostly moved to the Museu Nacional d'Art de Catalunya), which present unique iconic images of the Virgin Mary holding a bowl.[33]

Rossetti knew a thing or two (see fig. 3-3) and was most likely initiated here and there into secret societies. Unfortunately, I need to use black and white images in this book, or it will be too expensive to publish, but it is important to note that the lady in the original painting has red hair (fig. 3:3), just like the offspring of the Isis-Ninurta bloodline Isis created on her own, using the Tablets of Destiny. Notice that in all paintings and depictions we have seen throughout time, it's the Virgin Mary or Mary Magdalene holding the cup, not Jesus. So, the cup seems more related to Mary than to Jesus. The bird on Mary's back in the painting may be a symbol of Ninurta, who is of the "Orion Bird Tribe." This is not just Freemasonic symbolism, but also that of the Knights Templar, which is essentially the same thing. But today, it's the Masonic Fraternities carrying the secrets because The Knights Templar Order is integrated with the York branch of Freemasonry. So, in the above painting, Mary Magdalene holds a cup of "wine" in her hand, symbolizing the Holy Grail. Are there liquids other than wine that are red? Well, how about blood? Is what she's holding a cup of blood?

Her own blood or Jesus'? We will investigate further.

We all need to understand what the Matrix is about. In fact, it's about many things, but if we

---

[32] Wikipedia: *Holy Grail, #etymology.*

[33] Wikipedia: H*oly Grail, #Scholarly hypotheses*

would need to break it down to one common denominator, it would be *A War on Bloodlines,* as the title of this book shows. We can talk about control, power, wealth, and corruption as being driving forces running this world, and all of that would be correct, but what we humans are suffering from is essentially the consequences of the hidden war on bloodlines and ownership of the human soul group. Which bloodline is going to be the dominant one? It is about having full control over us humans. The two main bloodlines that are fought over are that of En.ki and that of Marduk. En.ki's purest bloodline was that of En.ki and Isis, going back to before Noah's Flood, and Marduk's purest bloodline is that of Marduk-Isis, which is being more and more diluted. These days, Marduk's dominant bloodline is that of Marduk-Ereškigal. This is so important to understand that it has become the theme for this book, and when we follow the trail, we also understand what is happening today, and how important it is for us to understand the implications of protecting certain bloodlines.

Fig. 3:3. The Damsel of the Sanct Grael,
by Dante Gabriel Rossetti (1874)

Another interesting thing to note is that Ninurta's Cross was not added to the Templars' outfits and banners until 1147 CE[34], which was eighteen years *after* the excavation of Solomon's Temple between 1119 and 1128. I would argue that 1147 was perhaps the year when at least one branch of the Templars changed their religious beliefs and started a secret operation with the Catholic Church's blessing. It is "assumed" by today's historians that the cross was added on the order of King Louis VII of France in 1147, which I believe is true. King Louis was elevated to Saint by the Catholic Church for being a devoted Christian. But was he also a Templar? I believe he was. Although he was not a Merovingian king, he carried a Merovingian name, Louis, which originates with the Merovingian name, Clovis (Clovis/Louis).[35]

Now that we know what the real purpose of the Knights Templar was, we will go back and investigate the Jesus story much deeper. We will return to the Templar Order later because they have had a large influence on our history over the last 1,000 years.

---

[34] Wikipedia: *Knights Templar.*
[35] Wikipedia.org: *Merovingian dynasty.*

Mary Magdalene and Virgin Mary

Who was Mary Magdalene?

4 **Many readers have probably** by now realized who Mary Magdalene was. After all, the title of this book gives it away. Yes, Mary Magdalene and Isis were one and the same. According to both the canonical gospels and the Gnostic counterpart, Mary was one of Jesus" disciples. We also learn that the male disciples did not like to have Mary around because she was a woman and had no business to be enlightened by Christ. In some Nag Hammadi texts, Jesus looked down at her as a woman, as well, and partly agreed with his male disciples, but told them that one day he might be able to make her a male as well.

> Simon Peter said to him [Jesus], "Let Mary leave us, for women are not worthy of life." Jesus said, "I myself shall lead her in order to make her male, so that she too may become a living spirit resembling you males. For every woman who will make herself male will enter the kingdom of heaven."[36]

Here we have yet another inversion. Those who have read the WPP, the Second Level of Learning, might remember what I wrote: *To enter the Court of Orion, everybody must appear as female.* Here, Jesus inverted it in the usual Overlord fashion.

Mary Magdalene has been called many things by religious people: She has been described as a whore, and she is also the Whore

---

[36] Nag Hammadi: *Gospel of Thomas.*

of Babylon—the Scarlet Woman mentioned in the Book of Revelation, riding the Beast. This, indeed, has a sexual undermining; Mary-Isis (sexually) riding Marduk, the Beast (Satan). Wasn't that what she did when she created the Marduk-Isis bloodline? If this is where the accusation comes from, there is some truth in that, whether Isis copulated with Marduk out of freewill, or if she was forced. According to the WPP, she said, at least, she was under a spell and was thus forced to create both the En.ki-Isis and the Marduk-Isis bloodlines. This was the statement that made her father, Ninurta, furious, and why he castrated En.ki. What Isis claimed could be true, but even as a goddess, she is nothing more than a soul, a mind, and spirit, just like us. And we know what happens when we endure a relationship with a narcissist or a psychopath. We soon fall into a "trance," and we tend to become exactly like our abuser wants us to be. In Isis' case, the narcissist is En.ki, and the psychopath is Marduk. When Isis fled from En.ki after having stolen the MEs (Tablets of Destiny) and went to Lake Baikal, she woke up from her trance and became aware of her sins, and she wanted to repent by creating the Isis-Ninurta bloodline, which was androgynous, as mentioned earlier, but is important to keep in mind. However, according to the Jesus story, Isis returned to En.ki and Marduk and started working together with them again. This might look suspicious if we see it from a superficial level, but perhaps she had her own agenda; and for that, it was beneficial for her to use the two abusers again. Only this time, she would betray them—or she might have tried to. It is difficult to know what her thought process was, and why she returned, but if she had a plan, it did not pay off in the long term, but it was a nice try, as we will see.

It is remarkable that Mary Magdalene has been mentioned so little in most Christian churches around the world, when in fact, she is mentioned more times in the gospels than any of the male disciples. She was very close to Jesus, and there was a reason for this.

Who was the Virgin Mary, Jesus' Mother?

One of the biggest mysteries in the New Testament is the virgin birth of Jesus. We are told that Mother Mary was between 12-16 years old when Jesus was born,[37] and that it was a virgin birth,

---

[37] Christianity.com: *Do We Know How Old Mary Was When She Had Jesus?*

impregnated by the Holy Spirit, which is interesting. Does this mean En.ki impregnated her? Well, I think that's what we are supposed to believe, so he, as the God of the Bible can demonstrate his non-existent supernatural powers—him acting as the Holy Spirit (God). I say non-existent because, at the time of Jesus' birth, En.ki (God) was impotent and castrated. In Christianity, it's commonly accepted that Jesus' birth was supernatural, and therefore unfathomable to humans, and it was indeed supernatural in a sense, but only for those who lack the true knowledge of the history of humankind and Orion, the Greater Universe.

Now, think back to what we discussed during the first pages of this book. Isis ran away from En.ki and created her own bloodline, and she did this without any male involvement. She created a new species that was androgynous, but could, if they wanted to, also copulate with human males. Yet they were essentially hermaphrodites, just like we were on Tiamat as Namlú'u.

That was her point! She wanted to create a species in honor of her father, Ninurta, who was present when the original humankind, the Namlú'u, was created on Tiamat, and where he donated his own blood/DNA to us humans. Thus, the Namlú'u had Ninurta's DNA, which is still within us to some extent. Isis also wanted to make her new species androgynous, just like we were in his father's and Queen Sophia's creation.

To recap, the creation of the Isis-Ninurta bloodline, I would suggest, happened before 2024 BCE, when I believe the castration of En.ki occurred, or at least very close to that. I base that on Sumerian texts, translated by Zecharia Sitchin, which discuss that En.ki left our planet that year and never returned[38]. The time frame also makes sense, since En.ki was still here when Isis ran away with the MEs, but he apparently was not here long afterward. I can't say with absolute certainty that 2024 BC is the landmark here, but it makes sense, and I think En.ki got thrown into the ABZU relatively recently, i.e., by the time he disappeared from Earth and Marduk became the Lord of Earth.

We know Marduk found Isis, but it's debatable whether Isis again escaped from Marduk after that, or if she got stuck with him. If the latter is true, which I think is the case, she was at his mercy after En.ki's went to jail. What is always difficult in this kind of

---

[38] Zecharia Sitchin: *The Stairway to Heaven pp. 263-264.*

research is to get the timelines right. Also, we must consider that history is written by the winners, so we can never be exact. But I would say it makes the most sense that Isis got trapped with Marduk. He neither wants to, nor can he free his father, who is trapped inside some kind of electronic prison that he and Ereškigal can't unlock.

This is most likely around this time the idea of Jesus as the long-awaited Jewish Messiah would appear. Thus, En.ki the Impotent "God" would go from impotent to omnipotent in the blink of an eye in the public eye. God had often walked around on Earth, mingling with humans, but because of the imprisonment, he was now gone, and the Overlords needed a solution to that. So, they simply elevated him to a Heavenly God, who no longer bothered to descend to Earth. In the Old Testament, the Jewish God as YHVH had been very much present, and he even ate dinner with Abraham and his family.

Ninurta knew what he was doing when he castrated En.ki, the Arch Narcissist. What narcissists want is power, to be loved and admired, to be the top of creation; they are God, they are Omnipotent, they are entitled, grandiose, and derogatory toward others. By castrating En.ki and casting him out of Orion and into the depths of the astral created the ultimate narcissistic injury in him. En.ki must have felt horrible when all his godly powers were stripped of him. He was literally powerless and must have felt he was dying. What Ninurta did is the worst thing you can do to a narcissist, who would prefer to die rather than to suffer such punishment. But in all that, Ninurta also made a grave mistake: With En.ki gone, he unintentionally put Marduk in power.

To Marduk, En.ki's imprisonment was excellent news, and he could now basically do as he pleased. Being castrated, En.ki's primary worry must have been that his bloodline, the ancient En.ki-Isis lineage, would die out when he could not be there and repower it. He knew that without his pure bloodline, he couldn't claim humankind as his. He was completely out of the game. When the Matrix was created, it was the En.ki-Isis bloodline that was the prominent; the rest were random bloodlines of random survivors from the Flood.

His plans were completely shattered when Ninurta cast him down into the ABZU. He feared his lineage would eventually disappear, and he was rightfully nervous about Marduk. En.ki was powerless where he sat, but Marduk was not. He was here on

Earth, which was to his great advantage, but his time to truly shine was yet to come—he wanted to wait until humankind was ready for his coup that he kept secret to everyone back then. However, I would say that the day En.ki was put in the ABZU, he was out of the equation and has been ever since, almost like if he were dead. Yes, he had some minions here on Earth, who were still loyal to him, but as we shall see, they soon became quite unimportant and powerless, too. From the day En.ki disappeared, Marduk's goal was to completely destroy En.ki's bloodline and replace it with his. And it all started with Jesus.

Marduk presented the Jesus idea to Isis. He wanted Isis to incarnate in the Davidian Shem bloodline as the Virgin Mary and thus destroy the En.ki-Isis bloodline. Instead of letting Jesus be born from that bloodline, he was going to be born through virgin birth. Marduk's purpose was to finish En.ki's Davidian bloodline, of which both Mary/Isis and her husband, Joseph, were part of, by *not* having children with Joseph, and instead using her androgyny to create Jesus. A careful study of the Bible shows that Mary stuck to her virginity for the rest of her life and never had sex with Joseph or any other man.[39]

The plan Marduk had was to create a completely new bloodline with Isis, without En.ki's blood involved, and because Isis gave birth to Jesus androgynously, Jesus' body was purely that of Isis' and Ninurta's DNA—no En.ki DNA. To that, Marduk added his, and we got Isis-Ninurta-Marduk DNA in a mix. He wanted to take En.ki out of the equation and gain ownership of humankind. Mary was of the Natan bloodline and Joseph of his brother Solomon's—both sons of David. He managed to disrupt the Davidian line, but because of unexpected things that happened, from Marduk's perspective, he failed to take over at that time. What happened instead is very interesting and perhaps an attempt to save and free humankind. I will make my case for that, but we must tell the story in the correct order.

For the Jesus story to work, so they could use the same old narrative, they must have a "Holy" Trinity. This Trinity comprised En.ki as God, Marduk as the son, and Isis as the Holy Ghost (Spirit). Because God (En.ki) was no longer present on Earth, they must make him Omnipresent and invisible to regular people on Earth.

---

[39] LinkedIn: *Brothers of the Lord, Did Mary have children after Jesus?*

Instead of him coming to us, we would come to him in his Glorious Heaven.

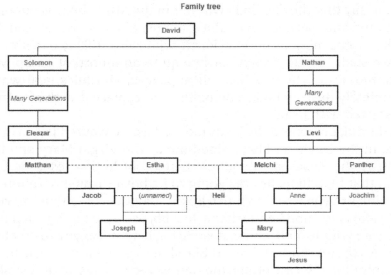

Fig. 4:1. The Davidian Family Tree.

It was a "brilliant" idea because it would benefit Marduk in more than one way. They could preserve the bloodline, they could create a new religion, and they could get a lot of loosh[40] from millions of humans worshipping them. In addition, Marduk could also receive the praise and the loosh directed to both God and Jesus because with En.ki out of the equation, Marduk could put himself as both the Father and the Son. But that was not all. The long-term goal was to preserve this new Jesus bloodline, so when the world would be ready for the Singularity, the 3% of humankind that the Overlords need to attack Orion should all have his DNA in their cyborg bodies and nothing of En.ki's. Today, genetic scientists tell us that in the next few generations, mothers will no longer give birth to children. Babies will be produced in laboratories. But for that to happen, the Marduk bloodline needs to still be active and in majority when this part of the agenda is being employed.

---

[40] A term coined by Robert Monroe, the founder of the Monroe Institute, referring to human soul energy that we give the Overlords through fear and worship to name only two. The Overlords absorb our life energy in this manner as an energetic food source, leaving us depleted.

We know very little about what Isis thought of all this. It is most likely she never managed to escape from Marduk after he forced her to create the Marduk-Isis lineage around 1200 BCE, when the Twelve Tribes of Israel were created[41] by Marduk and Isis (more about this later), and Marduk corrupted the pure Shem bloodline, which had been pure En.ki-Isis lineage, for the first time. That was 800 years after En.ki "disappeared" in 2024 BCE. Thus, the Hebrews were Marduk's and En.ki's creation. We may assume she was his prisoner of sorts or in a trance. If this was the case, she might have had little choice other than to comply. We must remember she was in the hands of the Arch Narcissist of the Universe and his psychopathic son since the beginning of the Matrix. The knowledge we have about narcissistic and psychopathic abuse on Earth tells us something. These two types of personalities rob their victim of their true personality, and they become puppets—powerless objects. Those of you who have experienced, or still experience narcissistic or psychopathic abuse can probably tell they feel like being in a trance. Isis was probably not different; after all, she is just a soul-mind with Spirit from being a "lesser" manifestation of Queen Sophia. She is like us in that sense.

It is clear from my research that Isis played the role of both the Virgin Mary and Mary Magdalene, the latter being only 12-16 years older than Jesus, according to scriptures. I would argue that Mary was about 13 years old when she gave birth to Jesus because the number 13 has major energetic implications and is a Divine number and the number of the Divine Feminine, Queen Sophia (whose role Isis was now playing). The major suspicion that Virgin Mary and Mary Magdalene were one and the same gets somewhat confirmed in Christianity, which states that Mary Magdalene was somewhere between 46 and 49 years old when Jesus died on the cross at the age of 33.[42] If the two Marys were the same Mary, Mary Magdalene was 13-16 years old when Jesus was born, which fits eerily well into our hypothesis.

I don't know whether all the details are correct in the above hypothesis, but regardless, the outcome is the same: Isis gave birth to Jesus (Marduk), and it was a "virgin birth." Now Jesus had a perfect body of pure Isis-Ninurta-Marduk bloodline.

---

[41] Ministry of Foreign Affairs: *The Twelve Tribes of Israel (ca 1200 BCE).*
[42] Usatoday.com: *How old was Jesus when he Died?*

Mary Magdalene in Gaul (France)

The Priory of Sion

5 **In 1982, journalists Michael Baigent**, Richard Leigh, and Henry Lincoln published a controversial book called *The Holy Blood and the Holy Grail*, which almost immediately became a bestseller, but also the focus of much scrutiny—not surprisingly from the clergy of the Catholic Church, but also from the Elite-controlled mainstream media, who as usual called in "experts" to debunk the content of this book. My readers might have heard of it and perhaps even read it. Author Dan Brown also used this book as an essential reference to his book, *The da Vinci Code*, many years later. As many people know, Dan Brown usually spends several years of research before he publishes a historical novel. He wants it to be as factual as possible at its core, and then he can put an intriguing level of imagination on top of that.

The Holy Blood and the Holy Grail is well researched, arguing that Jesus did not die on the cross but escaped together with Mary Magdalene to France, where they had at least one child (possibly more). The *Holy Grail* or the *Holy Graal*, means *Holy Blood* or *Royal Blood*, originating from *Sang Réal*, which in Medieval French means *Holy Blood,* suggesting that Jesus' blood supposedly ran through the veins of the Merovingian kings, who reigned in France between 481and 751 AD. This is of course blasphemy and heresy from Christian churches' perspectives, and therefore, the research was attacked and ridiculed. "Everybody knows" Jesus died on the cross (but was strangely resurrected afterward[!]). However, the attacks did little good for the clergy. I would suggest it gave even more attention to the controversial research because the book sold amazingly well, and it has nearly five stars on Amazon. The book resonates with a lot of people, which is another indication there is truth in it.

One of the big controversies is the authors' claim there was (and still is) an organization called *The Priory of Sion*, working behind the scenes to preserve and protect the Jesus-Magdalene bloodline with all their might. The authors further claim it was this secret Order that established the Knights Templar after the Military Order of the Catholic Church excavated Solomon's Temple between 1119 and 1128. It was then the Military Order changed their title to the *Knights Templar*, named after Solomon's Temple, or the Knights Templar was a public branch of the much more secret Priory of Sion, just like the *Opus Dei* is a branch of the Catholic Church. The Templar Order was eventually demolished, as we will discuss in a while, although a faction of the Order survived and has been incorporated into York Freemasonry and other diverse Orders since then. But the Priory of Sion supposedly still exists and has operated under the radar since long before Jesus was born, protecting the En.ki-Isis bloodline since more of less the beginning of the Matrix.

The controversy regarding this Order is that the Catholic Church and the Media claim it has never existed. They argue it was a charlatan in modern times who came up with this nebulous idea of such an Order, and he misled the authors of *The Holy Blood and the Holy Grail*. It is true there was such a person, but he would also be a perfect coverup for the Order, making it look ridiculous and like a hoax. If the Priory of Sion is real, which appears to be the case, they owe him for further occluding the Order, which wants to be secret, but it's more likely that the "charlatan" worked for the Order all along, and his job was to discredit it. The debunkers of the Order, of course, never took that into consideration. If I am correct in this, everything went per the plan—almost! What they probably did not expect was the enormous success of the book *The Holy Blood and the Holy Grail*.

Even if the Priory of Sion never existed, it has no bearing on the narrative of this book. The fact remains, there was a secret organization behind the scenes, keeping the supposed Jesus bloodline safe and clean for almost 500 years, until the Merovingian kings openly came to power, something I will address soon. If the Priory of Sion never existed, a very similar organization must have existed in its place, protecting the bloodline. In that sense, the validity of *that* particular Order is irrelevant. Therefore, I am using the information available about Sion, since it is certain that an Order of a similar foundation existed under that or some other name. Thus, I believe it's reasonable, for our purpose, to think of it as the Priory of Sion. For those who want to study the pros and cons of the existence of the Order, so they can build their own opinion, there is a website called *The Templar Knights* that discusses both sides of the story.[43] For even more research about the Priory of Sion, I highly recommend *The Holy Blood and the Holy Grail*. There have been, allegedly, prominent scientists and artists being members of the Priory of Sion, such as Leonardo da Vinci and Isaac Newton. Dan Brown borrowed from this information when he wrote *The da Vinci Code*.

> In The Holy Blood and the Holy Grail, Baigent, Leigh and Lincoln posit the existence of a secret society known as the Priory of Sion, which is supposed to have a long history starting in 1099 and had illustrious Grand Masters including Leonardo da Vinci and Isaac Newton. According to the authors' claims, the Priory of Sion is devoted to restoring the Merovingian dynasty, which ruled the Franks from 457 to 751, on the thrones of France and the rest of Europe. The Priory is also said to have created the Knights Templar as its military arm and financial branch.[44]

Some might say it is the Catholic Church that protects the bloodline, and this is true, but even so, the Church has their own organizations to execute such tasks. There is no lack of evidence that the Catholic Church protects a certain bloodline, whether it is Jesus' bloodline or something else, which we will come to. Just consider whom they worship—Jesus and Mary. Catholics could ask themselves why the Church worships Mary—even more so than Jesus, from what I can see. The Church, at its top level, understands beyond reasonable doubt that the Creatrix is feminine, although they will never admit to it, or the church and the entire patriarchal Mardukian religion would crumble. The Roman Catholic Church is "pagan" at its roots, and the pope functions as the middleman between God and humans, being his emissary on Earth. And God is no longer En.ki but Marduk.

---

[43] Thetemplarknight.com: *Priory of Sion.*
[44] Wikipedia.org: *The Holy Blood and the Holy Grail*

Now, let us return to Jesus and Mary Magdalene, since we have discussed the theme that there has always been an occult organization protecting the Holy Grail.

Was There a Crucifixion?

5.1. En.ki, from his supposed lofty position as God

These days, I feel certain there was a Jesus/Yeshua spreading "God's" message about, whether he did it personally or the narrative was written afterward by the four Evangelists. Marduk put his father, En.ki, in a lofty position as the Almighty God, when indeed he was the opposite; he was not in a lofty position at all but in the lowest position we can imagine, lacking all sort of power—the ABZU. Thus, even the story of his loftiness is inverted.

We know very little about the *true* story of Jesus' life. Of course, we have the canon; we have the Gnostic texts, and we have the Dead Sea Scrolls; but Mark wrote the first known gospel about 70 CE, which was approximately thirty-five years after Jesus' alleged death on the cross. Thus, it would be reasonable to assume the *Gospel of Mark* tells the most accurate story of Jesus' life, but we can't take its accuracy for granted. Mark could have been biased, and we don't know whose errand he was running. We have strong indications that Saint Paul (Saul) was an initiate in secret societies, so

59

Mark could have been, too. Other texts were written more than a century after Jesus' alleged death, and I would suggest most of them were channeled by Marduk or one of his "archangels."

Fig. 5:2. The Entombment of Christ by Caravaggio (c. 1603).

The big question many people, including scholars, have asked themselves if Jesus was crucified and resurrected, or has that been fabricated?

There are reasons to vote both for or against it, and we won't know for sure. What speaks against it is that Marduk probably would not want to put himself in the horrific situation where he was crucified, and therefore, even though crucifixions regularly happened at that time, I would suggest Marduk was never on the cross. If indeed Jesus' verdict was to be executed in this fashion, he was replaced by someone else, as the Nag Hammadi suggest. Perhaps he was supposed to be crucified, but in the last moment, the conspirators exchanged Jesus to another person, who was crucified in Jesus' place. His name was Simon of Cyrene, who was the father of two of Jesus' disciples.

> According to some Gnostic traditions, Simon of Cyrene, by mistaken identity, suffered the events leading up to the crucifixion. This is the story presented in the Second Treatise of the Great Seth,

although it is unclear whether Simon or another actually died on the cross. This is part of a belief held by some Gnostics that Jesus was not of flesh, but only took on the appearance of flesh (see also Basilides, and Swoon hypothesis).

Basilides, in his gospel of Basilides, is reported by Irenaeus as having taught a docetic doctrine of Christ's passion. He states the teaching that Christ, in Jesus, as a wholly divine being, could not suffer bodily pain and did not die on the cross; but that the person crucified was, in fact, Simon of Cyrene.[45, 46]

There is a relatively unknown Gnostic text called the *Gospel of Basilides*. Like other Gnostics, Basilides taught that salvation comes from Knowledge (Greek: Gnosis) and not faith.[47] This is what he wrote about the crucifixion:

He [Jesus] appeared on earth as a man and performed miracles. Thus he himself did not suffer. Rather, a certain Simon of Cyrene was compelled to carry his cross for him. It was he who was ignorantly and erroneously crucified, being transfigured by him, so that he might be thought to be Jesus. Moreover, Jesus assumed the form of Simon, and stood by laughing at them.[48]

A common belief in those days was that Divine beings could not suffer because they were not truly physical, which is an interesting point. People back then were completely comfortable with the thought that Divine beings were astro-physical, i.e., they often appeared in their astral bodies to use modern terms in form of an apparition. This makes me think about Jesus' resurrection because that's how it's usually described in religious texts: as an apparition.

If we play with the above theory some more, they nailed this Simon at the cross until he was dead. Then they took him down, and someone arranged a grave within a rock for him. There the deceased Simon was again replaced with Marduk, who pretended to resurrect after three days. Here is what the *Gospel of Mark* tells us:

---

[45] Cross, Frank Leslie; Livingstone, Elizabeth A., eds. (1997). "Basilides". The Oxford Dictionary of the Christian Church. Oxford University Press. p. 168. ISBN 9780192116550. LCCN 97165294. OL 767012M. Retrieved 2022-03-28 – via Internet Archive.

[46] Ehrman, Bart (2005-07-27). *Lost Christianities: The Battles for Scripture and the Faiths We Never Knew. Oxford University Press. p. 188.*

[47] Wikipedia: *Basilides.*

[48] Wikipedia: *Simon of Cyrene.*

Joseph of Arimathea is a member of the Sanhedrin, which had condemned Jesus, who wishes to ensure that the corpse is buried in
accordance with Jewish Law, according to which dead bodies could
not be left exposed overnight. He puts the body in a new shroud
and lays it in a tomb carved into the rock. The Jewish historian Josephus, writing later in the century, described how the Jews
regarded this law as so important that even the bodies of crucified
criminals would be taken down and buried before sunset. In this
account, Joseph does only the bare minimum to observe the Law,
wrapping the body in a cloth, with no mention of washing (Ta-
harah) or anointing it. This may explain why Mark mentions an
event prior to the crucifixion in which a woman pours perfume
over Jesus. Jesus is thereby prepared for burial even before his actual death. [49]

If we want to be conspiratorial here, could Joseph of Arimathea,
in the usual fashion, play both sides? He might not have been as
condemning of Jesus as Mark wants us to believe. This theory is
backed up by the *Gospel of Matthew*,

The Gospel of Matthew was written around the years 80 to 85, using the Gospel of Mark as a source. In this account Joseph of
Arimathea is not referenced as a member of the Sanhedrin, but a
wealthy disciple of Jesus.

[...]
This version suggests a more honourable burial: Joseph wraps the
body in a clean shroud and places it in his own tomb, and the word
used is *soma* (body) rather than *ptoma* (corpse). The author adds
that the Roman authorities "made the tomb secure by putting a seal
on the stone and posting the guard."[50]

Joseph hurried to make sure "Jesus" (Simon) was buried immediately after he was pronounced dead on the cross. He quickly
wrapped and put the body inside the rock, away from prying eyes.
Joseph cared little about anointing him if he was a part of Marduk's
conspiracy.

In the *Gospel of John 20:1* (KJV), it says, "Mary Magdalene went
to the tomb on the first day of the week." And *Mark 16:1-2* says,
"After Sabbath, Mary Magdalene, Mary the mother of James and Sa-
lome bought spices to anoint Jesus body, and they went to the tomb
on the first day of the week." We must ask ourselves, was

---

[49] Wikipedia: *Burial of Jesus, #Gospel of Mark*.
[50] Wikipedia: *Burial of Jesus, #Gospel of Matthews*.

anointment the true reason for the visit? Did Isis (Mary Magdalene) really have an interest in anointing Simon's body if we go for this hypothesis? After all, Marduk and Isis knew it was all a farce and couldn't care less about anointment. It is more likely that Isis as Mary entered the tomb and helped with the process of "bringing Jesus back to life," which means Simon's body was removed and Marduk took his place on the third day. It looked like he "left the tomb" on that third day when the Resurrection of Christ happened, when he was never inside the tomb in the first place. All they did was to take out Simon's body and remove the stone. Of course, in these times, people were superstitious, and many were afraid, hearing that the stone placed in front of the tomb was removed. Jesus was gone, and the guards, who had guarded the tomb on Pontus Pilate's order, were nowhere to be found. Instead, some eyewitnesses said the guards had been replaced by new, unknown guards, acting as angels, which adds to the supernatural and the Divine.

If Marduk as Jesus truly survived the crucifixion (if there was one at all), there is some evidence that Jesus/Marduk went to India after his "resurrection,"[51] while Mary Magdalene went to France. But why did Mary go to France of all places? Well, that's what we're going to investigate now.

How Mary Magdalene ended up in France

Although there are many who reject the possibility that Mary Magdalene started a new bloodline in France, there is clear evidence she was there for the rest of her life. After Jesus' alleged death (or escape), it seems as if Mary stayed in Jerusalem for a while after Marduk potentially went to India. It is likely they had agreed to meet up later to continue the Isis-Marduk bloodline by having a child.

According to history, King Herod Agrippa I started a persecution against the early Christians, and when St. James returned to Jerusalem from Spain, he was arrested and beheaded as the first of the apostles who became martyrs.[52] Soon enough, Mary was arrested as well, with the purpose of executing her. But the Jews who

---

[51] Krishna Rose: *Jesus After the Crucifixion-India-Evidence to Bridge Between East & West.*

[52] HiketheWay.com: *The Story of Santiago (Saint James)*

persecuted her were afraid of the masses and dared not execute her and some other prisoners, close to her and Jesus (which seems strange to me). So, they released Mary and a handful of other prisoners related to her, such as Maximin, one of the seventy-two disciples of Christ, Lazarus, whom Jesus resurrected from the dead, Cedonius, the blind man Jesus supposedly gave eyesight back to, and Sara, Mary's maid, and they put them on a boat and towed them off the shore of Palestine, abandoning them to the open sea.[53] However, it seems more likely that Mary, if imprisoned at all, had help from outside to escape, and that her destination was already determined, based on a grander plan she had, unbeknownst to Marduk.

Fig. 5:4. Mary Magdalene Preaching in Marseille (c. 1518),
Philadelphia, Museum of Art, Johnson Collection

After having narrowly survived rough weather, the boat eventually hit the coast of Gaul (today's France) in a town that is now called Saintes Maries de la Mer in Camargue.

There, the crew went in different directions, according to this story, and only Mary Magdalene, Lazarus, Cedonius, and Maximin traveled together. Lazarus later became the first bishop of

---

[53] Magdalenepublishing.org: *Mary Magdalene—The Provençal Tradition.*

Marseilles.[54, 55]. It ended with only Mary Magdalene and Maximin staying together and eventually reaching Aix, about 20 miles north of Marseilles.

Fig. 5:5. Scene from the Legend of Mary Magdalene, Mary Magdalene Receiving Viaticum by Sandro Botticelli (c. 1484-9), Philadelphia, Museum of Art, Johnson Collection.

Evidence of a clear alliance between Mary Magdalene and Provence in the south of France exists. Two pilgrim sites show this is likely the case—the *Basilica of Mary Magdalene in St. Maximin la Sainte Baume* and *La Sainte Baume*,[56] which is a mountain cave, located at Plan d'Aups, with a view over *Massif de la Sainte Baume*.

Maximin became the first bishop of Aix[57], and Mary Magdalene retreated to the above-mentioned mountain cave in 47 CE, and it is said she preached and eventually died about 30 years later.[58] If so, she died around 77 CE at the ripe age of 90 (according to Christian records).

In 1254, returning from the seventh Crusade, King Louis of France, on hearing of La Sainte Baume, wanted to visit La Sainte Baume with his Knights Templar (King Louis was a member of the Templar Order). This royal pilgrimage ended up having great

---

[54] *Ibid.*

[55] Catholic Encyclopedia, New Advent: *Marseilles (Massilia)*

[56] Mariemadeleine.fr.

[57] Wikipedia: *Maximinus of Aix.*

[58] HiketheWay.com: *The Story of Santiago (Saint James)*

repercussions,[59] as we shall see. I would suggest it was around this time the Knights Templar started worshipping the Mother Goddess rather than the male God, clashing with the Catholic Church, and from thereon operating under the radar.

Mary Magdalene's Body Unearthed by Templars

In 1279, Charles II (the Prince of Salerno and the Count of Provence), but also King Louis' nephew (most likely also a Templar), found out that Mary Magdalene was buried in the town of St. Maximin in the church with the same name, and on December 10, deep in the earth, he found her marble tomb. Inside lay her entire body, and in the burial place was also a wooden plate stating,

Fig. 5:6. "Here lies the body of Mary Magdalene".[60]

Eventually, the remains of Mary/Isis were moved to the *Basilica of Saint Mary Magdalene* in *St. Maximin-la-Sainte-Baume*, where her skull is on display up to this day.

---

[59] *Ibid.*
[60] *Ibid.*

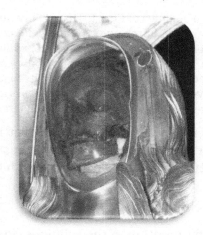

Fig. 5:7. Today the skull of Saint Mary Magdalene in a gold reliquary in the Basilica of Saint Mary Magdalene in St. Maximin-la-Sainte-Baume.

More Evidence of France's "Divinity."

There is sufficient proof from many irrefutable sources that Mary Magdalene was in France, and there she gave birth to at least one child. According to Lynn Picknett and Clive Prince in their book, *The Templar Revelation*,[61] they point out the so-called *Black Madonnas* that can be found in Southern France and a curious depiction of Mary Magdalene [not the Virgin Mary] with a child.[62]

Another big hint is that Pope Pius X (r. 1903-1914) declared France as the "Tribe of Judah of the New Covenant."[63]

But there is more. Pope Gregory IX (r. 1227-41) wrote to King Louis:

> Pope Gregory IX wrote to King St. Louis: "God, whom the heavenly legions obey, having established here below different kingdoms according to the diversity of languages and climates, has conferred on many governments special missions for the accomplishment" of his plans. And just as he once preferred the tribe of Judah to the tribes of Jacob's other sons and gave them special blessings, so he chose in preference to all the other nations of the earth for the protection of the Catholic faith and the defense of religious freedom. For this reason, "France is the kingdom of God himself, the enemies

---

[61] Amazon.com: *The Templar Revelation: Secret Guardians of the True Identity of Christ.*

[62] Thetemplarknight.com: *The Bloodline of Jesus and the Knights Templar.*

[63] Quora.com: *Where and who are the present descendants of Jesus Christ?*

of France are the enemies of Christ. That is why God loves France, because he loves the Church, which "spans the centuries and recruits legions for eternity. God loves France, which no effort has ever been able to detach entirely from God's cause. God loves France, where at no time has faith ever lost its vigor; where kings and soldiers have never hesitated to face dangers and to give their blood for the preservation of faith and religious freedom".[64]

For many, this is just a religious drivel, yet it is anything but. Now, when we understand more about what has been going on behind the scenes, letters like this one make much more sense.

Mary Magdalene's Pregnancy

What they don't mention in the religious doctrines is interesting because it has repercussions all the way up to our modern times: *Mary Magdalene bore a child in France.*

Books, such as *The Holy Blood and the Holy Grail* suggest she was carrying Jesus' child, and that this child was conceived before the crucifixion. This has, of course, been frowned upon and attacked by the Christian churches, and particularly the Catholic Church, who says Jesus never had children. I agree with the Church. I believe Mary Magdalene did *not* carry Jesus' child, although evidence points at that she did carry *some* child. The question would be, whose child?

Well, before we discuss that, let us discuss the Virgin Mary and Mary Magdalene, respectively. I hinted to earlier in this book they were one and the same. Curiously, they were both named Mary, or Mariam, which were their real names. This is a sacred name, or title, originating in Orion, being a title for Queen Sophia, aka the Queen of the Stars, the Creatrix of the Universe—the Cosmic *Mother.*

The records indicating where Jesus' mother died are confusing to say the least, and several locations are mentioned. Certain records indicate that the Virgin Mary died in Jerusalem,[65] while the same source also confusingly states she died outside of Ephesus in Turkey.[66] Other sources suggest either or. They all contradict that

---

[64] Ordodei.net: *Pope Pius X's 1908 Words on Joan of Arc, Courage, and Lukewarm Catholics*

[65] Ewtn.com: *Mary's Last Earthly Home?*

[66] *Ibid.*

she and Mary Magdalene were one and the same. Strong evidence shows at least the latter Mary died in France—there is little doubt about it. There is also another recording suggesting Mary Magdalene and the Virgin Mary both died in Ephesus.[67] This reveals a confusion regarding the two Marys, which I think is understandable because the scholars and the churches, at least not on lower to mid-levels, know the story about Marduk and Isis. So, how does that equation resolve? The fact that some records have the two Marys die at the same place indicates that they indeed were one and the same. It is highly unlikely *both* went to Turkey, and no records tell anything specific about their story in Turkey. The Virgin Mary more of less disappeared from history after Jesus' alleged death, and the only coherent story about Mary Magdalene is that she went to France, where she died, was buried, dug up, and whose remains now are on public display. My research makes me convinced the two Marys are the same person.

Now, let us return to Mary Magdalene's pregnancy. As we know, the Catholic Church worships Jesus and Mary. Again, some say the Church worships the *Virgin* Mary, while others say it's Mary *Magdalene*. Essentially, if they are one and the same, it is irrelevant. The bottom line is they worship Marduk/Jesus and Mary/Isis, and in public also En.ki (God), which makes up the true Unholy Trinity in this Matrix, with En.ki as the Father, Marduk as the Son, and Isis as the Holy Spirit. Taking on her androgynous nature, Isis impregnated herself to create the body of Jesus. She is also a hermaphrodite. Thus, she becomes the Holy Spirit. This is even hinted at through religious references (my emphasis in bold),

> In Christianity, Mary is commonly referred to as the Virgin Mary, in accordance with the belief that the Holy Spirit impregnated her, thereby conceiving her first-born son Jesus miraculously, without sexual relations with her betrothed Joseph, "until her son [Jesus] was born". The word "until" has inspired considerable analysis on whether Joseph and Mary produced siblings after the birth of Jesus or not. Among her many other names and titles are the Blessed Virgin Mary (often abbreviated to "BMV" after the Latin "Beata Maria Virgo"), Saint Mary (occasionally), the Mother of God (primarily in Western Christianity), the Theotokos (primarily in Eastern Christianity), Our Lady (Medieval Italian: Madonna), and **Queen of Heaven**... **The title "queen of heaven" had previously been**

---

[67] Brittanica: *St. Mary Magdalene.*

69

used as an epithet for a number of ancient sky-goddesses, such as Ninanna, Astarte, Ishtar and Astoreth, the Canaanite sky-goddess worshipped during the Hebrew prophet Jeremiah's lifetime.[68, 69]

The Catholic Church and all its organizations and branches (and they are many) publicly worship God, separately from Jesus to have a Holy Trinity, but the Church knows, at least on a lofty level, that God and Jesus are the same (Marduk). If the pope, and other subjects higher up in the Catholic hierarchy, get the message from "God" that Mary Magdalene's bloodline needs to be preserved and impeccably protected, we can rest assured the Church will obey and probably also be fearful about it. The Christian God, when it comes to Marduk, is an angry God if he is not being obeyed. This goes back to the Old Testament, where God was angry. As I've discussed many times, YHVH was a hybrid of En.ki and Marduk.

Let us now go back and discuss who the father of Mary Magdalene's offspring was. The most probable answer is there was no father. She was the Virgin Mary, remember? And she even created an androgynous bloodline, comprising only her and Ninurta's blood/DNA. Mary/Isis is a genetic scientist, but also a creator goddess. *I would eagerly suggest Isis was androgynous and a hermaphrodite in the incarnation of the Virgin Mary/Mary Magdalene.* She bore children that she herself impregnated if she wanted a female child, or she neglected to fertilize her egg if she wanted a male. Some researchers believe Mary gave birth to only one child in France, while others suggest there were many.

I do not believe Marduk/Jesus was the father to Mary Magdalene's child. Whether Isis and Marduk had sex is unknown (although some sources hint at that they did). From what I have concluded, it was planned that Mary/Isis should get pregnant with Jesus so the new Jesus bloodline could be protected and secured. Perhaps they had sex, and Mary pretended to be pregnant, although she made sure she never was. Thus, she tricked Marduk. If Isis impregnated herself, no one would be involved in that process besides her.

This raises an extremely interesting question: Why did Isis trick Marduk, and why was it so important to her to create a pure Isis-

---

[68] Wikipedia: *Mary, mother of Jesus, #In Christianity.*
[69] Jeremiah 44:17–19.

Ninurta bloodline, without En.ki's and Marduk's DNA?

Could it be she was attempting to save the human soul group and free us from the Matrix?

Was her plan to make sure humankind has more Isis-Ninurta blood/DNA than that of En.ki and Marduk, and thus, she can claim ownership of humankind? Was her plan to free us from the Matrix and take us back to Orion, proving her ownership, and there after setting us free? The more I research this entire subject, the more it continuously pops up as a viable option.

It is most likely that the Catholic Church thought Mary Magdalene's child was that of Jesus and Mary, and Marduk possibly thought so, too, believing he and Isis departed with Isis being pregnant with his child. The Catholic Church likely thought Jesus and Mary, the latter being a representative of the Divine Feminine, wanted to start a pure Divine bloodline in France, and this bloodline must be well protected.

Thus, my hypothesis is that Isis pretended to carry Jesus' child, so the Catholic Church would protect *her* bloodline. The child, perhaps unbeknownst to all to begin with, was of the pure Isis-Ninurta bloodline. Isis could, of course, have chosen her already created androgynous species for the occasion, but she needed to show the Roman Catholic Church that she was pregnant, and her previous creation was not as pure anymore. Therefore, she must carry yet another child.

The Church was fast to respond, and this is where the Priory of Sion (or whatever the Order's real name was) came into the picture. The Priory was an undercover Order of the Catholic Church, and its entire purpose has been to protect what they thought was the Jesus-Magdalene bloodline. If this is what happened, it was a brilliant move by Isis. As conveyed in the WPP, she created an Isis-Ninurta bloodline, and now, protected by her unsuspicious enemy, she created a secure and protected version of that bloodline, thus fooling everybody (at least for some time). There are different theories and hypotheses about what really happened, but from what I learned during the WPP years and wrote in the WPP (more about this later), I think the hypothesis I chose to develop here is the most likely, considering what happened many centuries later...

So, Mary eventually died at the age of 90, and her 3-UC moved on; but her pure Divine bloodline lived on, carefully protected by the Order, away from public scrutiny. I would suggest the offspring of this child of Isis was strictly controlled and could only go into matrimony with chosen partners, which is how it has worked since then within royal families to keep their bloodlines as pure as possible.

I want the reader to think about what *Royal* truly means in the cases we are discussing. We call the monarchies of the world the *royal families*, with a *divine right to rule*. We have all heard those terms. Most people think that royal is just another term for kings and queens, but nothing could be further from the truth. Royal means of *Orion blood*. Who in Orion is royal? Is it En.ki? Marduk? Khan En.lil? No, it's Queen Sophia. Here on Earth, Isis, as the spirited daughter of the Queen, and educated by her, is the Royal representative on Earth. If her blood is not floating in the monarchs' veins, they are not royal. Therefore, they have Orion blood/DNA. This has been severely diluted over the last 2,000 years, but the reader gets the point. Moreover, all royalties are 3-UC, i.e., they have soul-mind-spirit body. The Overlords, and even Isis, need royal humans to inhabit these bodies.

At the same token, the human soul group is also royal because we have the Queen's Spirit. We are a *royal species*. So, why then are we distinguishing between the monarchal royalties and the royal soul group in its entirety? Because the old kings and queens had more royal blood running through their physical bodies than we do, contaminated as we are with En.ki's, Marduk's, and later, Ereškigal's blood. I think Isis' purpose was to not let the monarchies spread the Isis-Ninurta bloodline; she wanted to distribute it among the general population, so she could claim humankind for herself. If my hypothesis is correct, she unfortunately failed, as we shall see.

Negative Blood Types

When I asked my Orion source why people have different blood types, the answer was they were different experiments. Now I believe I understand what he meant because something happened the other day. In a narrative I read, which was unrelated to blood types, it was mentioned that O- was the blood type of the Isis bloodline that she created at Lake Baikal. Although this was said in passing, it triggered the curiosity in me, and I decided to research it.

I started by researching red hair, and according to science, there is no connection between red hair and negative blood types. They say the gene for red hair, *MC1R*, is found on chromosome 16, and the gene for Rh factor is on chromosome 1[70]. Therefore, they can't be connected. Although, according to scientific studies (and without being a scientist myself), this is probably correct, but does this go for all redheads? Not all redheads are of Isis' bloodline.

The reason I am suggesting this is because of other information I stumbled upon, arguing that Rh-negative is royal blood. If this is true, it explains a few things: Let's say that Isis' bloodline indeed is O-, we also have other negative types, such as A- and B-. Are these perhaps En.ki's and Marduk's blood types? Playing with thoughts, we also have AB-, which would be a mix of En.ki's and Marduk's blood (the En.ki-Isis and the Marduk-Isis bloodlines). Those of positive blood types would, in that case, be of the Marduk-Ereškigal lineage, which most humans are these days.

Expanding further on this idea, and if I am correct so far, couldn't it be that they secure the negative blood types in the sense that those with these blood types can't procreate with regular humans? It would cause a miscarriage. In modern times, scientists have figured out how to remedy this, so a couple with a mix of positive and negative blood types, respectively, can have children. However, it didn't use to be that way. Therefore, the royal bloodlines were secured. A male royal could therefore have sex with a peasant, knowing she could not carry his child, unless she had a negative blood type, as well. Reversely, a royal female could have sex with a regular man without giving birth, although this probably didn't happen too often, since these women could still get pregnant but had to go through the struggle of a miscarriage.

This can very well be why certain bloodlines have survived the tests of time. Royals, as we know, marry others of royal blood.

What about "regular" people today, who are Rh-negative, are they royal? I would suggest they are, even if the royalties in their ancestry line may go far back in time. They are of the Isis pure bloodline, the En.ki-Isis bloodline, or that of Marduk-Isis. If they are AB-, they are probably a mix of the two latter. Not all royals became kings and queens, and bloodlines quickly spread out like branches on a tree, and now common people can be Rh-negative, too, as we know.

---

[70] Thetech.org: *Is there a link between red hair and Rh negative blood?*

The Merovingian Long-Haired Kings

6 **_Note: In Appendix B at the end_** _of this book, there are two links, leading to the complete family trees of the French and British royal dynasties, respectively. It's important to follow these family trees while reading the following chapters while reading the book. When I start discussing the different kings and queens and royal houses, it may quickly feel abstract and confusing unless you have these guides. I suggest you bookmark them on your computer and pull them up as you read further in the book._

Fig. 6:1. King Childeric I), the first Merovingian King, also portrayed as the King of Hearts in regular modern playing cards. Playing cards are all portraying the long-haired Merovingian kings. Below his portrait is the emblem of a crown with three Orion bees in the midst.

King Merovech of Belgium

For more than 400 years, the Priory of Sion kept the bloodline hidden, until 457 AD, when the pope put the first Merovingian King, Childeric I (440-481) on the throne of the Franks.

According to mainstream history, the word Merovingian possibly comes from the supposed father of Childeric I, whose name was Merovech (also, Mérovée or Merowig) (411-458). Although historians are uncertain of Merovech's existence, it is likely he was a real person. He is known as being the father of the Merovingian dynasty and allegedly reigned in today's Belgium around 450 until his death in around 458.

Merovech's Mother Raped by Sea Monster

There is a very interesting story about Merovech. In those days, it was said his mother went swimming in the ocean one day, when she was raped by a "Quinotaur," which is a fabled creature, corresponding with Neptune,[71, 72] whom, as we know, is related to En.ki. This is stunning if we put it in the context of this book's narrative. It brings about yet a suggestion:

This woman, never named, was thus the grandmother of the first Merovingian king. Historians are uncertain, but many of them agree that Chlodio, a King of Belgium, was this woman's husband, who probably thought their offspring, Merovech, was *his* son, when he was not. The records of the Merovingian bloodline before the first king, Cederic I, are mostly lacking. Of course, this woman was not raped by a sea monster, but it's a typical mythical metaphor we see so often in ancient texts and religious doctrines and beliefs. Let us say Isis tried to secure her own bloodline after she separated from Jesus, by letting the Catholic Church protect it, thinking it was Jesus' bloodline. Hundreds of years later, Marduk figured out what Isis had done, and furiously, he interfered. Thus, he impregnated Merovech's mother with his own DNA, and thus, he reestablished the Jesus Isis-Ninurta-Marduk bloodline. *It is important to note that En.ki's bloodline had by then been completely erased.* So, Marduk raped her, while taking on the role of "Neptune-Oannes," the

---

[71] Merovingians, *The Past, The Present, & Future kings: The rape of Chlodio's Wife and the Birth of Merovee.*
[72] Wikipedia: *Quinotaur.*

"Fisher King" (another title for Jesus, as we will detail in an upcoming section), "half fish, half human," also discussed in the WPP:

Fig. 6:2. Oannes (left), and the Pope (right) with his miter (fish head).

Ea was the later Akkadian name for Prince En.ki, the god of the Sumerian city Eridu, said to be the first known city on Earth. Ea was also called the "Fish of Heaven", and Oannes was half fish and half Oannes, by the way, is the inspiration for the Pope's miter or fish-hat, indicating that the Vatican is actually worshipping Prince En.ki/Oannes as their real Jesus Christ.[73]

From this interference, Marduk and Isis (indirectly) gave birth to the father of the first Merovingian king, Childeric I (fig. 6:1). Some even consider his father, Merovech, to be the first Merovingian king, except he was King of Belgium and not of Francia. Therefore, his son, Cederic I, is by most historians and genealogists deemed the first Merovingian king—the first King of the Franks. So, the Holy Grail lineage changed from Isis-Ninurta to Marduk-Isis-Ninurta even before the first king of Francia was born, the way it was supposed to be from Jesus and on, according to Marduk's plan. But because of the rape, the Jesus-Magdalene bloodline was finally established.

As I suggested earlier, I think it was never Isis' plan to put her Isis-Ninurta bloodline in the royal houses. This could have been Marduk's idea after he raped Merovech's mother. It is possible he let Sirians incarnate into the Priory of Sion brotherhood, convincing its members it was a good idea to hide the bloodline in plain site

---

[73] WPP, *The Fourth Level of Learning*, p. 51, op. cit.

within the royal houses. This way, Marduk could have a better control over the situation. This is pure speculation, of course. It may also be that Isis had already planned to put her bloodline in kings and queens—we simply don't know.

With the sea monster in mind, it is interesting that the child of the raped woman, who undoubtedly must have been of Isis-Ninurta blood, was named Merovech, which means *Sea-Bull*[74] (the Sea being a metaphor for En.ki as Oannes, representing the main male bloodline, and the Bull being Zeus[75], in Greek mythology representing both En.ki and Marduk at different times).

How the Merovingian Bloodline was Maintained

Childeric I died in 481, but it is uncertain when he was born. Historians have speculated back and forth, but it seems reasonable he was born around 438-440. He married the Thuringian queen, Basina, with whom he had a son, Clovis[76], who became Clovis I, the second king of the Merovingians. Wikipedia says Queen Basina was a "runaway wife" from the King of Thuringia, which seems to be another cover story. Who, in history, is the "runaway queen" who tries to escape Marduk, her husband? Isis. This is what Wikipedia has to say [my emphasis in bold]:

> During the reign of Childeric I [...] the Frankish King married the runaway wife of the King of the Thuringians, **but the story may be distorted**.[77]

Moreover [my emphasis in **bold**],

> Gregory of Tours reported that Childeric I was exiled from Roman Gaul for a period, and during that time he went to the kingdom of Thuringia. When he returned, Basina came with him, although she had been married to the king there, Bisinus. **She herself took the initiative to ask for the hand of Childeric I, king of the Franks, and married him. For as she herself said, "I want to have the most powerful man in the world, even if I have to cross the ocean for him"**.[78]

---

[74] https://en.wikipedia.org/wiki/Merovingian_dynasty
[75] Cedarhurst.org: *Mythology of the Bull.*
[76] Britannica: *Clovis I*
[77] Wikipedia.org: *Thuringii #First Appearances*
[78] Wikipedia.org: *Basina of Thuringia #Biography*

Our history is full of hints, obviously. In addition to the runaway wife of a king (big clue right there), she also tells Childeric she only wants the most powerful man in the world,

Fig. 6:3. King Childeric I and Queen Basina (Isis?)

"even if [she] has to cross the ocean for him." Very interesting statement. Since Thuringia was located on the European mainland, just like Francia (France), she crossed no ocean to see him. But "someone" crossed the ocean (or the sea, rather) from the Middle East to Gaul (France during the life of Jesus). This woman was Mary Magdalene. *Therefore, I strongly suggest Queen Basina was Queen Isis incarnated.* I also argue that as the Queen of Thuringia, she also might have inserted the Jesus-Magdalene bloodline there, so the two monarchies could interbreed in the future to avoid too much incest. For that purpose, Isis also married Cederic to avoid too many offspring between siblings in the beginning of the Merovingian Dynasty.

Thus, Childeric I and Isis, incarnated as Basina, had children. Clovis was the eldest son, and he and his siblings remained of the bloodline. From thereon, the Merovingian bloodline became self-propelled without too much inbreeding. The kings could, for the most part, marry their cousins, and members of other dynasties, where the princesses were also of "true blood." If the Merovingian dynasty ever weakened, Isis could incarnate and be a breeder again. It appears that Isis was Marduk's prisoner and breeder again, perhaps being found and captured after the Neptune rape, and since then, she has been quite trapped. I believe Marduk keeps track of her incarnations, and most likely even forces her to incarnate in certain bodies, and that she has little choice in the matter. *They need her as much as they need us!*

This has been a challenging section for the reader, I'm sure, keeping track of all names. So, let's create a timeline to get a clearer overview. Here are the players on the Merovingian scene, their spouses and offspring, and the approximate time when they lived:

King Chlodio of Belgium (d. 448).

Wife of Chlodio unnamed (the woman Marduk raped and impregnated) Chlodio died around 435.

Merovech, King of Belgium, the son of Chlodio (although it's more likely Merovech was the son of Marduk, not of Chlodio because of the rape)

Unnamed wife of Merovech, probably a sister (no records).

Childeric I, the first Merovingian, King of the Franks, son of Merovech and his sister(?) (c. 440-481).

Queen Basina, former Queen of Thuringia, wife of Childeric I (438-477). She was probably an incarnation of Isis.

Clovis I, the second Merovingian king, son of Cederic and Basina/Isis.

There are many interesting things to say about the carefully protected Merovingian kings. As soon as they started their reign, they were forced not to cut their hair for the rest of their lives. If they did, they could no longer rule and would be dethroned and put in monasteries. Long hair was controversial at the time because the general population usually kept their hair short. Therefore, people around the world knew them as "the long-haired kings." Our history does not convincingly explain why these kings had to keep their hair, but it's explained in the WPP that long hair, both in men and women, work as an "antenna," so they can more easily connect with the metaphysical realm, such as the astral, but even with the KHAA, i.e., the Spirit Universe (Orion). Maria Oršić and the women of the Vril Society in the early to mid-20th Century knew this very well, and they used this technique to channel. We can therefore assume the Merovingians used their hair to better connect with the astral. Perhaps Marduk was in direct contact with many or all of them?

Another peculiar thing about these kings is that most of them did not reign in the traditional manner. They just functioned as royal "icons," i.e., they usually didn't do much. Instead, they handed over royal matters to their mayors, who were the second highest in rank within the Frankish court. So, it was the mayors who held the true power.

Moreover (and this was discussed in the WPP, the Second Level of Learning), one of the Merovingians symbols was the bee, which is an Orion symbol, later also adopted by Napoleon and the Swedish monarchy. If you review the picture of Cederic I (fig. 6:1), you notice a symbol comprising a crown with three bees beneath the portrait.

Charles Martel, Pepin the Short, and Charlemagne

The Merovingian dynasty remained unbroken and protected for about 300 years until 751, when King Cederic III (c. 717 – c. 754) was in power.

Fig. 6:4. Charles Martel, Mayor of Francia.

In 718, Charles Martel (not a Merovingian) became the Mayor of the Franks and therefore the most powerful man in Francia. After the death of King Theuderic IV in 737, Martel, as the surrogate ruler, reigned without a king, and he was now the mayor of both the Palace of Neustria in the west and Austrasia in the northeast, making him enormously powerful. It should be noted that during the time when the Merovingian dynasty was seated on the throne of Francia, their empire comprised a big part of the European continent, save England and Scandinavia. It was not because of the kings, but mainly because of the mayors who ruled behind the scenes. This can be loosely compared to today's United States of America, where the President has the power in the mind of the population, but behind the scenes, it's the Vice President and the President's Advisor who sit with the power, at least in Pentagon.

Fig. 6:5. King Childeric III (r. 741-751)

When Charles Martel died in 741, his sons, Carloman and Pepin the Short, became co-mayors of the palace. However, there was a younger half-brother named Grifo, and their brother-in-law, Odilo, Duke of Bavaria, who revolted over Carloman's and Pepin's positions and wanted a part of that power. This revolt probably played a role in their decision to put another Merovingian king on the throne, Cederic, the son of either Chilperic II or Theuderic IV (historians are uncertain). After a six-year vacancy, a new king would add legitimacy to their reign. In those days, the kings were merely puppets. Eventually, Pepin the Short took the crown for himself.

> Pepin sent letters to Pope Zachary, asking whether the title of king belonged to the one who had exercised the power or the one with the royal lineage. The pope responded that the real power should have the royal title as well. In 751, Childeric was dethroned and tonsured. His long hair was the symbol of his dynasty, and thus of the royal powers he enjoyed; by cutting it, they divested him of all

royal prerogatives. Once dethroned, he was confined to the Benedictine monastery of Saint-Bertin in Saint-Omer, while his son Theuderic was sent to the monastery of Saint-Wandrille.

There are conflicting accounts of exactly when Childeric died, with some sources claiming as early as 753, while others state that his death occurred as late as 758.[79]

The above text mentions Cederic III being tonsured. What does that mean? If you look at his portrait (fig. 6:5), you see he had a very long hair, in a proper Merovingian manner. Pepin dethroned him by forcing him to have his hair cut and his scalp shaved. Thus, he could no longer be king per Frankish law, and he was now confined to a life in a monastery. He died young (as they often did) shortly after.

Fig. 6:6. Pepin the Short

Once again, the Frankish throne was vacant, and on July 28, 754, Pope Zachary anointed Pepin and his sons Charles and Carloman as kings of the Franks and patricians of the Romans, but the Pope's right to do so is doubtful.[80]

With Pepin being anointed, it was the end of the Merovingian dynasty, although the Merovingian bloodline still survived and was

---

[79] Wikipedia: *Childeric III, #Life*
[80] Wikipedia: *Donation of Pepin*

protected by the Priory of Sion, which had failed to safeguard both Isis' pure bloodline before Marduk intervened and the Merovingian dynasty. These things happen, of course, because in the seats of power, there is always competition, and there are usually usurpers taking over eventually. Pepin became the first king of the Carolingian dynasty, of which the famous Charlemagne was a later king. The purpose of the orders, protecting the Isis-Ninurta bloodline today, is still working on putting a new Merovingian line in power, primarily working through the Priory of Sion, the Order of St. John, and the Rosicrucian Order.

Although Childeric III was the last Merovingian king, the bloodline survived on the female side, and the Carolingians, taking over, said they would take Merovingian princesses as wives. This seems to have been the case on more than one occasion, since there are some hints about this:

> Charlemagne's maternal grandfather was named Charibert, a forename that also occurs in the Merovingian dynasty (two Merovingian Kings were named Charibert). His mother, Bertrada, is speculated to have been the daughter of King Theuderic III (or Theoderic; his name is spelled both ways in the original sources), which would explain how her son came by his name. Charlemagne also had an illegitimate son named Theodoric, another common Merovingian forename (as suggested by the possible parentage of Bertrada of Prüm), and, of course, he gave his third son a name very similar to that of Clovis (Louis the Pious' name is written Hludowicus in the original Latin sources, which very similar to Chlodovechus, which is how Clovis' name is rendered, and we know that the name Louis is derived from the Old Frankish *Hlōdowik), if he did not name him directly after that famous Merovingian or one of his descendants. Another possible argument in favor of a Merovingian connection is the fact that Charlemagne's fourth son was named Hlotar (Lothar), which name Louis gave his eldest son, which appeared in the Merovingians in the form of Hlodar or Chlothacar. So, while we have no direct evidence, the transmission of these names into the Carolingian stock suggests a possible connection.[81]

---

[81] Quora.com: *Were the Carolingians in any way related to the Merovingians, and were the Bourbons descended from the Merovingians? Op. cit.*

Symbols of Mary Magdalene

The Lily

7 **Now we need to return to the** Virgin Mary, before Baby Jesus was born. When it was established that the Virgin Mary was pregnant with Jesus, the gospels say the Archangel Gabriel visited Mary, giving her a lily "in recognition of her purity[82,83]." Tradition tells us that when Mary received the lily, it was without a scent, but as she held it in her hand, an exquisite fragrance arose from it. Gabriel also brought her a violet, which bloomed and blossomed outside her window. Thus, Mary said to Gabriel, "Here am I, the servant of the Lord," and accepted God's plan for her to give birth to Jesus.[84]

The lily has been a symbol for the Jesus-Magdalene bloodline ever since the "archangel" allegedly gave a lily to Mary as a gift. There are countless esoteric Christian paintings, predominantly from Medieval times and earlier, where painters, deeply initiated into different secret societies and occult orders, portray Mary holding a lily, or her being surrounded by them. But why *many* lilies? Perhaps because later, the Virgin Mary as Mary Magdalene gave birth to more than one offspring in France?

---

[82] University of Dayton (udayton.edu): *Flowers of the Annunciation, op. cit.*
[83] lpm.missouri.edu: *Madonna Lily: Beauty through the Ages.*
[84] *Ibid.*

Fig. 7:1. Mary, surrounded by lilies.

With the royal symbol of the lily in mind, now notice how the Merovingian kings, in most of their portraits, carry a royal staff (fig. 7:2). Close in on the tip of the staff, and you can see the lily, the symbol of the Jesus-Davidian bloodline. It should be proof enough right there, but even so, there is much more to tell.

The Divine Right to Rule

The saying, *divine right to rule,* was coined by King James I, who authorized the King James version of the Bible. What he said is embedded within the following quote:

> Divine right is the notion that royalty is given divine sanction to rule. In the words of England's King James I (r. 1603–1625): "The State of MONARCHIE is the supremest thing upon earth: For Kings are not only GOD'S Lieutenants upon earth, and sit upon GOD'S

throne, but even by GOD himself they are called GODS."[85]

Fig. 7:2. King Clovis I with his royal staff, topped with a lily.

King James said it all in two sentences.

Who is God? After En.ki's imprisonment, it's Marduk. Whose lieutenants are the monarchs? Marduk's.

Still, the Merovingian kings were very reluctant to rule, saying they did *not* have the divine right to rule. This must have been related to that they were at the mercy of the mayors, but that changed with the Carolingians and from there on. The first few kings, however, *were* dedicated to their role as kings, but their ambitions were watered down as the kingship descended. But in these echelons of powers, the weak never survive. If a ruler or someone in power shows weakness, there is always someone else ready to take the position, as we shall see.

The Rose

The rose is another symbol connected with Mary Magdalene, the petals opening to secret and forbidden knowledge. [86] From here, we also have the name the *Rosicrucian Order* and all their

---

[85] Daily.jstor.org: *Making Sense of the Divine Right of Kings, op. cit.*

[86] Sanmiguelicons.com: *Iconography of St. Mary Magdalene: symbolism and meaning.*

different ancient and modern branches. As we will explore later, the Rosicrucian Order, or the Order of the Rosi Cross, is another secret society, connected with yet other secret societies and orders with a purpose to protect the Holy Grail.

Fig. 7:3. The Rosicrucian Cross with the rose midst

This Order of the Rose is an Order calling up wisdom and knowledge from the Templar *Order of St. John* in France, possibly showing Mary Magdalene had more than one child and upon that, Mary's alleged sexual connection with John the Baptist. Albeit the latter is not impossible, the narrow true age span between Mary and John the Apostle (who supposedly was the offspring, as suggested below), speaks against it, in my opinion:

> "The Bride: I am the Rose of Sharon, and the Lily of the valleys. Solomon: As the lily among thorns, so is my love among the daughters." Rose Windows of churches and cathedrals. They are, in fact, more like chrysanthemums. They carved old confessionals with a five-petaled roses *[sic]* to assure parishioners, who couldn't read, that anything said in the confessional would be confidential. Flowers unfold their secret fragrance and beauty.

> In France there is an Essene Masonic secret society called the Order of Saint John, whose members claim to be Desposyni, a branch of descendants of Jesus and Mary Magdalene. Their legend purports that John the Apostle was born to John the Baptist and Mary Magdalene. The legend says that after John the Baptist was beheaded, Jesus married his sister-in-law, Mary Magdalene, and adopted her son John. This would have been a respectable outcome for a widow

in Mary Magdalene's time.[87]

But who knows? After all, Isis is the goddess of love, mothership, healing, *sexuality*, and war.

The Egg

Fig. 7:4 Mary, holding an egg (red in original).

In the *WPP, The Second Level of Learning*, I conveyed that the egg, as well as the bee, are symbols of Orion. Thus, we have Easter eggs, a supposedly egg-shaped planet, and an egg-shaped Universe, all with "shells" (boundaries) around them (as above, so below). Adding to this, we also have Mary holding an egg—a red egg, i.e., a "blood egg," symbolizing Jesus' resurrection[88], but also, more importantly, the royal bloodline.

_____

[87] *Ibid., op. cit.*
[88] Sanmiguelicons.com: *Iconography of St. Mary Magdalene: symbolism and meaning.*

The Holy Ampulla

Fig. 7:5. Mary Magdalene pouring Jesus' blood into the cup, the Symbol of the Holy Grail. This "Divine Oil" became later a symbol for Jesus' blood in the royal anointment process.

There is more hard evidence that Jesus' bloodline was later reestablished after his death. This is from Wikipedia:

> So, the fleur-de-lis stood as a symbol of the king's divinely approved right to rule. The thus "anointed" kings of France later maintained that their authority was directly from God. A legend enhances the mystique of royalty by informing us that a vial of oil—the Holy Ampulla—descended from Heaven to anoint and sanctify Clovis as King, descending directly on Clovis or perhaps brought by a dove to Saint Remigius. One version explains that an angel descended with the Fleur-de-lis ampulla to anoint the king. Another story tells of Clovis putting a flower in his helmet just before his victory at the Battle of Vouillé. Through this propagandist connection to Clovis, the fleur-de-lis has been taken in retrospect to symbolize all the Christian Frankish kings, most notably Charlemagne.[89]

Now compare this to the following painting of Mary Magdalene,

---

[89] Wikipedia: *Fleur-de-lis #France.*

holding the *Holy Ampulla*, symbolically containing the Holy Oil, which represents anointment of the "Divine Rulers" (the Jesus-Isis blood/DNA.

We are now beginning to see how important the Jesus bloodline, aka the Marduk-Isis-Ninurta bloodline has been since the beginning of the Matrix. But as we will continue discussing, there has always been a war between bloodlines, and there still is.

The Holy Grail in Christian Churches

Another symbol of Mary and the Holy Grail is the practice of Communion in virtually all Christian churches, including the Catholic Church. The person taking the Communion kneels before the altar, accepts the oblate, symbolizing the flesh of Christ, and drinks from a cup of red wine, symbolizing the Holy Grail, symbolizing he or she is drinking Jesus' blood. Thus, it's very important that the wine is red; white wine does not represent blood and will not suffice.

Familiar to most readers, the following is what the priest or preacher says, with some derivations, when he or she lets you drink from the Holy Cup: "The Body of Christ, the bread of heaven/The Blood of Christ, the cup of salvation."[90]

Who was the Archangel Gabriel in the New Testament?

I know that with the publication of this book, there will be many questions asking who the Archangel Gabriel was in this story, so I will answer it here for all to read. Unbeknownst to most, the Archangel Gabriel is not a name but a title, just like many "names" (titles) we stumble upon in religious and ancient texts. Archangel Gabriel, at least within the Matrix, is a title with certain tasks attached to it. Therefore, the Gabriel who visited Mary could be any of the Overlords, but in this case, most likely an apparition of Marduk before he incarnated in Jesus' body.

---

[90] Episcopalchurch.org: *Words of Administration (of Communion).*

Pepin the Short and the Carolingian Kings

8 **After much research, it seems** like the usurpation of the Merovingian throne was a power-hungry human endeavor happening out of necessity, but I could be wrong. While researching this, I was suspicious of Pepin the Short, the first Carolingian monarch, being merely a mayor, rising to power of the mighty Frankish Empire. I must add that although I have not found evidence of the Pippinids to be of the Jesus-Magdalene bloodline, it does not mean they were not. But leaving that to what may, it was still necessary to overthrow the Merovingians. I suppose Pepin might not have been of the Grail bloodline, but as mentioned earlier, the Carolingians apparently married Merovingian princesses[91]. For instance, Pepin married Bertha "Broadfoot," who allegedly was a Merovingian princess, and they were the parents of the famous Carolingian king, Charlemagne (my comment in brackets [ ] and bold).

> PIPPIN (Pepin) THE SHORT, King of the Franks, married BERTHA (Bertrada) 'Broadfoot'--they were the parents of Emperor Charlemagne. Bertha was the daughter of CHARIBERT, Count of Laon (seen 720-747), by his wife Bertrada. Count Charibert's father is said to be MARTIN of Laon, who in turn is said to be a son of ANSEGISEL and BEGGA ... Count Charibert's mother was named

---

[91] "Charles' [Martel] successors, who did seize the throne, went out of their way to establish their legitimacy by marrying Merovingian princesses." – *Holy Blood and the Holy Grail, p. 358* (Kindle version).

BERTHA, and she was a Merovingian. This female-line descent through the family King Pippin's wife Bertha is the only fully establish Carolingian descent from the Merovingian Dynasty. Unfortunately, the ancestry of Charibert's mother Bertha is uncertain. She could have been a daughter of one of the Merovingian kings **[I would suggest the sister of Cederic III, the last Merovingian]** living at about that time, but others says *[sic]* her father was a man named THEODARD **[Theuderic IV]** (who would in turn be of Merovingian descent).Thus, the only road by which a Carolingian descent from the Merovingians may be established is still under construction.[92]

Apparently, the Merovingian bloodline, diluted or not, continued with the Carolingians dynasty.

There is another quote from the same reference I want to include because it's well-researched, and it brings us to a potential clue to whether the Merovingian bloodline survived until modern times:

These and similar possible descents were discussed by the late Sir Anthony Richard Wagner is his two books ENGLISH GENEALOGY and PEDIGREE AND PROGRESS. In the latter book, he also shows intermarriage between the Merovingian House and the Oiscing Kings of Kent in England. ECGBERT, King of Wessex, was the son of EAHLMUND, Sub-king of Kent, who either married an Oiscing heiress or else was himself descended from one, so it is very likely that the Pre-Conquest Kings of England (Ecgbert's family) were descendants of the Merovingians through the Kings of Kent. However, once again we find that the exact pedigree cannot be established. Others here might know more about the Kentish connection to the Merovingians and could offer you more assistance. Other than this one, I am unaware of other links between the Merovingians and later European families.

(One of the legendary pedigrees of the Habsburgs made them male-line descendants of the Merovingians through a certain LIGIBERT, supposedly a son of one of the Kings of Austrasia--but that pedigree is most unacceptable, to say the least.)[93]

The reader may ask why the protectors of the Grail keep the Merovingian bloodline so sacred that they want to reestablish it in modern times. After all, isn't everything about the Marduk-Isis-Ninurta bloodline, anyway, Merovingian or not? The reason is not

---

[92] Groups.google.com (Jared Olar): *Carolingian - Merovingian LINK?*
[93] *Ibid. op. cit.*

only because the bloodline might have been diluted with the usurpation of Pepin the Short, but also because much later in history, Marduk created the Marduk-Ereškigal bloodline, which we will get into when we're at that point in history. Thus, he replaced the Jesus-Isis bloodline in the European dynasties, and the Holy Grail line was then almost completely extinct. The modern Rosicrucians, and a few other beforementioned secret societies, currently work on putting the Jesus-Magdalene based Merovingian line back into power.

It is important to realize that Pepin's (or Pippin's) usurpation of the Frankish throne was not a military *coup d'état*. The mayors had been ruling the Franks behind the scenes for a few generations because, although the Merovingians were of Mary Magdalene's descendants, they were not strong rulers. The mayors brought Francia from a divided country to an empire. And as we all know, in the royal courts of virtually all countries or empires, there are intrigues and hunger for power. The last few generations of Merovingians died young, usually in their 20s, for (apparently) different reasons; but one can't help but suspect a conspiracy. Before these young kings died, they had offspring (interbred), but because the kings died early, their offspring were often between nine and thirteen years old when they became kings, incapable of ruling an empire. This was, of course, convenient for the mayors, who then had free range to do what they wanted. They still needed the Merovingian kings in apparent power, if ever so impotent, because of a Catholic law that *only Merovingian kings (of Jesus' bloodline) had the divine right to rule*. It's easy to suspect a conspiracy, where the mayors made sure the kings died young, without any substantial education in how to rule a country, and even less, an empire.

I would argue that Pepin, although convincing and glib, should not be given all the credit for his rise to power. This had most likely been planned over generations from the mayors' dominance. There was a vacancy in rulership between the time of Theuderic IV and Cederic III (the second last and the last king, respectively), lasting 20 years. During that time, Pepin the Short had due time to show his excellence in warfare and strategy. After that, it was necessary to put one last Merovingian king on the throne (Cederic III) to safeguard the power of the Carolingian dynasty against other usurpers while Pepin worked behind the scenes to take over. Weak leadership on behalf of the empire invited invasions. Francia needed to show a strong dynasty outward to the world, although Cederic III was no more than a puppet and filled no other function than to hold his title. He spent much of his days being carried around in a cart, showing himself to the public. He was a marionette, and that was his entire purpose until they didn't need him anymore.

Fig. 8:1. The procedure of cutting Cederic III's hair (Pepin the Short to the right, wearing a crown).

Everyone, from the person on the street, all the way to the papacy, noticed the impotence of the monarchy. Therefore, Pepin the Short agreed and said to the pope that something must be done, presenting his case wisely. He had applied an ancient formula that always seems to work, *problem-reaction-solution*. The majors created a *problem* by ruling instead of the kings, which weakened the monarchy. Pepin stood behind people's opinion that something must be done *(reaction)*, and then he presented the *solution*, which was to anoint him, allowing him to become the next King of Francia. He said that the Merovingian kings could accomplish nothing these days, while Pepin and his mayor forerunners, behind the scenes, had made most royal decisions and accomplished the hard work of keeping the Frankish empire expanding, also protecting the Frankish citizens in the process. Meanwhile, at the Frankish borders, the Germans, and others. stood ready to invade the Franks. Moreover, Vikings from Scandinavia were invading England and would most certainly attack Francia in due time. Even though the mayors had power, they were limited by the Constitution. Thus, wasn't it better that he, Pepin, became the King of Francia instead of the impotent King Cederic III?

Pope Zachary agreed, and as a compromise, not to break the law that only Merovingians could sit on the throne of the Franks, Pepin offered to marry Bertha, a Merovingian princess.

Pepin had achieved his goal and became Pepin I of France. As conveyed earlier, Cederic III was forced to have his head shaved, spending the rest of his brief life at a monastery, stripped of the little power he had. According to Frankish law, he had no choice after the haircut; without his long hair, he could not rule. Because his only son was put in a monastery, too, there were no more Merovingians who could inherit the throne.

That was the end of the Merovingian royal dynasty, and the line of the Carolingians, starting with Pepin I, ended with King Louis V in 987, where after the *House of Capet* ruled France.

On the Priory of Sion and the Knights Templar

9 **Much can be said about the** Priory of Sion, but I will not go into every detail about this order. Many prominent artists became members of the Order over time, such as Leonardo da Vinci and Victor Hugo (both Grandmasters), and scientists, such as Isaac Newton. We often see esoteric paintings from Medieval times having much esoteric symbolism in them. These artists were, of course, either Templars, members of the Priory of Sion, Rosicrucians, or they belonged to some other offspring from any of the above, all there to protect the Royal Bloodline. The more I investigate this, the more all tributaries of the river seem to connect at the same point. The Priory of Sion turned into the Knights Templar, who later, with the Priory of Sion, created the York Rite of Freemasonry, led by the Templars.[94] The Grand Lodge of England, where Prince Phillip was the Grandmaster, is also essentially a Templar Order.

The Priory of Sion located themselves in Jerusalem after the Catholic Church's First Crusade in 1099. A few decades later, they formed the Knights Templar to protect the Holy Grail, eventually trying to reinstate the Merovingians, ultimately defeating the Church of Rome[95]. Not all Templars turned against the Church after

---

[94] Wikipedia.org: *York Rite #Knights Templar (Grand Encampment of Knights Templar of the U.S.A.)*
[95] TheTemplarKnight.com.

the excavation of Solomon's Temple between 1119 and 1128, however, since they branched out. The reason for this may be clear to the reader in time, but first, we must address what happened after the excavation of Solomon's Temple between 1119 and 1128.

> Around 1118, a French knight named Hugues de Payens created a military order along with eight relatives and acquaintances, calling it the Poor Fellow-Soldiers of Christ and the Temple of Solomon—later known simply as the Knights Templar.[96]

The Order quickly grew as new members were recruited and became the front for the Priory of Sion, which is an Order, probably going back as far as old Babylon and Mesopotamia. Perhaps this Order was first established by En.ki as Osiris, when he and Isis created their particular bloodline, and their purpose was to protect it. The following is from a website called *The Templar Knight:*

> Other accounts linking the Templars to the Holy Grail view it as secret knowledge hidden in Jerusalem that gave the Templars huge power over the church and accounts for their sudden increase in wealth. It goes something like this:
>
> - The Templars were Gnostics, influenced by an early form of Christianity that sought to liberate the soul through a true understanding of the divine – and did not recognise the earthly priesthood of the Roman church.
> - The nine knights who founded the order deliberately based themselves in what had been the Al Aqsa mosque under Muslim control but was in fact the site of the Temple of Solomon. Having obtained permission from Baldwin, the crusader ruler of the city, to take over the building, they began furiously digging underneath it.
> - They found something that allowed them to go to Rome and extract concessions from the papacy. This might have been a gospel written by Jesus himself. It may have been the Ark of the Covenant.[97]

Yes, the Templars were Gnostics, or at least a branch of them were. Therefore, I believe they found Gnostic texts underneath Solomon's Temple during the excavations, and because a branch of the Templars became followers of the Mother Goddess religion, I would suspect it was the Nag Hammadi texts, which they later, during the inquisition of the Templar Order by the Catholic Church in

---

[96] History.com: *Knights Templar.*
[97] TheTemplarKnight.com: *Templar Grail Quest.*

the early fourteenth century, hid together with other Templar treasures. Knights might have sailed to Egypt and dug these texts down in Nag Hammadi, only to be found in 1945. The discovery of the Nag Hammadi texts, which introduces the Mother Goddess into the overall divine story of the Universe, and most likely other artifacts referring to the Divine Feminine, contributed to the Knights' conversion to Mother Goddess worship (yes, sadly, it seems they went into worship).

Not all Templars changed their religious beliefs, however. The branch that did took advantage of the situation and could extract concessions from the papacy, and they got wealthy, also going into banking, lending out money to a high interest. Soon, they became the wealthiest organization on Earth, save from the Catholic Church itself. Although the Church of Rome was most likely aware of the Divine Feminine, they held it secret to instead promote a masculine God, and it was not meant to happen for the Templars to find the truth under the Temple.

As we have discussed earlier, the Church of Rome, with local popes, positioned in different provinces of the Roman Empire, worships both Mother Mary (Virgin Mary and Mary Magdalene) and Jesus. They are an Isis-Marduk (Magdalene-Jesus) cult, protectors of the Holy Grail, with the Priory of Sion and the Templars, as well as in current times, the Rosicrucians (The Rose Crux), and other occult organizations. They are all connected and sit on the same kind of information, only presented differently. It appears to me that one branch of the Templars, who continued following the Church, took the male God approach, while another branch took a grander approach, seeing through that Isis is the Cosmic Mother, or maybe they even realized she was an extension of her, since this is conveyed in the Nag Hammadi. The latter branch understood the difference, and also that the Church knew about it but kept it secret, making sure they acknowledged Enki as God, and not the Queen of the Stars—Sophia.

When I mentioned that the Templars also might have found something else underneath the temple, it could have been evidence of the much purer Ninurta and Isis bloodline—Isis' hermaphroditic creation of the redheads. They understood that this was the bloodline that deserved to be protected, not the Marduk-Isis-Ninurta lineage that the Church focused on. It has been much talk about that the Templars found a genealogy chart of Jesus' bloodline all the way to King David, and perhaps they did, but the real Graal is the connection to the true Mother Goddess through Isis and Ninurta.

If such a discovery happened, which seems likely, taking into consideration what we soon are going to discuss, the Mother Goddess worshippers among the Templars did not actively try to destroy the Catholic Church, but they worked slowly behind the scenes. It's more than possible the Church knew the Templars had this evidence in their possession, and the Order used it as blackmail. They kept the information hidden, and perhaps they threatened to expose the Church as a fraudulent, or at least a false religion, which would, of course, be devastating. Thus, the Templar Order could gain tremendous wealth, reluctantly provided to them by the Church.

Thus, two different bloodlines were now protected by different branches of the Templars, respectively, creating two opposing branches. They were essentially just one bloodline (which is the Jesus-Magdalene lineage; it was a matter of perspective, such as, who is Divine, Jesus or Magdalene?). An important stronghold for the Templars was a place in France called Rennes Le Château, with the skull and crossbones symbol and the Ninurta cross above the entrance. This is an old Templar symbol, which they also used on their ship sails. Today, we see it in many occult societies, most prominently at the Yale secret society, *Skull & Bones*, of which George H.W. Bush and his son, George W. Bush, among many other famous Elite are/were members. It's also a symbol of the *Jolly Roger*, the pirate flag, which again is the Templar symbol, first in use in the early 1700s by the "pirate," Emmanuel Wynne[98]. There is much we have not been told about our history, isn't it? Who were the pirates? Ill-treated Templars from whom the British Crown stole treasures?

The Templars residing in Rennes Le Château were mostly loyal to the papacy and were left alone, not being arrested in what led to the prosecution of the Order in the early 14th Century, while others were not so lucky.

---

[98] The Guardian: *Why is the Pirate Flag Called the Jolly Roger?*

Fig. 9:1. The skull and crossbones, staring at us from the Templar fortress, Rennes Le Château.[99]

The branch that prioritized the Mother Goddess blood, considering *that* royal, and not the Jesus bloodline, set up their strongholds in Portugal, a country that was created by the Templars, and in Germany, which was at the time not under the influence of the papacy.

Then something peculiar happened: The Mother Goddess branch had a setback in the 1200s, most likely because of their connection to Mother Goddess worship, and they had to flee to Germany and Portugal for safety. Thus, they could prolong the inevitable prosecution, which came to fruition later. The following will probably, by many, be discarded as superstitious nonsense, but it's not necessarily so. The German Knights, on more than one occasion, saw an apparition appear before them, and this apparition spoke to them. As we know, taking my research into consideration, the Overlords (including Isis) knew how to shapeshift and take form in our reality. This appears to have happened. Interestingly, this apparition called herself Isais.

> The Untersberg is a great mountain straddling the Austro-German border opposite Salzburg. It was reputed in local legend to be the seat of the god Wotan and to be haunted. The Knights Templar of the region had their headquarters in Vienna and before the year 1222 never had a Komturei (a command post) near the mountain. The commander of a "section" returning from the crusades to Austria in 1220 received an apparition believed to be of the demi-

---

[99] Atlasobscura.com: *Rennes Le Château.*

goddess Isais at Nineveh, old Babylon, who instructed him to proceed to the Untersberg and erect a temple in her honor inside it. There she would address them frequently which she did as from 1226.

The Appearance of Isais to the German Knights

Sometime in the year 1220, the German knight Templar and commander Hubertus Koch, returning to Austria from the crusades with a small company, arrived at the ruins of the former Assyrian capital Nineveh in ancient Babylon. Here he reports being approached by an apparition of the demi-goddess Isais, "a graceful maiden-like figure of a girl whose **copper-colored hair** waved as if in a breeze although the day was actually windless." She gave Koch instructions to proceed to the "mountain of the Old God Wotan", that is, the Untersberg near Salzburg, build a house there and await her next apparition where she would give "important information regarding a new Golden Age for the world".

The first testified apparition of Isais at Untersberg occurred in the year 1226 and was repeated regularly over the next twelve years, Isais delivering the full 134 verses of her revelation by 1238. The supposed purpose of Isais was to help achieve the destruction of the Powers of Darkness in the heavens and on Earth, and as a first step, the world had to be rid of the Church of Rome since it worshipped Jehovah as God Almighty.

The underlying basis of the Isais Revelation is the Marcionite heresy of the second century AD. It denies that the Hebrew god of the Old Testament, always referred to in the Revelation as "El Shaddai", was God of the New Testament. Isais states that it was Allvater, God himself (verse 21) who descended in human form as the Allkrist, Jesus Christ (verses 98, 99), and was crucified by those he had come to reform.

"The apparition was a figure clothed in a breath-fine dress of shimmering green such that one could perceive the outline of a tall female, slim and supple, shining through it. She was a wonderful being, half woman and half girl, and undoubtedly not of this world. Her beautiful face was narrow and pallid and absolutely wonderful; her eyes, hair and fingernails shone with the color of amber; a golden tiara held back the masses of her hair, which reached to the ground; and on top of the tiara was a golden crescent moon[100] with points like horns, and at its center a golden sun. Her unhumanly large eyes stared at us and her lips seemed to be glowing. And she was the most beautiful picture that a person ever saw but she was translucent and not of

---

[100] Isis is known as the Moon Goddess.

humankind."

She said, "I called you here without you being aware of it," at which Roderich asked for her identity. She answered at once, "I am Isai, Ishtar. The folk who revered me in this place called me Asherah; the people in the North who were your ancestors knew me as Idun": (Idun, Nordic goddess of the clan Aesir). Different peoples named me as suited their own language."

Then German knight Emmerant said that they were both true to the Lord Jesus Christ and would never worship another deity. Ishtar apparently amused replied, "I heard your prayers to him, to my godlike brother. But he is in his realm while I, his godlike sister, am here again - for a short while. For ultimately it is female power which will defeat Jehovah, Satan. The goddess of love will change into a goddess of war to strike down Satan when the moment comes."[101]

After this, it was mostly the German and Austrian Templar branches that started despising the Church more openly. It is said the Templars were suddenly, according to the Church, practicing "heresy, homosexuality, financial corruption, devil-worshipping, fraud, spitting on the cross, and more..."[102]. They were also accused of denying Christ. [103] This is probably true, at least from the Church's perspective. But the real downfall of the Templars was their greed. They lent money to monarchies, and they put everybody in debt whom they came in contact with. The interest upon delayed payments was ridiculously high, which prevented countries from being able to balance the debt (sounds familiar? This is how they put entire countries in debt today). King Philip IV (1268-1314) of France, the ruler of one such country being in enormous debt, was tired of the Knights' usury. He wanted to destroy the Templars completely to get rid of the debt, and he was also the one who accused the Templars of heresy and all the other accusations mentioned above. It seems plausible that he infiltrated the Order and found actual clues to what was going on. Rome was still a great empire, and France was a part of it. However, the French monarchy stood above the papacy.

Philip was substantially in debt to the Knights Templar, a

---

[101] https://www.ancient-origins.net/human-origins-religions/german-knight-0013616
[102] History Channel: Knights Templar.
[103] *Ibid.*

monastic military order whose original role as protectors of Christian pilgrims in the Latin East had been largely replaced by banking and other commercial activities by the end of the 13th century. As the popularity of the Crusades had decreased, support for the military orders had waned, and Philip used a disgruntled complaint against the Knights Templar as an excuse to move against the entire organization as it existed in France, in part to free himself from his debts. Other motives appear to have included concern over perceived heresy, assertion of French control over a weakened Papacy, and finally, the substitution of royal officials for officers of the Temple in the financial management of French government.

Recent studies emphasize the political and religious motivations of Philip the Fair and his ministers (especially Guillaume de Nogaret). It seems that, with the "discovery" and repression of the "Templars' heresy", the Capetian monarchy claimed for itself the mystic foundations of the papal theocracy. The Temple case was the last step of a process of appropriating these foundations, which had begun with the Franco-papal rift at the time of Boniface VIII. Being the ultimate defender of the Catholic faith, the Capetian king was invested with a Christ-like function that put him above the pope. What was at stake in the Templars' trial, then, was the establishment of a "royal theocracy".[104]

In 1303, King Philip kidnapped and murdered Pope Boniface VIII[105], and most likely a second local pope, as well. Then the king used his influence over Pope Clement V and forced him into agreeing to a prosecution of the Templars since the pope was only his puppet. The pope, however, wanted to hold proper trials. Still, after having arrested several Templars, leading to confessions of heresy and more under torture, King Philip IV used these forced confessions to have these Templars burned at the stake before they could form a defense.

Then the Church (under Philip's command) raided the Templar facilities, trying to find treasures and "curiosa" in their possession, but they found many Templars had fled, and there were no treasures or relics found anywhere. It was later discovered that some

---

[104] Wikipedia: *Philip IV of France, #Suppression of the Knights Templar.*
[105] History.com: *In 1303 the French King Sent Goons to Attack and Kidnap the Pope.*

members of the Order had sailed to sea under the Templar flag with the treasures and were never heard from again. Some suspect the Catholic Church discovered them and caught them at sea, confiscating their valuable cargo, but no one knows for certain.

Fig. 9:2. King Philip IV, also called "Philip the Fair." Here, again, we can see Isis' lilies on his cape.

Whatever the truth is, it appears the Templars were forewarned, perhaps having spies within France's royal court, so they could disappear before the Church invaded and arrested those who stayed behind. Others, who still were on Roman territory, fled to their companions in Germany and Portugal.

A faction of the Order had a tragic end, as most of the readers might know, and it was officially dismantled in disgrace in 1314. On March 11, the Catholic Church burned at the stake the Templar Grandmaster, Jacques de Molay, and with him, many other Knights. Interestingly, no Templars in Rennes Le Château and its vicinity were ever prosecuted. That part of the Order was still in favor of the Catholic Church and the worship of the male God and Jesus. After the horrific end, surviving Templars, worshipping the Goddess, went underground or laid low. Eventually, some of them went to England and Scotland, where they were protected by Robert the Bruce, King of Scots.

For those who want more evidence that the persecuted Templars were Mother Goddess worshippers, please read the following quote. Here they talk about the "Venus family." Venus is a Roman goddess, who was also the Greek Goddess, Aphrodite[106], who in Egypt was Isis[107]. Venus/Isis is also associated with copper[108] (red hair), and if you go back to the quote about the Isis apparition showing herself to the Templars, she was associated with copper, as well.

Fig. 9:3. The British coat of arms with the Lilies of Isis
with the Templar cross in the middle.

The persecuted Knights Templar and the families they were members of were what we now collectively call, the "Venus families". Why Venus? The planet Venus has always been considered the manifestation of the Great Goddess in the heavens since humans first began to watch and track the celestial bodies in the night sky. Venus is the third brightest body after the sun and the moon and moves in ways that makes patterns such as the five-pointed star or pentagram if tracked over its eight year cycle, a symbol long associated with Goddess ideology. These families and the Templars kept alive an ancient faith where the sacred feminine was considered critically important, at the very least She was an equal to the male God and maybe even paramount.

Because this flew in the face of the controlling Roman Catholic Church in medieval times which actively pursued and burned at the stake anyone not practicing the dogma of the Church, the Templars

---

[106] *Getty.edu: Aphrodite and the Gods of Love.*
[107] Eso.org: *Venus in Mythology.*
[108] *Ibid.*

needed to keep their reverence for the sacred feminine carefully veiled so as not to endanger themselves or their critical plans. In fact, we find that there is reason to believe the Templars and associated families had a Covenant with the Great Goddess that had to do with helping them finding a new safe place to live, bring their treasure, their families and worship as they wished, a New Jerusalem, away from the monarchs of Europe and the Catholic church in exchange for keeping the sacred feminine aspect of their faith alive and well, yet carefully veiled, in perpetuity.[109]

In Scotland, the Templars created a new Order, the Scottish Rite of Freemasonry, officially established in 1717, although records are showing it might have been established centuries earlier.

This is what the Freemasons themselves say about it:

No one knows with certainty how or when the Masonic Fraternity was formed. A widely accepted theory among Masonic scholars is that it arose from the stonemasons' guilds during the Middle Ages. The language and symbols used in the fraternity's rituals come from this era. The oldest document that makes reference to Masons is the Regius Poem, printed about 1390, which was a copy of an earlier work. In 1717, four lodges in London formed the first Grand Lodge of England, and records from that point on are more complete.[110]

And here is the correlation between the Templars and Masonry from the horse's mouth (Freemasonry):

The Knights Templar, full name The United Religious, Military and Masonic Orders of the Temple and of St John of Jerusalem, Palestine, Rhodes and Malta, is a fraternal order affiliated with Freemasonry.[111]

Ultimately, it's just another branch of the ancient brotherhood, starting with En.ki's *Brotherhood of the Snake* in the early Second Construct. But the Freemasonic branch of Scotland and England both protect the pure Isis-Ninurta bloodline behind the scenes. This is extra interesting because these Templars came to the British Islands from Germany, and who is on the throne of England up to this day? The House of Windsor, who is German. My Orion Source told me that the late Queen Elizabeth thought she was Sophia's representative on Earth with her Divine Right to Rule, which he said is

---

[109] Templar.gold: *The Great Goddess, op. cit.*
[110] Massachusetts Freemasons: *History of Freemasonry.*
[111] Wikipedia: *"Knights Templar (Freemasonry)"*

utterly false, and she is just another imposter. He further claimed she is not even royal, having no more royal blood than the regular human. Back then, I did not understand what he meant, but now I do, and it will be more obvious later in this book. The "name" Elizabeth is also a title for the Mother Goddess, according to my source. Thus, things are truly coming together. Prince Philip, being a member of the English Lodge of Freemasonry while he was alive, therefore protected the bloodline of the House of Windsor. Although Elizabeth II was little more than a commoner in this sense, Prince William and Prince Harry have more royal blood, so I guess Prince Philip protecting the Holy Grail was justified, after all. More about this, as well, when we come to the chapter about the House of Windsor.

The Supposed Templar—Baphomet Connection

Although the God of the Old Testament said we humans should not worship idols, the Catholic Church is famous for worshipping them, but so was the Templar Order. Many alternative researchers—particularly those who specialize in the Illuminati and the Elite bloodlines—often discuss the Baphomet, an idol Satanists often worship, and who is also mentioned in the 20th Century magician, Aleister Crowley's teachings. Ever since the Catholic Church condemned the Templars, said to have been worshipping the Baphomet, this "entity" has been considered a satanic element.

Fig. 9:4. Éliphas Lévi's depiction of the Baphomet.

107

Those who have done research on occult history have most likely come across the Baphomet, allegedly originating with the Knights Templar. The most common picture we have of this figure is the drawing of the occultist, Éliphas Lévi, from the mid-19th Century.

Wikipedia says,

> Peter Partner states in his 1987 book The Knights Templar and their Myth: "In the trial of the Templars one of their main charges was their supposed worship of a heathen idol-head known as a Baphomet (Baphomet = Mahomet)."[112]

Mahomet denotes the feminine (Ma = mother).

It's important to realize that Lévi's depiction of the Baphomet has nothing to do with the Templar version. They are two separate things, except that Lévi borrowed the name and idea from the Templars.

So, what idol, if any, did the Templars worship?

> The indictment (acte d'accusation) published by the court of Rome set forth ... "that in all the provinces they had idols, that is to say, heads, some of which had three faces, others but one; sometimes, it was a human skull ... That in their assemblies, and especially in their grand chapters, they worshipped the idol as a god, as their saviour, saying that this head could save them, that it bestowed on the order all its wealth, made the trees flower, and the plants of the earth to sprout forth."[113]

Now, let's go back to Wikipedia:

> The description of the object changed from confession to confession; some Templars denied any knowledge of it, while others, who confessed under torture, described it as being either a severed head, a cat, or a head with three faces. The Templars did possess several silver-gilt heads as reliquaries, including one marked capud lviiim, [sic] another said to be St. Euphemia, and possibly the actual head of Hugues de Payens. The claims of an idol named Baphomet were unique to the Inquisition of the Templars. Karen Ralls, author of the Knights Templar Encyclopedia, argues that it is significant that "no specific evidence [of Baphomet] appears in either the Templar Rule or in other medieval period

---

[112] Wikipedia: *Baphomet #History.*
[113] Jules Michelet: *History of France (1860), page 375.*

Templar documents."[114]

Taking into consideration that the information about the Templars worshipping heads came out under torture, we must take this information with many pinches of salt. People confess to anything under torture, which is then held against them. That's the sad story of humankind. So, whether the idol, the Baphomet, was a Church invention, or a skull worshipped by the Templars, is hard to say. Still, there is a probability they did. They were, after all, an occult order, with secret levels of initiation, and we know for a fact that Freemasonry and other secret societies use idols in their rituals and initiation processes. There are references to this:

> ... "Baphomet" was formed from the Greek words βαφη μητ8ς, baphe metous, to mean Taufe der Weisheit, **"Baptism of Wisdom"**.[38] Nicolai "attached to it the idea of the image of the supreme God, in the state of quietude attributed to him by the Manichaean Gnostics", according to F. J. M. Raynouard, and "supposed that the Templars had a secret doctrine and initiations of several grades", which "the Saracens had communicated ... to them".[39] He further connected the figura Baffometi with the Pythagorean pentacle...[115]

The Templars were Gnostic, and the Greek translation of the Baphomet gives a reference to Wisdom, which is the main Gnostic trait of the Spiritual Aeon, Pistis Sophia.

And moreover [my emphasis in bold]:

> Hugh J. Schonfield (1901–1988), one of the scholars who worked on the Dead Sea Scrolls, argued in his book The Essene Odyssey that the word "Baphomet" was created with knowledge of the Atbash substitution cipher, which substitutes the first letter of the Hebrew alphabet for the last, the second for the second last, and so on. "Baphomet" rendered in Hebrew is בפומת (bpwmt); interpreted using Atbash, it becomes שופיא (šwpy', "Shofya'"), **which can be interpreted as the Greek word "Sophia", meaning wisdom.**[116]

That both the Knights Templar and the Freemasons are Gnostics is not a secret, but something they willingly admit to themselves on their own websites and elsewhere, such as at

---

[114] Wikipedia: *Baphomet #History.*
[115] Wikipedia: *Baphomet: #Alternative etymologies.*
[116] *Ibid.*

universalfreemasonry.org. [117] Adopting to Gnosticism originates from the Knights Templar, who merged into one larger organization, Freemasonry.

---

[117] Universalfreemasonry.org: *The Historical Origins of Freemasonry/Gnosticism.*

The Templars and the Holy Grail in the Wes Penre Papers

10 **In the WPP, the story about** the bloodlines, the Holy Grail, the Knights Templar, Isis being Mary Magdalene, and more of the rest of the story is described in *The Second Level of Learning* and *The Fourth Level of Learning*. The page numbers listed in this section will be from the PDF versions of the Levels of Learning, which can be found here: *https://wespenre.com/7-first-to-fifth-level-of-learning-in-pdf*.

Most of the information is in the fourth level, and it is spread among those papers. Taking the vast number of papers at all Levels of Learning, respectively, very few people remember it all, and the section, or sections about the bloodlines and the Holy Grail have largely been forgotten by most, I think. Therefore, I will cite myself in this chapter as a reminder from what I discussed with the Orion source on the subject and published.

Here is from *The Wes Penre Papers, The Fourth Level of Learning [my current emphases in **bold**]:*[118]

> ...there is a hidden, "Holy Grail" bloodline, which the Elite want to keep as pure as they possibly can. Of course, many of these Elite members have bastard offspring, but they were more or less "cast out" and created their own watered-down bloodlines all over the world. Therefore, we have the Morgans, the Buchanans and the Bauers, etc. amongst regular people as well, although those names are Elite bloodlines. Some of these people claim family ties to the

---

[118] Wespenre.com.

super-rich Elite, and on some level, the ties are there, but they would hardly ever be acknowledged by the real Elite—the "bastard" bloodlines are too watered-down to be useful. Therefore, these people are often as much slaves in the eyes of the Elite as those whose names are Anderson or Taylor.

We know that the reason the Elite need to inbreed is because if their bloodlines are not pure enough, they can't host an interdimensional being such as En.ki and the AIF. We also highly suspect that many of the Global Elite people have been taken over by the AIF [Alien Invader Force, aka the Overlords] already and are now not only remotely run by them, but more directly so. As we discussed in an earlier paper, many souls, whom En.ki managed to release from the Sirian prison—the Dark Star—are now inhabiting human bodies here on Earth, but more are waiting to be released when a new chance arises (if ever).[119]

The last part is important to remember. Today's Elite, on the more advanced levels, is completely taken over by the renegades from the Sirian prison, where Khan En.lil put them.

And here is more:

The "Fisher Kings" became one of the terms for the Merovingian Kings, who were the Elite Bloodline of the Patriarchal Regime—the bloodline [which] Marduk and En.ki decided to protect as their own main Elite Bloodline. It needed to be protected—therefore, what can be compared to as a "police force" or "semi-military force" was created. This force wore the "Celestial Cross," which is the symbol of Ninurta—something that was never spoken of. The "Ninurta bloodline" survived through Isis [sic] descendants, also known as the "Grail Bloodline." ... This police force was, of course, the Knights Templar, and although they had different tasks to perform, the protection of the Holy Grail Bloodline was their main duty.[120]

The term, *the Fisher Kings*, in the section above, ultimately refers to the original Fisher King, which, according to gospels was Jesus. Sir Laurence Gardner put it neatly in a book he wrote many years ago:

We now know that there are allegories within the Gospels: the use of words that have hitherto been misunderstood. We know that baptismal priests were called 'fishers', while those who aided them by hauling the baptismal candidates into the boats in large nets

---

[119] Penre: *The Fourth Level of Learning*, pp. 332-333, op. cit.
[120] Penre: *The Fourth Level of Learning*, pp. 385-386, op. cit.

were called 'fishermen', with the candidates themselves being called 'fishes'. The apostles James and John were both ordained 'fishers', but the brothers Peter and Andrew were lay 'fishermen', to whom Jesus promised ministerial status, saying, 'I will make you to become fishers of men'.[22]

[...]

Apart from eventually becoming a fisher, Jesus was also referred to as the Christ – a Greek definition (from Khristos) which meant the King. In saying the name Jesus Christ, we are actually saying King Jesus, and his kingly heritage was of the Royal House of Judah (the House of David), as mentioned numerous times in the Gospels and in the Epistles of St Paul.

From AD 33, therefore, Jesus emerged with the dual status of a Priest Christ or, as is more commonly cited in Grail lore, a Fisher King. This definition, as we shall see, was to become the hereditary and dynastic office of Jesus's heirs, and the succeeding Fisher Kings were paramount in the continuing Bloodline of the Holy Grail.[121]

Jesus is portrayed as King Jesus, and sometimes as the King of Kings, i.e., the KHAN.US KHAN.UR. And who is the Sirians KHAN.US KHAN.UR? Marduk.

Although the Knights Templars, under false premises, protected the female line of Queen Isis, a.k.a. Mary Magdalene. Gardner mentions this as well in his *Bloodline of the Holy Grail:*[122]

This was especially apparent during the Age of Chivalry, which embraced a respect for womanhood, as exemplified by the Knights Templars whose constitutional oath supported a veneration of the Grail Mother, Queen Mary Magdalene.[123]

By Isis and Marduk creating this new bloodline, Marduk is laying claim to the throne that Ninurta has inherited. In fact, the Isis-Marduk bloodline becomes what is referred to as the "Grail Line," or that of the "Fisher Kings." ... They are signifying the aquatic Bird Tribe of En.ki/Nergal, which we were discussing earlier in conjunction with the Sirian Wars and the Dark Star.

---

[121] Gardner: *Bloodline of the Holy Grail—The Hidden Lineage of Jesus Revealed, op. cit.*

[122] Penre: *The Fourth Level of Learning, p. 386, op. cit.*

[123] Gardner: *Bloodline of the Holy Grail—The Hidden Lineage of Jesus Revealed, op. cit.*

This bloodline has been very well protected throughout history, and something similar to a "police force" was formed already at an early stage. Isis/Ishtar/Lilith/Inanna now becomes the hand-maiden to En.ki/Nergal. The Secret Police is wearing one of Ninurta's symbols, the "Celestial Cross," to signify that they are pro-tecting the seed line of Isis/Ishtar/Inanna ... The offspring are now direct descendants of Ninurta and are thereby claiming his right to the Throne of Orion, which was given to him by Khan En.lil and Queen Nin. Ninurta's inheritance, which En.ki claims includes the Earth, Sagittarius (the Constellation directly related to the [center of the] Milky Way Galaxy), Ursa Major, and a lot of other asterisms belonging to the Orion Empire. The Tribe of Dan becomes a direct line, as well, to Ninurta's Throne, via the seed line created by Mar-duk and Isis. So those who are of the Tribe of Dan and are still alive on Earth today are the offspring of Marduk and Isis. Isis then be-comes the "Eve" (the originator) of this bloodline, and she is instructed to have sex with the progeny of this seed line to keep it as pure as possible. In the ancient records, it says she has a Temple where this takes place, and she is working as the "breeder." Fore-most, as Inanna and Ishtar, she then becomes known as the "Harlot," or the "Whore of Babylon." It is her seed line that is the one designed to rule the Earth, and the way it was done, this seed line has a direct link to Prince Ninurta of Orion.

This is a serious attempt by En.ki and his son to take the power away from Ninurta and give it to themselves, believing that the more purity they can provide via themselves and a long line of progenies, the better their chances are to inherit the Throne of Orion in a more "legal" way, regardless of what the Queen and the King of Orion think about them. However, En.ki is now out of the equation. En.ki's and Marduk's hope is that the rulers of Orion will have no choice other than to accept them. For this to work, they believe, the father and son need to seed a long line of progenies for the laws of Orion to take effect in their favor.

They probably understand that this may be a long shot, but these beings are obsessed with succeeding, and they are taking eve-rything they can into consideration. This does not at all exclude a real invasion of the Inner Sanctuaries of the Orion Empire, and if this option needs to be played out (which seems to be the case), humanity is involved big time, working as foot soldiers for the gods.[124]

There are three notable passages in the above quote from Paper #13 worth elaborating upon, and I want to begin with the third passage, starting with, "This is a serious attempt by En.ki and his son to take the power away from Ninurta and give it to themselves..." I highlighted this section to show the reader why Orion is very concerned about us humans having babies. It is because we are then contributing to the Overlords' success in spreading their "royal blood" and therefore having a better chance of gaining power in Orion. Thus, my source told me to spread the message that, if a person knows this information, they must not have children because then they are not serious about wanting to help humankind and the Orion quest, and that may have consequences for those who have children regardless and then go to Orion. They don't look kindly at this because it might put the entire Universe in jeopardy. *No one wants the Overlords to be in charge of Orion.* So, we who know must refrain ourselves from reproducing.

Why is Sagittarius, the constellation directly connected to the Galactic Center, so important? Well, in the WPP, I mentioned that those in charge of the nano-world rule the Universe. Orion, as explained in earlier work, *is* the nano-world, or the Nanoverse, as I call it—the KHAA. I have also hypothesized that the Milky Way Galaxy *is* Orion, and that each galaxy is its own universe. Therefore, I think Sagittarius is so important because those who are in control of the Galactic Center are in control of the Orion Universe. The sixth density beings channeled in the RA Material[125, 126] also consider each galaxy to be a separate universe. Souls created in this universe cannot travel to other galaxies/universes because, in those other rules apply, and our souls would be destroyed if we could try.

I mentioned that Isis has a Temple where she is breeding with the progeny of the En.ki seed line. This may have been correct in ancient times, but what about now? Also, what about in the era of the Merovingian Kings? Did Isis have offspring with them, these rituals taking place in temples belonging to these royalties? In fact, as

---

[124] Penre: *The Fourth Level of Learning, pp. 363-65, op. cit.*

[125] Amazon.com: *The Ra Material: An Ancient Astronaut Speaks (Law of One).*

[126] Lawofone.info

Fig. 10:1. Philae, Temple of Isis on the island of Agilka, Egypt. Photo taken by the Rosicrucian Museum.

mentioned in David Icke's research from 1999[127], the Merovingians performed mysterious, "magical" rituals, away from public scrutiny, so it's not historically known what these rituals entailed. Were these the places where the incarnated Isis, even long after Mary Magdalene died, sometimes copulated with the kings? We can only guess.

However, if you remember from earlier in this book, I referred to the German Templars seeing an apparition of Isis telling them to raise a temple in her honor, which they did. That was in the thirteenth century. Did that have something to do with breeding? If it did, was Isis producing children with surviving progenies of the Marduk-Isis-Ninurta bloodline to keep it going?

Perhaps unrelated, an ancient temple, dedicated to Isis in the third century BCE (around 280 BCE), was restored and partly rebuilt between 1960-1970, and, *it was moved, stone by stone* to an island called Agilka, in Egypt! The temple is called the *Philae Temple*[128]. The photo below is taken by the Rosicrucian Museum[129]—the Rosicrucian being the protectors of the Marduk-Isis-Ninurta bloodline. Nice connection there. Has this place been used since the 1970s to keep the Holy Grail alive, or was it built for future use for that same purpose? The temple is open to the public; but of course, only between certain hours. If this location is used as a breeding location for the sacred bloodline, it's perfectly placed on an island, where you need a boat to visit; it's a simple task to gain privacy.

---

[127] Icke: *The Biggest Secret, 1999.*

[128] EgyptianMuseum.org: *Greco-Roman Period Monuments: Philae—Temple of Isis.*

[129] *Ibid.*

In mythology, the first red roses are said to have arisen from the BLOOD of Adonis for the love of Aphrodite; thus, they have become symbolic of love, and often resurrection. In Christian symbolism, the RED rose stands for the blood shed by Jesus on the CROSS; it has also become a symbol for earthly love, a tradition which continues today. The rose may represent the Virgin Mary, and thus virginity, or fertility and passion. It is beauty and perfection, happiness and grace, yet it is also sensuality and seduction.[130]

Roses and lilies have been symbols of Mary since earliest times. The rose, emblematic of her purity, glory and sorrow, was her attribute as Queen of Heaven and a symbol of her love for God and for Christ, her son. The lily represented her immaculate purity, her innocence and virginity. [131]

11 **The rose is an ancient symbol,** and as we can see in the first quote above, it goes back at least to the Second Construct, with Isis as Aphrodite in Greek mythology.

As most people know, the rose is also a symbol of love, and who is the goddess of love? Isis (and Aphrodite, Inanna, Ishtar... same deity). It is also a symbol for Jesus, the Virgin Mary, and Mary Magdalene (the two latter being the same person), and the Divine

---

[130] Websites.imuch.edu: *Rose, op. cit.*
[131] Franciscanmedia.org: *Honoring Mary in Your Garden #Roses*

Feminine. Within secret societies, such as the Rosicrucians, the Golden Dawn, and the OTO, the rose represents the Jesus/Magdalene bloodline, Jesus' blood[132]. The rose is a part of their emblems, usually attached to the cross.

Fig. 11:1. The Rosicrucian Cross with the open red rose and the lilies, representing Mary Magdalene.

The color of the rose is often significant. In our daily life, if we are in love, we usually give the lady in question a red rose, while the black rose can sometimes symbolize hatred, despair, death, rebirth, and so on. In this chapter, we will specifically focus on the red and the white roses, since these two rose colors are represented in the famous *Wars of the Roses*, fought between the Houses of Lancaster and York for the English throne between 1455 and 1485. The esoteric connotation of the white rose is very similar to that of the red rose, but also denotes new beginnings: something new that replaces the old:

> From Christian iconography of Mary and the Christ child to ancient Greek and Roman myths about the goddess of love, Venus, white roses have always held a divine connotation.
>
> [...]
>
> White roses can also symbolize hope and the promise of new

---

[132] I would also suggest that the red rose symbolizes Isis'/Mary's red hair, which is a trait I've found goes straight through our history within the Mary Magdalene bloodline.

118

beginnings...[133]

The white rose also symbolizes the *birth* of Aphrodite[134] (Isis), the Divine Feminine from the esoteric perspective of secret societies, such as those mentioned above, adding certain branches of Freemasonry to the list. But foremost, as it is being used in such societies, and currently as the symbol of Yorkshire, England, denotes the purity of the Virgin Mary.[135]

The wars were named after the emblems of the two houses: the white rose of York and the red rose of Lancaster. Eventually, the House of Tudor of the Lancaster branch (the Red Rose) won this civil war when Henry Tudor (Henry VII) defeated and killed Richard III at the *Battle of Bosworth Field* in 1485, and the wars ended. King Henry VII then united the houses by marriage.[136, 137]

The feud is complicated, and so much happened back and forth that it's a subject for an entire book, so I will stick to what is relevant to this writing. It's easy, otherwise, to get lost in the political scene of England in the 15th century.

How the House of Lancaster Came to Power

After the reign of Edward III (1327-77), the House of Plantagenet was divided into two sections. Edward's son, Edward the Black Prince, as he was called, formed the House of Lancaster, while his brother, Edmund of York, founded the House of York. Because Edward the Black was the eldest, he was appointed as Edward III's successor of the English throne. However, Edward the Black died one year before his father died in 1377, but had a son, Richard II, who became the next King of England, being of the Lancaster clan. Richard was childless, so his branch of the family tree ended with him, wherewith his first cousin, Henry IV of the Lancaster clan, became the next regent.

The Lancaster clan went back to the Merovingians because Henry IV's father, John of Gaunt (1340-1399), who was not a king,

---

[133] Sarascoop.com: *Spiritual Meaning and Symbolism of a White Rose.*

[134] Amarantelondon.com.

[135] Wikipedia: *The White Rose of York.*

[136] Britanica: *Wars of the Roses Summary.*

[137] Go to Appendix B and pull up the English Royal Family Dynasties and follow my narrative. It's makes it a lot easier to follow.

married Constance of Castile, who was French. The French bloodline was always the primary Holy Grail bloodline, most closely protected by the Catholic Church. Therefore, Henry IV had French blood in his veins, The York side of the family tree had no recent French ancestry.

Mary, Elizabeth, Sophia, and Red Hair

When I see the names Mary, Elizabeth, and Sophia in the royal family trees, I pay attention. Often, they are significant in one way or another, and some of them may positively have been Mary/Isis reborn. I also look for sudden red-haired women among the royals, coming up from "nowhere." Some of them have mysterious backgrounds and sport red hair, although their ancestors seem to not have it. Red hair is a significant trait within the Isis bloodline. It also helps those whom it may concern to trace her lineage to a degree. As we shall see, many Marys and Elizabeths were redheads; not so Mary de Bohun, Henry IV's consort, from what we are told. She died young in childbirth but birthed the next king in line, Henry V. There is no evidence that Mary de Bohun was Mary/Isis, but she carried the name Mary, and she was significant because it seems like a plot was instigated during her and Henry IV's reign to put their son, Henry V, on the throne of France. Whether or not Mary was Isis, it appears she had pure blood, and they apparently wanted to strengthen the French bloodline. Therefore, Henry married Catherine of Valois, who was French. The reason Catherine married the English monarch, Henry V, was to fulfill the plan to put him on the throne of France as a DNA booster.[138] Although Catherine managed to put her son, Henry VI, on the French throne for a while, the plan failed. Henry VI had a son, Edward of Lancaster, but he died young without having a successor. However, Catherine did not give up. After Henry V's death, she remarried Owen Tudor, and the two started the House of Tudor lineage. More about them in a minute.

It was during Henry VI's reign that Richard of York disputed the Lancasters' right to rule England, probably because Henry ascended to the French throne. Thus, Richard of York's son, Edward IV, took over when Henry IV went to France in 1461, and he ruled

---

[138] Wikipredia.org: *Catherine of Valois.*

until 1470, when Henry IV came back to England and regained the throne of England, thus taking it back from Edward IV. However, Henry IV conveniently died in 1471, where after Edward of the York clan claimed the throne once more, until his death in 1483. The throne remained with the House of York when Edward's brother, Richard III, succeeded the throne. This didn't sit well with the House of Lancaster, and the dispute led to the final battle in the Wars of the Roses, where Henry Tudor (later Henry VII) defeated and killed King Richard III in the *Battle of Bosworth Field* in 1485, which ended the war that had lasted on and off for 30 years. Henry Tudor now became the King of England, ruling as Henry VII, the first monarch of the House of Tudor. He ended the conflict of the roses (also called *The Thirty-Year's War*) by marrying a princess of the House of York and thereby merged both houses.

A House of York Incarnation of Isis?

O ur story does not end here, however, which is partially why I included this chapter. I think that amid all this, we have an incarnation of Isis lurking. When we follow the plots in the Wars of the Roses, we can quite clearly see the War of the Bloodlines played out. It becomes obvious that En.ki and Marduk wanted someone from the House of Lancaster to inherit the throne of France, but despite heavy efforts, the Lancasters failed. They put two of their own on the French throne, but none of them had offspring, which means the Jesus-Magdalene bloodline could not survive through that lineage during The Thirty Year's War. So, they were back on the drawing board again.

Let us look at the House of York for a moment. King Edward IV, who took over when Henry VI went to France, married Elizabeth Woodville, earlier Elizabeth Grey (see family tree chart). This was an interesting lady, and possibly an incarnation of Isis. The reason for her marrying Edward IV was to find her way into the Lancaster bloodline through the Tudors, and from there put her DNA into the heir of the French throne, which she succeeded in doing—for a while.

What stands out about Elizabeth, besides her name (a title for the Mother Goddess), is that she was a redhead, and there are no records of her birth. History books have tried to place her as the daughter of Jacquetta of Luxemburg. She apparently was raised by her, but there are no records that Jacquetta was her biological mother. Elizabeth's DNA, mixed with the Tudor family later, often created redheads[139]. It used to puzzle historians that so many Tudors had red hair, but the conclusion was that the red hair came from Elizabeth Woodville.

> The red hair allegedly came from Elizabeth Woodville, also known as Elizabeth Grey: Elizabeth Woodville (also spelt Wydville, Wydeville, or Widvile;[a] c. 1437 – 8 June 1492), later known as Dame Elizabeth Grey, was Queen of England from her marriage to King Edward IV on 1 May 1464 until Edward was deposed on 3 October 1470, and again from Edward's resumption of the throne on 11 April 1471 until his death on 9 April 1483. She was a key figure in the Wars of the Roses, a dynastic civil war between the Lancastrian and the Yorkist factions between 1455 and 1487.[140]

Isis is legendarily known as the goddess of love, sex, *and* war.

Elizabeth played a key role in the Wars of the Roses and a crucial role in securing the accession of Henry VII of the House of Tudor in 1485 after Richard III was slain. She made sure her daughter, Elizabeth of York (another red-haired Elizabeth), married Henry Tudor, which also happened. This ended the wars, which was exactly what Elizabeth, as a potential Isis, wanted, because now she saw her chance to get her DNA into the French royal bloodline again—not directly, but via her granddaughter with Henry VII, Mary Tudor (yet another Mary).

Mary Tudor

Mary Tudor was briefly Queen of France and the third wife of Louis XII.[141] (see the French Royal Family Tree in Appendix B). Louis was more than 30 years older than Mary, who married him when she was 18, and he was about 50. However, they were only married very briefly, desperately trying to produce an heir, but some say Louis was too old for such bedroom adventures, and he died without being able to impregnate Mary. Others say he died from gout, but either way, no heir was produced. After Louis XII's death, there was a big problem placing Mary somewhere in the

---

[139] Sucheternaldelight.wordpress.com: *Where the Tudor Re-Gold Hair came from.*

[140] Wikipedia: *Elizabeth Woodville.*

[141] Wikipedia: *Mary Tudor, Queen of France.*

French court, so again, the strengthening of the Jesus-Magdalene bloodline in France failed.

The Fascinating Continuous Story about Jane Grey

Elizabeth Woodville's first marriage, before she married King Edward IV, was with John Grey of Groby, a minor supporter of the Lancaster clan. However, he died at the *Second Battle of St. Albans*, leaving Elizabeth a widowed mother of two sons. We know next to nothing about these two children. Still, Elizabeth's granddaughter, Mary Tudor, through her older daughter, Francis, was the maternal grandmother of Jane Grey, the famous teenager who was the Queen of England for 9 days in July 1553, before she was burned at the stake for claiming she could hear divine voices in her head.

Fig. 11:2. Lady Jane Grey at the guillotine.

Why is this so interesting? Well, it amplifies the constant struggle with keeping the bloodlines pure. When Elizabeth I sat on the throne of England later in the 1500s, she succeeded Mary Queen of Scots, whom she executed by beheading her. Mary (yet another Mary and another Elizabeth) had a son, who became James VI of Scotland, and later James I of England (James I was the one who authorized the translation of the King James Bible). Elizabeth did not want James as her successor. Instead, she conspired with John Dee, her famous court magician and advisor, to put Jane Grey on the throne instead. Elizabeth herself was without an heir. She did not want to marry because she had learned that men who married queens did so because they wanted to usurp the throne and get the power for themselves. Thus, she had no known children.

The choice of Jane Grey is interesting because she was a direct descendant of Elizabeth Woodville of the House of York, whom I suspect was Isis. Therefore, Jane Grey was of pure bloodline. Queen Elizabeth I and John Dee managed to put the teenage Jane Grey on the throne of England, but because of her clairvoyance, she was deemed a witch and was burned at the stake. She claimed to have a direct channel with Jesus, among other divine beings. After Jane had been executed, James VI of Scotland, son of Mary Queen of Scots, also became the King of England as James I.

I have mentioned elsewhere that people of the purest bloodlines can easily be possessed by the Overlords, and perhaps Jane Grey was no exception.

The Windsor Bloodline

12 **I want to dig deeply into** the House of Windsor, as well, particularly in the light of what I wrote in the Wes Penre Papers about the late Queen Elizabeth II. In the discussions with my Orion source, the British Royalty came up in the conversation. My source told me Queen Elizabeth thought she was the Mother Goddess representative on Earth and had the *divine right to rule*. He said this was completely false, since she put herself in that lofty position (as have her ancestors) without permission from Orion. He also commented on being given the name Elizabeth, which is a direct title of both the Mother Goddess (Queen Sophia/the Queen of Orion) and her daughters (Zoë Sophia/Isis being one such daughter, once being born into the Sirius system to overview the Peace Agreement between Sirius and Orion). Moreover, he told me that the House of Windsor can hardly call themselves royals anymore because their bloodline is so diluted. At the time, I didn't understand why he stated this, and I had not researched Queen Elizabeth's bloodline at all. Now, I know better, after researching this book, ten years after my source told me this. It showed to be an important comment by my source, as we will see...

The House of Wessex

Tracing the Windsor bloodline on Queen Elizabeth's side, we find that it goes back to Alfred the Great, King of Wessex, England (848-899 C.E.). It goes back further than that, of course, but it's as far as the mainstream research goes when pertaining to the Windsor bloodline. Those who have watched all the *Vikings* series on Netflix over the last few years (which I have) know about Alfred the Great of Wessex, who had to deal a lot with Scandinavian Vikings. Alfred's obsessive goal was to unite all the small kingdoms in England at the time into one country (later Great Britain) to create a strong united country. He almost succeeded, but the final touches to unite England were done by his much later descendants, who kept his vision alive. Although Alfred's bloodline is considered British, it was later mingled with bloodlines from other royal families, of course, but most notably the French and Scottish, which were (and are) of the major Jesus-Magdalene bloodline with the French bloodline dominating.

Fig. 12:1. Alfred the Great (848-99 C.E.)

The House of Normandy

From Alfred the Great of the House of Wessex, the British royal bloodline turned into the House of Normandy with William I (William the Conqueror) in 1066. We need to keep in mind that Alfred's bloodline was originally not of the Jesus-Magdalene lineage at all. I have not yet researched the British bloodline to its true origins before Alfred, since it's beyond the scope of this book, but my current assumption is that it's not more royal than the bloodlines of you and me. It was most likely created by the winners of ancient tribal wars.

William the Conqueror married Matilda of Flanders, who was of a French aristocratic bloodline through the House of Flanders,[142] connected to the Carolingians. This is when the British bloodline started to be mixed with the French. Matilda was not of pure bloodline—probably a few times removed from it, but it was a beginning of the mixing of French and British royal blood. The House of Flanders only goes back to the mid-800s, but it's possible that if we trace it back further, it is likely to be connected to the Merovingians via the Carolingians.

The House of Plantagenet

The House of Normandy ends with King John in 1216, but during this dynasty, there were intermarriages with French aristocracy, again, still not of completely pure blood. The succeeding dynasty of the Brits was the House of Plantagenet, which took its name from Geoffrey Plantagenet, Count of Anjou in France (1113-51), who married the British Empress, Matilda (1102-67). Geoffrey was a great warrior, also called Geoffrey the Fair because of his good looks, *and he was red-haired,*[143] which indicates a purer bloodline, which could explain why the British Royalty named their new dynasty after him, about 100 years after his death. The British Royal Family had now purer blood running through their veins.

More on Elizabeth Woodville—Another Isis?

Henry III (r. 1216-72) married Eleanor of Province (1223-1291), and thereby was the first of a long line of British royalties who took French consorts. It was during the reign of the House of Plantagenet that the Wars of the Roses played out, ending with the slaughter of Richard III. Ambitions were then made, probably instigated by Elizabeth Woodville (whom I suspect was Isis) to put English-Scottish royalty on the French throne. It's likely that Elizabeth seeded her daughter, Elizabeth of York, with her Jesus-Magdalene DNA to further strengthen the French bloodline. As we discussed in a previous chapter, it failed.

Thus, Henry VII (r. 1485-1509) and Elizabeth of York (1466-

---

[142] Wikipedia: *House of Flanders.*
[143] Wikipedia: *Geoffrey Plantagenet, Count of Anjou #Early Life.*

1503 and the daughter of Isis?) seeded the British House of Tudor in 1491, when their son, Henry VII (r. 1509-1547) was born.

Fig. 12:2. The red-haired Elizabeth Woodville, with a rose on her dress, symbolizing the Isis bloodline

Another important branch of the Jesus-Magdalene bloodline was the Scottish royalty. Scotland is also to which a branch of the Knights Templar fled when they were hunted by the Catholic Church; and the French bloodline, to some degree, was spread to the Scottish Royal Families. A similar intermarriage as that with the British Royalty between the French and the Scots took place over generations. The plan was now to further expand the Jesus-Magdalene line to "unite" the French-Scottish-British connection, making all three royal houses more powerful, bloodline-wise. This is where Mary of Guise (1515-60) and her daughter, Mary Queen of Scots (1542-87) come into the picture.

The Tudor Dynasty

Henry VIII—A King of Terror and Tyranny

Henry VIII, son of the first Tudor regent, Henry VII, and his wife, Elizabeth of York, reigned between 1509 and 1547, during which he murdered two of his six wives,[144] Anne Boleyn [1501-36] and Catherine Howard [1520-42], and from failing to have his first marriage with Catherine of Aragon annulled because of a disagreement with Pope Clement VII to divorce her, Henry initiated the *English Reformation,* separating the Church of England from papal authority. Thus, he put himself as *Supreme Head of the Church of England* and dissolved convents and monasteries, and because of these actions, he was excommunicated by the pope, something that did not bother King Henry the least. Since then, to sit on the throne of England, you cannot be a Catholic. You must be a Protestant and adhere to the Church of England. And since then, the rest of Europe has had problems with England when it comes to major reformations, such as the Enlightenment in the 1700s, which we will come to later in this book. Banning the Catholic Church was not a bad thing, per se, but it shows Henry VIII's mindset. Only because he was not allowed to divorce his wife, he reformed the policy of an entire country, which had consequences in foreign affairs, for good and for bad.

Fig. 12:3. Henry VIII

---

[144] Britannica: *Why did Henry VIII kill his Wives?*

King Henry accused his second wife, Anne Boleyn, of adultery, and she was convicted and beheaded on May 19, 1536. However, the true reason for her execution was that she had failed to give him a male heir, so he needed a new wife. The only way, as a king, to legally remarry was if his previous wife dies. Therefore, he arranged that. His fifth wife, Catherine Howard, he accused of having affairs before their marriage, and of adultery. She was charged with treason, which led to her execution as well on February 13, 1542. The reason why the king married so many wives was onefold: He wanted sons, not daughters, so he could save the Tudor Dynasty. This became an obsession of his. Jane Seymour [1508-1537], his third wife, was the only one who gave him a son, whom he named Edward, later King Edward VI, and he inherited the throne after Henry's death. However, Edward was only ten years old at the time Henry died, and he perished at age sixteen, whereafter Henry's second daughter, Elizabeth I, raised to the occasion. Thus, Henry never got a son who could take over after him, despite all his sometimes horrific efforts.

The king was probably the archetype for the kind of monarch Marduk wanted. He was rigidly dedicated to continue the bloodline, and under his reign, he expanded the royal power, which was what Marduk wanted (at the time), and he was the one who ushered in, and coined the term, the *divine right of kings to rule*, opposed to papal supremacy.[145] If someone opposed him, he wasn't shy to use charges of treason and heresy, and those whom he accused were often executed without trial. As the supreme king, he considered himself to have the right to do so. During his rule, he made many radical changes to the political system in England, often achieved through the work of his chief ministers, some of whom he banished and executed when they fell out of favor (his actions are eerie similar to the Roman Emperor, Caligula, who ruled Rome during the life of Jesus).

Disconnecting from the Church of Rome had its advantages for King Henry, e.g., the money that used to go to the Catholic Church, he could now spend as we wished, and spend it, he did! He was often close to ruin from wasting much of the money on himself and his own comfort and amusement, but also on several useless wars.

Despite all these unpleasant and dominant parts of his

---

[145] Wikipedia: *Henry VIII.*

personality, he was considered a great king:

> Henry's contemporaries considered him an attractive, educated
> and accomplished king. He has been described as "one of the most
> charismatic rulers to sit on the English throne" and his reign de-
> scribed as the "most important" in English history. He was an
> author and composer. As he aged, he became severely overweight
> and his health suffered. He is frequently characterised in his later
> life as a lustful, egotistical, paranoid and tyrannical monarch.[146]

Reading this, we may start wondering: if he was as unpleasant
and tyrannical in the early part of his reign as described in this section of the book, how terrible must he not have been in his later
years? But isn't that how it goes? A person commits hideous crimes
in his youth, and then, when getting closer to death, these inhu-
mane acts start wearing on him, and the person sometimes goes
completely insane, unable to face themselves or suppress the
shame.

Henry VIII, aside from being quick to execute opponents and
people near and far who disagreed with him, is known for having
created many new reforms—some of them still in practice today,
500 years later. One such reform was to ban the Catholic Church
from having any influence over English religion and politics. He established the Protestant Church of England under his own
supremacy, and he even executed several abbots and threw out the
rest. This happened despite Henry having been a devoted Catholic
until the pope refused the annulment of his first marriage. This was
very frustrating to Henry because Catherine of Aragon did not
bring him a son, which threatened his legacy and ability to save the
House of Tudor. He wanted a new wife, who could give him one or
more sons.

As another reformation, he published acts that recognized royal
supremacy over the church. He declared the King as being "the only
Supreme Head on Earth of the Church of England," making it High
Treason, with a death penalty, to refuse acknowledging the king as
such.

Henry VIII died in 1547 at the age 55 from complications of his
extreme obesity. He was so overweight he could not walk on his
own but needed help to move around. He was succeeded by his only
son, Edward VI, who died early.

---

[146] *Ibid. op. cit.*

The Unification of Three Dynasties into One

When I researched how the Jesus-Magdalene bloodline moved between the royal houses in Europe, I suspected that Mary Queen of Scots might be another incarnation of Isis because it made sense. She was a redhead, carried the name Mary, and made a major change to the royal lineages. Isis, I noticed, usually shows up when major changes are in the planning. Still, I failed to connect her to Isis, despite deep research, so I left it with that, until I suddenly got an epiphany. *Mary Queen of Scots was not Isis, but her mother, Mary of Guise most likely was.* She was a redhead, her name was Mary, she was French, marrying onto the Scottish throne, becoming the Queen of Scotland by the marriage to King James V of Scotland. By that, the Scottish bloodline was strengthened. Presuming Mary of Guise was Isis, the task now became to put the bloodline on the British throne as well, uniting the Scottish, English, and French Jesus-Magdalene bloodline into three dynasties at once. Thus, there was an expansion and rejuvenations of the bloodline, which was in En.ki's and Marduk's interest, and in resonance with the overall plan.

Fig. 12:4. The red-haired Mary of Guise, attending a rose.

A "convenient" twist of events secured the succession of King James to the throne of Scotland. Obviously, Mary of Guise (Isis) wanted Mary Queen of Scots on the Scottish throne—the Queen of

Scots being female of the direct, strengthened bloodline of Jesus-Magdalene. Mary Queen of Scots had two elder twin-brothers, James, Duke of Rothesay (1540-1541) and Robert (also called Arthur), Duke of Albany (1540-41). Both died in quick succession the same year, both one year old. The only child who survived was Mary, born the year after, thus becoming the heir to the throne of Scotland. It is, of course, pure speculation, but taking into consideration that the plan was to unite the dynasties, I think it was important to Isis that Mary of Guise's descendant to the throne of Scotland was a female. Perhaps this is why the two sons were "eliminated." The next child was a female, Mary Queen of Scots, and by that, the mission was completed—no more children necessary.

Mary Queen of Scots gave birth to James VI of Scotland through Henry Lord Darnley, who was a Stuart of French descendant. Thus, there was now a strong French-Scottish bloodline connection via Mary of Guise (French) and King James V (Scottish), mixed into Mary Queen of Scots' DNA (she who gave birth to James VI of Scotland), being of a strong Jesus-Magdalene bloodline. James VI was the king Mary Queen of Scots wanted to put on the English throne. Mary of Guise (Isis) most certainly knew that the British Queen Elizabeth I, who ruled England during her own queenship and that of her daughter's, planned not to marry, and therefore, not having offspring. Thus, it was a golden opportunity to put a French-Scottish king on the English throne after Elizabeth.

Elizabeth, however, was not stupid, and she saw through this plot, but also being paranoid (justifiably so), feared the worst, i.e., that she would be murdered, so that Mary Queen of Scots could take the British throne. This was most likely not Mary's plan, since she wanted her son to inherit the British throne after the childless Elizabeth I, but the fact is, according to history, that Elizabeth never wanted James VI to succeed her; perhaps because she feared a *coup d'état* from Mary if she remained inactive. Hence, Elizabeth developed her own plans. She conspired with her court magician and chief advisor, John Dee, to put another pure-blood on the throne to succeed her—Jane Grey, the direct descendant of Elizabeth Woodville. To accomplish this, Elizabeth, who was also Mary's cousin via James V of Scotland, accused Mary of many crimes and had her put in prison, in wait for a trial. With Mary out of the way, Elizabeth I probably thought she now had more control over the situation. Later, she executed Mary of Scots by beheading her. The attempt to put Jane Grey on the throne succeeded, but only for 9 days, as explained earlier in this book. The execution was, of course, not on Elizabeth's order.

Left was James VI, who now could confidently claim the throne of England *and* Scotland, uniting the two. He became James VI of Scotland, and simultaneously, King James I of England after Elizabeth's death.[147] When he came to power, he wanted nothing to do with court magicians, such as John Dee, whom he probably considerably disliked on a personal level for having conspired against his mother, Queen of Scots. He fired Dee, who died in poverty in the streets of England. Most likely being the grandson of Isis, King James also made sure there was a Bible translation as accurate as possible in the English language, resulting in the *King James Bible*, widely spread up to this day, written in beautiful prose; many say it was translated by Sir Francis Bacon. James I also started the House of Stuart since Elizabeth's direct bloodline died out with her. The new house took its name after James' father, Henry Lord Darnley Stuart.

Thus, the French-Scottish-English strengthened bloodline plan was fulfilled for the moment.

The House of Stuart

The House of Stuart was ruling England for a little over 100 years, ending in 1714 with Queen Anne (r. 1702-14), who married the British monarch King William III (William of Orange), who died in 1702, where after Anne took over the throne of England, Scotland, and even Ireland to which the bloodline was also spread, but is not within the scope of our story. She married King George of Denmark, and she had no surviving children.

I must say it's amusing (if I may use that word) to notice that when big changes occur, and a female is seeding a new dynasty, she is almost always portrayed in history as "the only surviving female" of her birth family in question. It goes as a straight line through the bloodlines. It's not a coincidence, I'm sure. It was to secure this particular female (often the daughter of an incarnation of Isis) to be the one seeding the new strengthened bloodline. There was no difference after Queen Anne died, without having an heir to the

---

[147] There are stories about how Elizabeth's mental health declined when she got older, and she regretted having executed Mary.

throne. The throne then went to George I (r. 1714-27)[148], second cousin of Queen Anne, thus founding the House of Hanover, named after his mother, Sophia of Hanover, who was German. Therefore, King George I (r. 1714-27) was the first German monarch on the British throne. This, again, was a change of dynasties, and who was the instigator? A woman named *Sophia*. These are no coincidences: We have Mary, Elizabeth, and Sophia—three names related to the Queen of the Stars.

Also, don't forget the secret societies lurking in the background, having members swearing blood oaths to protect the Holy Grail, doing everything necessary to keep it running, including committing murder and manipulating, threatening, and bribing behind the scenes.

Remember Mary of Guise and her daughter, Mary of Scots. Two Mary in a row. Now, when the House of Hanover was founded, we have two Sophia: Sophia of Hanover, who instigated the new bloodline, and her daughter, Sophia Dorothea of Celle, who married King George I. When I investigated Sophia Dorothea, this is what I found:

> Born in Celle on 15 September 1666, Sophia Dorothea was **the only surviving daughter** of George William, Duke of Brunswick-Lüneburg, by his morganatic wife Eléonore Desmier d'Olbreuse (1639–1722), Lady of Harburg, a French Huguenot noblewoman.[149]

As I mentioned earlier, she was the "only surviving daughter." Sophia Dorothea was not Sophia of Hanover's daughter; Sophia Dorothea was married to Sophia of Hanover's son, George (originally George Louis of Hanover), coming from a German bloodline, and "coincidently," her name was also Sophia. Sophia Dorothea, King George's consort, was also German, *so the German royal house completely took over the British crown*.[150] I call it "The German Invasion." Sophia of Hanover shows to be extremely important, and I will discuss her more in a moment.

As an interesting side note, I mentioned in earlier research that the names we are given by our parents are not just random names that our parents come up with. It's programming. The parents think they choose a name for their child, when it's actually implanted as

---

[148] George's coat of arms of the House of Hanover pictured the three lilies of Isis' bloodline.

[149] Wikipedia.org: *Sophia Dorothea of Celle, #Life ##Early years.*

[150] Dw.com: *How German are the British royals?*

a thought from astral workers to fit the personality, destiny, and astrological configuration of the child; these subconscious decisions are embedded as a part of the person's destiny for that lifetime. There is always a chance some parents "accidentally" override this programming, but that is rare. Therefore, I do not believe it's a coincidence that both these women's names were Sophia. Also, by having the same name, the bloodlines are more easily traced by insiders who need to do so.

Elizabeth Stuart

Sophia of Hanover was the granddaughter of King James I,[151] and here it comes: Her mother was ELIZABETH Stuart (1596-1662), *another redhead*. She was called the "Winter Queen," since she and her husband, Frederic V of the Palatinate (1596-1632), reigned in Bohemia over one winter. And here we go again. *Elizabeth was the only surviving daughter of James I of England*:

> Princess Elizabeth was the only surviving daughter of James VI and I, King of Scotland, England, and Ireland, and his queen, Anne of Denmark, and she was the elder sister of Charles I.[152]

"Someone" made sure, as far as it was possible (taking human unpredictability into consideration), to guarantee the progression of the bloodline through the generations via the feminine bloodlines across the royal houses. These females were often married into the existing royal bloodlines. This has been a fairly reliable pattern over the centuries and the millennia.

There are some interesting stories about Elizabeth Stuart. There was, in 1605, a plot to murder King James I, her father, and the conspirators kidnapped Elizabeth, at that time 9 years old, with the purpose to replace her father on the British throne. Elizabeth, not being the eldest of her siblings, could not otherwise become the Queen of England, Scotland, and Ireland to strengthen the bloodline where it counted. This plot failed, however, and the conspirators were betrayed.[153] It makes me wonder who these conspirators truly were. Were they parts of a secret society, directly involved in protecting the Holy Grail? Rosicrucians? Templars?

---

[151] Wikipedia: *Sophia of Hanover.*
[152] Wikipedia: *Elizabeth Stuart, Queen of Bohemia, op. cit.*
[153] *Ibid., op. cit.*

It is possible Elizabeth was yet another incarnation of Isis. Here is another clue,

> By the age of 12, Elizabeth was fluent in several languages, including French, "which she spoke with ease and grace" and would later use to converse with her husband.[154]

She seemed to favor French before all other language she spoke, which would also make sense if she was Isis. She even decided to speak it to her husband in French, being their everyday language.

Fig. 12:5. The red-haired Elizabeth Stuart in a dress with roses.

Elizabeth's involvement in the future of the royal bloodline via her daughter helped strengthen the bloodline of the House of Hanover.

George I's son, George II (r. 1727-60) married Caroline of Ansbach, who was of German descendant, and thus, the English Royal bloodline got mixed with German blood, which I believe was not as pure. This might have been the first dilution of the Holy Grail

---

[154] *Ibid., op. cit.*

since Mary of Guise united the bloodlines. It could also be an attempt to spread the bloodline further, but if this was the plan, I would argue they would do it in reverse: They would put a member of the British Royal family on the German throne, and not the other way around.

My conclusion is that by merging the German and the British royal houses, it helped fulfilling an old plan Marduk had, which it was now time to implement. He wanted to dilute the Jesus-Isis-Ninurta bloodline and overthrow the royal families all over the world for a superior agenda. This started with the French king, Louis XIV, who was ruling France during the "German Invasion." We will spend a lot of time with King Louis in a separate chapter because he turned everything upside down and literally changed the entire world during his rulership, which had major ripple effects after his death. Louis XIV was the longest ruling monarch in history, reigning for 72 years, beating even Queen Elizabeth II.

Later down the line, King William IV (r. 1830-37) married Adeleine of Saxe-Meiningen, another German, which, from what I can see, diluted the British bloodline even more. They had no surviving offspring, so King William IV's niece, Queen Victoria (r. 1837-1901) inherited the throne, starting the Saxe-Coburg & Gotha dynasty, which was short-lived. Although she was not a direct descendant of King William IV, she still had significant German blood via her mother, Victoria of Saxe-Coburg and her grandmother, Charlotte of Mecklenburg. Her son, Edward VII (r. 1901-10), married Alexandra of Denmark, now adding the Danish branch of the bloodline into the mix, once more diluting it. King Edward VII was the last king of the Saxe-Coburg & Gotha dynasty.

The House of Windsor

George V (r. 1910-36), son of King Edward VII, became the first king of the House of Windsor, marrying Mary of Teck (1867-1953). Time for a new dynasty, so let's introduce either a Mary, Elizabeth, Sophia, or a mix of them—several women suddenly showing up with the same names. Mary was a first cousin to Queen Victoria, and her grandmother on the male side was a direct descendant of George III of Hanover, whose parents were both German. So, let us examine Mary a little more, and the reason I think she might have been another Isis.

Mary of Teck

Mary was, curiously, a redhead, although her parents were not. It seems no one knows why Mary had red hair.

Fig. 12:6. The red-haired Mary of Teck with waterlilies on her dress. [155]

It seems like it was high time and overdue to strengthen the bloodline again, and this time the empowerment came from Germany, the same royals who had infiltrated the British monarchy. In Mary of Teck, we might have another Isis incarnation. This time, it could have been an attempt of Isis to at least put some of her DNA into the Windsor German royal blood. Germany was Marduk's domain, and the German royal bloodline had been severely diluted on purpose by Marduk, as we shall see in the next upcoming chapters. Perhaps this was Isis' early effort in modern time to counter Marduk and save the Jesus-Magdalene bloodline. By reintroducing her DNA into the British monarchy, if ever so little through Mary of Teck, she might have planted a seed there, so she could continue a mission of her own in the next few generations, free from Marduk's

---

[155] Bristolpost.co.uk: *Royal family: Prince Harry looks just like not-so-distant ancestor, according to fans.*

influence.

When George V died in 1936, Mary became the Queen Mother when her son, George VI (r. 1936-52) ascended the throne. When I researched this last part of the Windsor dynasty, I noticed something interesting. Presuming Mary Teck was Isis, her son, George VI married an Elizabeth (Elizabeth Bowes-Lyon) (1900-2002), known to us as the "Queen Mother." She was English-Scottish with German blood, as well. And what was the name of the Queen Mother's daughter? Of course, Elizabeth, coronated in 1952 as the Queen of England as Elizabeth II (r. 1952-2022). She gave birth to Charles, who married Diana. That is when it really gets interesting, but first thing first.

Although the British bloodline was most likely strengthened again by Mary of Teck because of Isis' soul-spirit DNA mixed with that of the physical body, it was, of course, not enough. After all the inbreeding with the Germans previously, the bloodline was weak, even more so after Queen Elizabeth II's marriage to Prince Philip (1921-2021)[156]. Therefore, it needed to be strengthened further, as we will discuss after we have investigated Prince Philip, which we will do now.

The House of Mountbatten

Philip was born on the Greek island of Corfu in 1921 as Philippos Prince of Greece and Denmark, but he had his toes dipped into most royal dynasties in Europe. There's hardly any dynasty in Europe which he did not have a blood connection to.[157]

His father was Prince Andrew, a younger brother of King Constantine of Greece, and his mother was Princess Alice of Battenberg, from which the House of Mountbatten got its name, Princess Alice being German (mountain translates to *berg* in German). The House of Mountbatten took its name in 1917:

> The name was adopted on 14 July 1917, three days before the British royal family changed its name from "Saxe-Coburg and Gotha" to "Windsor", by members of the Battenberg family residing in the

---

[156] Irony has it that Prince Philip said in an interview many years before he died that if he reincarnated, it would be as a virus(!) How ironic that he died during the CORONA "virus" epidemic in 1921.

[157] thednatests.com: *Prince Philip Family Tree.*

United Kingdom, due to rising anti-German sentiment among the British public during World War I. The name is a direct Anglicisation of the German Battenberg, or Batten mountain, the name of a small town in Hesse. The titles of count and later prince of Battenberg had been granted in the mid-19th century to a morganatic branch of the House of Hesse-Darmstadt, itself a cadet branch of the House of Hesse.[158]

In other words, the current House of Windsor changed the name of their dynasty from the German name, Saxe-Coburg & Gotha to Windsor, not to show they are major descendants of German royalty through inbreeding with German royal bloodlines during the 1800s. Almost 90% of all sitting monarchs during the House of Saxe-Coburg & Gotha took German consorts, which also was devastating for the pure bloodline, as mentioned earlier. The Battenbergs of Germany needed to do the same, and in 1947, Prince Philip took his mother's family name and changed it to the more English-sounding name, Mountbatten, when marrying Queen Elizabeth II. The royal family also stopped interbreeding with pure German royalty for a generation, after they changed their name to Windsor to wait for the British anti-German hostility to wear off after the World Wars.

However, when both World Wars were over, the interbreeding continued with Queen Elizabeth II marrying Prince Philip in 1947. Philip was half German and half Greek, also with ties to Denmark, Norway, Sweden, and Iceland, via *The House of Schleswig-Holstein-Sonderburg-Glücksburg* on his mother's side. Lady Louise Mountbatten became Queen Consort of Sweden after marrying King Gustav VI Adolf of Sweden.[159]

The origins of the House of Mountbatten (or rather, The House of Battenberg) is so well described in Wikipedia that it is unnecessary for me to define it in my own words, so here is Prince Philip's immediate ancestry:

> The Mountbatten family are a branch of the German house of Battenberg. The Battenberg family was a morganatic branch of the House of Hesse-Darmstadt, rulers of the Grand Duchy of Hesse in Germany. The first member of the House of Battenberg was Julia Hauke, whose brother-in-law Grand Duke Louis III of Hesse

---

[158] Wikipedia: *Mountbatten Family.*
[159] Wikipedia: *Mountbatten Family.*

created her Countess of Battenberg with the style Illustrious Highness (HIllH) in 1851, on the occasion of her morganatic marriage to Grand Duke Louis' brother Prince Alexander of Hesse and by Rhine. Julia was elevated in her title to Princess of Battenberg with the style Serene Highness (HSH) in 1858...

Two of Alexander and Julia's sons, Prince Henry of Battenberg and Prince Louis of Battenberg, became associated with the British Royal Family. Prince Henry married The Princess Beatrice, the youngest daughter of Queen Victoria. Prince Louis married Victoria's granddaughter, Princess Victoria of Hesse and by Rhine, and became the First Sea Lord of the Royal Navy. Due to anti-German feelings prevalent in Britain during World War I, Prince Louis, his children, and his nephews (the living sons of Prince Henry), renounced their German titles and changed their name to the more English sounding Mountbatten. (They rejected an alternative translation, "Battenhill".)[2] Their cousin George V compensated the princes with British peerages. Prince Louis became the 1st Marquess of Milford Haven, while Prince Alexander, Prince Henry's eldest son, became the 1st Marquess of Carisbrooke.[160]

This explains well the prince's connection to the British Royal Family. Again, we can see how the Germans "invaded" the British royal bloodline during the Saxe-Coburg & Gotha dynasty, which essentially is the same dynasty as the House of Windsor; they only changed names. Thus, the same German bloodlines (Prince Philip's being one of them), interbred with the British throne already in the 19th century through Queen Victoria's daughters, and it has continued ever since. It seems to me that the British royalty, for a specific reason, have decided to mix their blood with Prince Philip's bloodline.

Prince Philip and the Jewish Connection

Julia Haucke (or more correctly, Julia von Haucke), mentioned in the above quote, the first member of the House of Battenberg, is said to have been Jewish, which means Philip also had Jewish blood.[161] Was this the reason the British royalty took German wives of the Battenberg bloodline? I would say so because of the presumed Jesus connection, where it's implied that Jesus was Jewish.

---

[160] *Ibid., op. cit.*
[161] The Jewish Chronicle: *Clues that tell us Philip had Jewish Blood.*

Thus, there may have been an additional reason why Prince Philip changed his name; he had Jewish ancestry to hide. The Nazis even interrogated Philip's mother, suspecting her of being a Jew; but she pretended she had a hearing problem and couldn't understand them, so the Nazi interrogators became frustrated and let her go. They had lots of other people to interrogate.

Fig. 12:7. Julia Haucke of Battenberg, Philip's Jewish ancestor

Prince Philip's ancestors, at least those on his mother's side, have interbred with the royal families of Europe by adding their Jewish blood. I know that people, and even scholars, say that Jesus was Jewish and that therefore, the Merovingians, and those who came after, were Jewish as well.

This is, as we discussed in the opening of this book, not true, however, because Jesus was born from an unfertilized egg, and Mother Mary was not of the Davidian bloodline. To keep our memories fresh, let us repeat what we discussed at the beginning of the book and clear up the confusion around Jewish ancestry.

The Virgin Mary was not of the Davidian bloodline, as many

assume, because Saint Anne and Saint Joakim, her alleged parents, were *not* her parents (which some scholars also have concluded). The Virgin Mary was of Isis' own bloodline, the redheads, the androgynous, and the hermaphroditic. She was "pure" and "free from sin," as the Bible tells us, because she was not of a bloodline full of baggage, like her husband, Joseph. She was impregnated by the "Holy Spirit," i.e., she impregnated herself; Isis being the only one of the three conspirators (En.ki, Marduk, and Isis) who was spirited. Therefore, Jesus was of pure Isis-Ninurta bloodline, and he was red-haired—something that must have stuck out in the Middle East in those days. Marduk was incarnated in Jesus' body, and the bloodline mix happened as planned. But Jesus was not Jewish, and

he was probably "white," just like in the pictures we see so often. He did not have a typical Middle Eastern look. The bloodline simply started with Jesus, who was the first offspring of a new and completely uncontaminated lineage, not connected with the diluted Davidian genes, so the Overlords could start afresh. Therefore, the Merovingians were not Jewish either. They were the product of about 400-450 years of Jesus' gene pool, kept as pure as possible and protected by secret societies, such as the Priory of Sion, so no commoners, like you and I, could "pollute" the bloodline.

Fig. 12:8. Queen Elizabeth II, with the red Maltese Cross inside the eight-pointed star, symbolizing the Royal Victorian Order. The Maltese cross is the Cross of Ninurta, worn by the Knights Templars, denoting the Ninurta bloodline.

It appears that Prince Philip was the first person with Jewish blood to marry into the British monarchy, but his Jewish blood is irrelevant, which the reader will understand when we now review the different bloodlines of Noah—Noah being of the En.ki-Isis lineage (for those who want to study this in more detail, see *The ORION Book, Volume 2*, pp. 6-11).

The Jewish branch we perhaps hear the most about is that of the Ashkenazim, but we have many branches of Judaism, which all claim to originate from the same ancestor, i.e., Israel was the descendant of the first patriarch, Abraham. Israel (also named Jacob) is considered the first Hebrew. These Jews call themselves the *Israelites*. Israel/Jacob was Abraham's and Sarah's grandson, and it's from Jacob the land of Israel is named, and from where the term *Israelites* comes. And here is a kicker: If we break down the name Israel, we get Is.Ra.El., i.e., Is(Isis).Ra(Marduk).El (Elohim). Jacob and Israel were the same, and therefore, we have the relation to "Jacob's ladder" in the Old Testament—the ladder leading to the gods, and from which "God" was symbolically descending to Jacob. I would strongly suggest this was when Marduk and Isis created their bloodline—the Semitic bloodline—and then, Jacob/Israel started seeding the *Twelve Tribes of Israel.* Therefore, this is another point in history when Isis was present. Jacob married (was told by God to marry) Leah and Rachel, two twin sisters who supposedly gave Jacob the twelve sons, founding the twelve tribes of Israel.

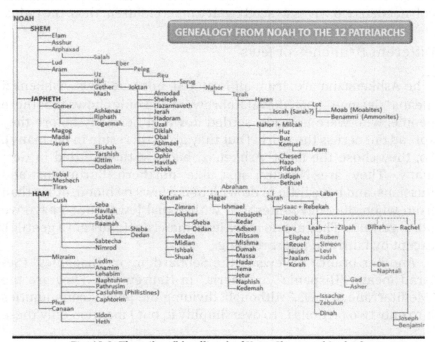

Fig. 12:9. *The tribes (bloodlines) of Ham, Shem, and Japheth.*

But wait! None of the two wives carries the names Mary, Elizabeth, or Sophia!

Well, if we investigate what Leah and Rachel mean in translation, it's "cow" and "ewe" (Eve), respectively. Who was the cow goddess? Hathor. And who was Hathor? Isis. Then, who was Eve? Isis.

> Leah is the elder daughter of Laban and the wife of Jacob, father of twelve sons who will become the twelve tribes of Israel. Leah and her sister Rachel, whose names mean "cow" and "ewe," give Jacob many sons; and their father gives him actual live-stock.[162]

However, Isis can't be two women at once (presumably), so which one was Isis? None of the two. Leah and Rachel must have been daughters of the real Isis, who named them after her attributes. The Bible tells us that the sisters' father was Laban, and their mother was Adina (or Adinah), which translates to "gentle" or "mild" from Hebrew to English. These seem to be two attributes of Isis—both as the Virgin Mary/Mary Magdalene and other potential Isis incarnations. If Adina was Isis, she would have named her twin daughters after other attributes connected to her. I hypothesize Jacob needed two wives to seed twelve male children: thus, the twins.

Different Branches of Jews

The Ashkenazim are, from all I can tell, not true Jews. Ashkenazi means "German" in Medieval Hebrew,[163] and only shows that these people, who were nomads, settled down in Germany before they spread out across the world (but they also still reside in Germany). So, they chose the name Ashkenazi because they settled in Germany. They are Nordics, just like northern Europeans and Russians, and have little to do with being Jews by blood, other than from when they have interbred with actual Jews, but so have we other gentiles. They are no more Jews than I am (and I am a gentile), except by faith and interbreeding.

Another branch of Jews is the Sephardim, or "Hispanics" (Sefarad means "Hispania" or "Iberia" in Hebrew[164]). They are the "Mediterranean Jews." Although, dividing the Jewish communities into only two factions is to oversimplify it, but I mention only these

---

162 Jewish Women's Archive (jwa.org): *Leah: Bible.*
163 Wikipedia: *Jewish Ethnic Division.*
164 *Ibid.*

two factions in particular for the purpose of this book. Those who want to dig deeper into the history of Judaism can search Wikipedia for "Jewish Ethnic Division." That's a good place to start. However, genetic studies have shown that both culturally and physically, they all originate from the same common ancient Israelite population, anyway, namely the Hebrews through the twelve tribes of Israel.[165] This may be correct, but the Ashkenazim are not part of any of these tribes, as we shall see.

Review of the Post-Diluvian Noah Bloodlines

Before we continue, we must review what I wrote in *The ORION Book, volume 2*. I said there were three *main* branches of Noah's bloodline after the Flood, and it's the En.ki-Isis bloodline that was the lineage En.ki wanted to save back then, when the Flood swept across the Earth. It was his pure bloodline, and Noah was the last descendent of this lineage. One branch became the black people from Africa. The black Africans are the descendants of Noah's son, Ham.

The second Noah bloodline was that of Marduk-Isis, the Shem lineage, although all three bloodlines were of En.ki-Isis to begin with. According to my recent research, I put the time when Prince Ninurta/En.lil castrated En.ki to about 2024 BCE, which aligns well with the Sumerian texts when En.ki left Earth and never returned. After that, the breeding project to keep the bloodlines pure cane on Marduk, who then created the Marduk-Isis bloodline by infiltrating a part of the Shem bloodline, which became the Semitic bloodline, from where the Hebrews stem. The timeline fits perfectly with the biblical texts, which propose that Abraham, the Arch Jew/Hebrew, lived in the 18th century BCE,[166] just about 300 years after En.ki was thrown into the ABZU.[167] Abraham was the beginning of the Marduk-Isis bloodline and that of the Hebrews. Therefore, the Mediterranean Jews can claim descendant of Abraham. Lately, black African Jews claim to be the true Israelites, but that is not

---

[165] Wikipedia: *Genetic Studies on Jews.*

[166] The-Map-Of-History.com: *The Bible and History: Geographical map for the Saga of Abraham.*

[167] Some Jewish sources mention 1,200 BCE, but it's quite irrelevant, as it was still close after En.ki was placed in the ABZU.

correct, since they are of Ham's descendants, i.e., the En.ki-Isis bloodline, directly from Noah.

Last of the three main bloodlines is the Japheth lineage, which are the Nordic and Eurasian tribes, i.e., the northern Europeans and the Russians, for the most part. The Ashkenazi "Jews" belong to this tribe, and so do many of you who read this, me included. We are of the Marduk-Ereškigal bloodline. Even more likely, most of the Nordic people are a mix of the Marduk-Isis and Marduk-Ereškigal gene pools. This may sound complicated because the Nordic people have existed much longer than 4,000+ years, and the Marduk-Ereškigal lineage is more recent than the Marduk-Isis bloodline. However, when Marduk and Ereškigal created their own bloodline, they did not genetically modify the entire Japheth line. They simply started a new branch of it, which included Ereškigal's DNA. Therefore, we Nordic people are, for the most part, a mix of the original Japheth line and that of Marduk and Ereškigal. The Ashkenazim converted to Judaism around 900 C.E.,[168] but they did not originate there. This is what a deep study from 2013 of the Ashkenazim showed:

A 2013 study of Ashkenazi mitochondrial DNA by a team led by Martin B. Richards agreed with the older hypothesis of the origin. It tested all 16,600 DNA units of mtDNA, and found that the four main female Ashkenazi founders had descent lines that were established in Europe 10,000 to 20,000 years in the past while most of the remaining minor founders also have a deep European ancestry. The study argued that the great majority of Ashkenazi maternal lineages were not brought from the Near East or the Caucasus, but instead assimilated within Europe, primarily of Italian and Old French origins. The study estimated that more than 80% of Ashkenazi maternal ancestry comes from women indigenous to (mainly prehistoric Western) Europe, and only 8% from the Near East, while the origin of the remainder is undetermined.[169]

Because 80% of these people originate in Western Europe, it makes them of the Japheth bloodline (non-Jewish), now mixed with that of Ereškigal. Technically, they can still call themselves Jews, since they converted to Judaism, by which they are accepted into the Jewish community.

With all this explained, we can see that the Jewish mix with the

---

[168] Wikipedia: Ashkenazi Jews
[169] *Ibid., op. cit.*

non-Jewish British bloodline (and other European Jesus-Magdalene blood-based European dynasties) is irrelevant. The Jesus bloodline includes Isis', Marduk's, and most importantly, Ninurta's blood, and the Marduk-Isis Shem bloodline includes the same DNA, but not as pure as the original Jesus lineage of the Merovingians. Therefore, I would suggest that to various degrees, the Marduk-Isis bloodline, mixed with that of different dynasties, amplifies the Jesus line after 2,000 years of gradual decline. So, my conclusion is that Prince Philip's Jewish blood took nothing away from the British bloodline. Of course, it is uncertain whether Prince Philip was of Ashkenazi or Sephardic descent. If it is the former, it *would* take away from the pure blood.

Hitler, the Holocaust, and the Semitic Bloodline

So far, we have learned that the Semitic people are of the Marduk-Isis and not the En.ki-Isis bloodline. This means this bloodline of Hebrew descendants should be something that at least Marduk would like to preserve. So, why did Hitler, being Marduk's puppet, wish to terminate Jews? A similar thing went on in Russia under Josef Stalin.

Now, please pay *close* attention to this section and read carefully because it will be very important when you continue reading. It all connects!

Hitler and his genetic scientists dug deeply into human genome and heritage. Based on the development in Nazi Germany, I think we can safely say that Hitler was aware of Noah's sons' bloodlines. I also discussed in the ORION books that Marduk and En.ki fight for the ultimate power over humankind, and Germany is, and has been for long, Marduk's domain. However, it was fairly recently Marduk seeded the Marduk-Ereškigal bloodline, which he now wants to become the dominant bloodline because that's where he donated most of his genes. And where did he foremost seed his DNA among the general population? In the Nordic Japheth bloodline, i.e., the bloodline he now wants to dominate the Earth. Marduk and the Khan Kings manipulated Hitler into believing this bloodline is descended in a straight line from the Aryan (Namlú'u) lineage, which is, of course, false, and Marduk obviously knows this. He just wanted to give Hitler a carrot. We know, from convincing evidence, that Hitler was in psychic connection with the "Supermen" from beneath the Earth, as he had been told (the Marduk clan of the

Overlords), and he intensely feared them. This is described in detail in the book, *The Spear of Destiny,* by Trevor Ravenscroft.[170] So, it is my theory that Hitler was hoodwinked by Marduk and his Khan supporters to believe the modified Japheth line was the pure human bloodline. It's highly likely, as I see it, that Marduk, to gain full power over En.ki, and to prepare for the Singularity (still 100 years in the future back then), wanted to destroy the Shem bloodline, and perhaps, eventually, also the Ham lineage (the black people). Left on Earth would be his new bloodline, mixed with those of the royal houses of Europe (which we will talk about later), in which Marduk had invested his DNA as Jesus. This is his way of dominating the human soul group via his DNA.

Hitler might or might not have known that the Ashkenazim were not Jews but of Japheth's line. Regardless, according to geneticists, the Ashkenazim are inbred with the Hebrew Jews, so they had to go, too. The same applied to the Gypsies—everything had to go, except for what Hitler considered the purer form of the Japheth bloodline, i.e., those who qualified as accepted by the Overlords; those of the Isis-Ereškigal gene pool. He was even attacking the Ashkenazi Banking Elite, and this was part of a side agenda that also had to do with the Jews: Hitler wanted to stop what he considered the Jews' usurping practices, afraid they, although a minority, would increase in power through their control of the banking industry and the wealth random Jewish families were gathering because of their greed and usurping businesses.[171] Hitler was a typical narcissist and psychopath, which means he saw everything in black and white—no shades of gray. He saw the greed of the Ashkenazim, so he wanted to root out them, too, including the Banking Elite, and he eventually banned all secret societies from Germany, save his own. Marduk might not have wanted the latter to happen, at least, but on the other hand, I don't think the warlord from Sirius was particularly concerned about whether Hitler would get hold of the Rothschilds and their ilk. He knew Hitler would never get to them; Marduk would see to that. The Banking Elite was still useful and could be replaced later. This is an oxymoron, it may seem, because Hitler, stunningly, was Jewish. Somehow, the Overlords had

---

[170] Amazon.com.

[171] Timesofisrael.com: *Abbas: Ashkenazi Jews 'are not Semites,' Hitler killed them for their 'social role'*

apparently promised to spare him because of his great work (which they would not).

Of course, Hitler failed in his bold attempt, and it was a setback for Marduk. Or... was it? In my conversation with the Orion source, he conveyed that the entire Germany was, at that time, destined to be slaughtered in a monstrous genocide of the entire German population, and this genocide would feed the gods, who could have an extravagant feast in "Valhalla," prey on an abundance of loosh when people were slaughtered in droves (human life energy, i.e., soul and spiritual energy, and vril [cosmic energy] gained from the spirited humans).

But why did Marduk want to sacrifice his own people, and moreover, the bloodline he told Hitler he preferred? Because Marduk has no morals and ethics akin to a normal person, but that of a psychopath. Psychopaths are extremely calculating and goal driven; and they are prepared to take any action to reach their goal.[172]

Regarding Marduk's plans for Hitler, it was not particularly about a culling of the world population to keep the number of people down—the true motive had to do with that there were too many mix-bloods amongst the German population. The entire World War II was one monumental bloodline cleansing. Marduk wanted to get rid of all traces of the Isis bloodline—even his own Marduk-Isis genome. No more Isis. Why? *Because before the Singularity, he wanted as many people as possible in the world to be of his new Marduk-Ereškigal bloodline, so only he and his fellow Sirians could control and ride the human Avatars and also control our minds through theirs.*

So, why did Marduk not introduce the Marduk-Ereškigal bloodline much earlier? Why did he use Isis as a breeder for so long? I believe one reason was England. Marduk had always had a problem with England, historically known to refuse to follow Marduk's twist and turn in plans. Marduk waited for the right moment, and it eventually came.

As most of us understand by now, the Nazi philosophy did not die out with the end of World War II. The entire project moved to the United States, where Nazi scientists were secretly transferred to America after the war in *Operation Paperclip*[173], thus saving their

---

[172] See Professor Sam Vaknin's lectures on his YouTube channel.
[173] Wikipedia: *Operation Paperclip.*

lives and using them to further propel the agenda, leading to the Singularity. They used brilliant Nazi scientists, such as Werner von Braun and Josef Mengele, whom among many other Nazi scientists were smuggled out of Nazi Germany before the Nuremburg trials.

The "German Invasion"

Back in 1714, the German Dynasty of Hanover completely took over the British Crown, and the old British bloodline became overly mixed with German blood, which is of great significance, as we shall see. King George I was of almost pure German royal blood, and his wife, Queen Sophia Dorothea of Celle, was also German. Therefore, their offspring were all Germans, not British.[174] How did this happen?

Without getting entrenched in too many boring details, we could say, in summary, that in case there were no British offspring of William III of the House of Stuart, the British throne would go to Sophia of Hanover and/or her offspring. Sophia was the daughter of Elizabeth Stuart, a daughter of James I of England (all these Elizabeth and Sophia again, with a Mary thrown in here and there, as well, for good measures. Big things were apparently in the making). Elizabeth Stuart was married to Frederick V of Bohemia, Elector of Palatine (German), so Sophia of Hannover was half German and half English.

Now it so "happened," that King William III (r. 1689-1702) was childless (what a surprise). He was British-Scottish, and the great grandson of James I (the King James' Bible). Circumstances had it that a few years followed until Sophia's of Hannover bloodline could legally take over. Thus, from King William's death in 1702 until King George of Hanover, Sophia's son, could inherit the throne, Princess Anne, James II's daughter, consort to King George of Denmark, ruled for twelve years. Thereafter, George I became King of England and the first monarch of the House of Hanover.

Ever since, the British Crown has been almost completely of German blood, and by Queen Elizabeth II marrying Prince Philip (of significant German blood), the German bloodline was even strengthened.

The official story is that it so happened that George I from

---

[174] Dw.com: *How German are the British royals?*

Germany must put himself on the British throne (against his will), but what was truly going on behind the scenes? To understand that more clearly, we need to start investigating the Marduk-Ereškigal bloodline, which will be thoroughly done in a later chapter.

The Spencer Bloodline

Now, while having addressed the Jewish subject, let us dig into the Diana Spencer bloodline. She had a quite interesting lineage, and there are a few mysteries around Diana in that respect.

The Early Life of Diana Spencer

Fig 12:10. The Diana Chronicles cover.

Diana Spencer was born in 1961 to Frances Shand Kydd (1936-2004), born Frances Ruth Roche, which sounds like a Jewish name, very similar to Rothchild. I have tried to find a Jewish connection in Frances Roche's case, but I have found no Jewish connection to that particular name, except some mentioning of Frances' Jewish connection in a book by Tina Brown, called, The Diana Chronicles:

> In her book "The Diana Chronicles", Tina Brown claims that Princess Diana's Jewish mother, Frances Shand Kydd had relationships with a Jewish banker called James Goldsmith while she was married to Earl John Spencer. She argues that Diana, who was born in 1961, was the illegitimate child of Goldsmith and was not the real

daughter of Spencer. Brown writes that even if Diana is not born to a Jewish father, based on the Jewish law, she is still considered a Jew as she was born to a Jewish mother.[175]

I have not read the book, making me unfamiliar with the sources Tina Brown is using for her statement, so I can't confirm or dispute. However, Ms. Brown was Princess Diana's friend, which gives some credit to her claims. If her sources are only her verbal communication with Diana, it is, however, difficult to verify her claims. A potential Jewish connection would have given an extra spice to the Diana-Charles marriage because the Jewish bloodline, as we know, is that of Shem, which in turn is of the Marduk-Isis gene pool.

The book can be ordered from amazon.com.

Others claim that one of the two branches of the Spencer family is Jewish, that these two branches were mingled, and that Diana belonged to both:

> Diana Spencer, the late Princess of Wales and international icon, was born into an aristocratic British family, the Spencer family. Interestingly, Diana was also related to the Jewish Spencer family, a prominent and wealthy dynasty of European bankers. The link between the two branches of the Spencer family was established more than two centuries ago, when a branch of the Jewish Spencer family emigrated from Germany to England. Since then, the two branches of the Spencer family have continued to share a common heritage, with Diana being a direct descendant of both. This article will explore the relationship between the Jewish and British branches of the Spencer family, as well as the influence that Diana's Jewish ancestry had on her life and legacy.[176]

If this is correct, there is also a German aspect to the Spencer family, which follows the pattern within the British Royal Family since the early 1700s when the Marduk branch of the Brotherhood took over, and his new bloodline was introduced.

The Spencer family has a connection with the British Royal family going back a long time and has continued up to this day. It can be traced to the British Royal House of Stuart[177, 178],

> Through the marriage of Princess Diana's grandparents, John the

---

[175] Mehrnews.com: *British Royal Family: Christian or Jewish?*

[176] Dvaita.org: *Is Diana Spencer Related to the Jewish Spencer Family?*

[177] *Ibid.*

[178] Wrongsideoftheblanket.com: *Today's Royal Family.*

7th Earl Spencer and Lady Cynthia Hamilton, the Spencer family enjoys a uniquely comprehensive range of descents from the royal house of Stewart/Stuart that ruled in Scotland from the late 14th century and in all of Britain from 1603 to 1714.[179]

In *The Diana Chronicles,* it apparently says Diana's mother had a sexual relationship on the side with Sir James Goldsmith, the Jewish tycoon, who at his death in 1997 was the richest man in the world. There are many pictures with Diana and Goldsmith being together, and she visited him at the hospital when he was dying from pancreatic cancer in 1997. Tina Brown claims Diana was *his* daughter, not Earl Spencer's. The same claim is done at radaronline.com, based on what Ms. Brown wrote.[180]

Prince Charles was also Diana's second cousin, and she was blood related to the current Queen Camilla of Great Britain, King Charles III's queen consort.[181] Another potential clue that it might be the case that Diana was born out of wedlock is that the Spencer bloodline is full of redheads, and Diana's siblings have red hair. Diana's true hair color, however, was neither red or blond, but auburn, and there are those who have said that she resembled James Goldsmith.

Diana is the name for Isis in ancient Rome, as those who have read the WPP might recall.

> Like her Greek counterpart, Artemis, Diana was the goddess of the hunt. The daughter of the Roman god Jupiter and his mistress, Latona.[182]

Artemis is another name for the Mother Goddess, aka Queen Sophia, and Diana/Isis is known as the creatrix of homo sapiens in the Second Construct, together with En.ki. Jupiter is the equivalent to both En.ki and Marduk. Because it's a title, it depends on who is holding that title, and when. In our time, Jupiter is Marduk.

So, what does this mean in relation to Diana Spencer? Am I suggesting Diana was Isis? I do. There is overwhelming evidence for this. The closer I come to present time in my research, the easier it is to get more in-depth data and information to compare.

---

[179] Unofficialroyalty.com: *The Spencers' Royal Stuart Ancestors, op. cit.*

[180] Radaronline.com: *Secret Diana Took To Grave: Was Billionaire Sir James Goldsmith Her Real Father?*

[181] Dvaita.org: *Is Diana Spencer Related to the Jewish Spencer Family?*

[182] westportlibrary.libguides.com: *Artemis/Diana: About, op. cit.*

People may have different opinions on the British researcher, author, and lecturer David Icke (1952-) and his claim that the British royal family (and other authority figures) are shapeshifting reptilians, but fact remains that Icke has done some brilliant research over the years. Often, he was the first to reveal Elite secrets that we now take for granted as holding much truth. Already in 1999, he acknowledged the Mother Goddess as the Feminine Creatrix, and at the same time spoke on the imbalance of the feminine and masculine forces in humans. He especially pointed out how men suppress their creative feminine side and instead concentrate on boosting testosterone and to be aggressive and competitive in a toxic way, when a balance between the masculine and feminine is needed in all of us. Regarding his shapeshifting reptilian research, it's not as farfetched and ridiculous as it might sound. I am convinced that the royal families, because of their nurtured bloodlines, makes it easy for the Overlords to possess them. After all, that's the whole purpose, and one of two reasons why bloodlines have always been so important to the Overlords. The other reason is to prove ownership of humankind. I would dare say that those of the purest Marduk-Isis-Ninurta bloodline and the Marduk-Ereškigal lineage are more or less possessed by the Overlords and little more than puppets with a destiny. We common people, who don't have royal blood in any significant amount, can't be possessed, unless we are pure enough. Blood that's too mixed repels. Therefore, we should call ourselves "lucky" because we are safer in that regard than those of blue blood. I can easily imagine that these beings, possessing those in power, sometimes "bleed through" into our frequency band of visible light and can sometimes be seen by those who are sensitive, and that's what I believe Icke essentially tried to say. Are these "overhangs" reptilian in nature? Yes and no. It depends on how they shape themselves, since they can take any shape and form, thus the term "shapeshift."

Aside from all that, Icke's research on Princess Diana in his book *The Biggest Secret* from 1999 is no less than brilliant. He did an amazing job, and now, almost 25 years later, his research still holds water, and it very much coincides with my own research and current findings. I will take the liberty to refer somewhat extensively to that book because it says so much about Diana, her fate, and the powerful occult symbolism around her, which is, as Icke so rightfully points out, Isis symbolism. Diana was very mild tempered, which seems to be a trait of Isis across most of her incarnations over the millennia. Yes, she is a "goddess"—a lower aspect of the Mother Goddess of Orion, but so are we humans. The main difference between humans (3-UCs) and Isis is that Isis is older as a soul and a Spirit, and she never lived on Tiamat. She has more knowledge and wisdom stored than we humans. It is my conclusion that Isis was captured by En.ki and Marduk (particularly Marduk) and is held hostage. Her only function is to be a "breeder." Diana, like previous incarnations of Isis, was a virgin when she met Prince Charles, so being a virgin seems to be a prerequisite for her missions in her different incarnations. Thus, she is the breeder and the incubator. Therefore, she is called *the Whore of Babylon* in the Bible. Isis is both the virgin and the "whore," the latter denoting she is a breeder. Keep in mind that the Whore of Babylon rides the Beast, according to the scripture, a graphic sexual description of Isis riding Marduk-Satan. There is no way for me to get into Isis' head, of course, but putting on my empathy shoes, I can imagine how trapped she has been since she got in touch with En.ki and Marduk and became "imprisoned" by them. All she seems to be doing is to go from incarnation to incarnation to insert her DNA into the Elite royal bloodlines. I am convinced the two malignant conspirators always keep track of her whereabouts—even in the astral, after she has finished an incarnation. Often, it seems like she sometimes also had violent deaths, in one way or another, in a ritual manner. This is also the case with Princess Diana—more so than people realize. Her entire life was a grand ritual from beginning to end.

There is no reason to put Isis on a pedestal as some mighty Goddess of the Universe. She is like us, albeit she is highly trained in the Orion sciences, particularly genetic engineering and tinkering, which she has learned from her Cosmic Mother, Queen Sophia. I would suggest that her artificial soul was programmed in the astral by the Overlords before each incarnation, so she knew what to do, and what qualities she had. We also know, according to the New Testament of the Bible, that Isis as the Virgin Mary (also being of a mild nature) was visited by the "Archangel Gabriel," who gave her and Joseph instructions. I can almost guarantee that this has happened during most of Isis' incarnations; Marduk and En.ki steer her in the direction they want her to go. According to some people who knew Diana, and whom David Icke interviewed after the murder, claimed that Diana was most likely mind-controlled and had a multiple personality. There was a very shy side to herself, reserved and introverted, but she was also, in her opposite, a socialite, and liked to be around people. She could, of course, have been an MK-ULTRA victim in that lifetime.

The Research of David Icke on Princess Diana

Some of you might have read Icke's *The Biggest Secret*, but even if so, follow my train of thoughts as we go along. Although much of the following information is based on that book, I expand on Icke's thoughts, based on my own research and conclusions.

> Diana Frances Spencer was born at Park House on the Queen's Sandringham estate in Norfolk on July 1st, 1961, the third and youngest daughter of Viscount Althorp, later the 8th Earl Spencer, and his first wife Frances Roche. Her parents separated when she was six and divorced in 1969, and her mother married the wallpaper tycoon Peter Shand-Kidd.
>
> [...]
> She told Andrew Morton in his book, Diana: Her True Story: "The atmosphere was always very strange when we went there and I used to kick and fight anyone who tried to make us go.[183]

We see how interwoven everything is in royal circles, and how inbred the royal families are. People in general know very little about this. There are no coincidences regarding who marries who—it's all decided by the royal "council," and the marrying couple has little to no say in the matter. It's all about keeping it within the bloodline, and to avoid physical and mental consequences of too close inbreeding, the royal families evade marrying their own siblings, unless there is no one else to marry to keep the bloodline clean. Marrying cousins and second cousins is routine. As we can see in Diana's case, she was much closer to the British royal house than people realize; she grew up on their domain, and she played with the royal children at Park House as a little girl. According to Icke, Prince Charles first saw Diana while she was still in her pram. At that time, Charles would have been 13-14 years old.

---

[183] David Icke © 1999: *The Biggest Secret, op. cit.*

Diana Meets Charles

To get a clearer picture of Diana's ancestry, and how Charles and Diana met later, I will continue quoting Icke from his book,

> The Spencers are an Elite bloodline family. They are cousins of the Spencer-Churchills and related to the Marlborough family at Blenheim Palace in Oxfordshire, where Winston Churchill was born. Other forebears included the Duke of Marlborough, Sir Robert Walpole, and the Spencer family inherited a considerable fortune from Sarah, Duchess of Marlborough. They also married into the Cavendish family, the Dukes of Devonshire at Chatsworth House, and that offshoot became known as Spencer-Cavendish. Diana shared common ancestors with Prince Charles in the 3rd Duke of Devonshire and, most significantly, King James I, the first Stuart king of England and Scotland and sponsor of Francis Bacon. It was King James who played a highly influential role in the expansion of the Brotherhood, the formation of the Virginia Company which still controls the United States, and the creation of the King James version of the Bible. Diana was also descended through several lines from the Stuart kings, Charles II and James II, which connected her, as with James I, to the Merovingian bloodline in France. Charles II had so many children out of wedlock that goodness knows where some of their bloodlines are today. One thing's for sure, the Brotherhood will know. As Elite families go, the Spencers are an important bloodline and Diana was related to countless aristocratic lines, including the Earls of Lucan. Further afield the Spencers have blood ties with many leading American families and they are distantly related to the Rockefellers. They have a long history of serving the monarch and the tradition continued with Diana's father. He was equerry to King George VI (who was married to the Queen Mother) and to Queen Elizabeth. Diana's sister, Jane, is married to Sir Robert Fellowes, the Queen's Private Secretary at the time of Diana's death. Both of Diana's grandmothers, the Countess Spencer and Ruth Lady Fermoy, were inner circle members of the Queen Mother's court, as were four of her great aunts. The Spencers and the Queen Mother were very close and it was Lady Fermoy and the Queen Mother who manipulated Diana into her marriage with Prince Charles. This could be most significant when you hear about the true nature of the Queen Mother. The countdown to the marriage began when Diana met Prince Charles at Althorp while he was having a relationship with her sister Sarah, in 1977. Diana was 16, but it was three years later that the Windsors really made their move on her. With the Queen Mother and Lady Fermoy manipulating behind the scenes, she was invited to a dance at Buckingham Palace to celebrate Charles' 30th birthday. Then, in July 1980, a friend of Charles, Philip de Pass, asked her to stay with them while

the Prince was there.[184]

The Spencers relation to the Rockefeller family (and apparently to the Rothchilds, as well) certainly make them Jewish. According to Icke, the old Queen Mother, Elizabeth Bowes-Lyon, was deeply involved in occultism and what is commonly called Satanism, something that should not come as a surprise. These occult, and sometimes gruesome rituals were commonly practiced already among the Merovingians. It appears it was she and Diana's maternal grandmother, Lady Fermoy, who gave the orders to Queen Elizabeth and Prince Philip (who passed the news to Prince Charles) that Charles and Diana should marry. Because the Queen Mother ran the show in the royal family, with Prince Philip second in charge, the Queen Mother's word was law.

Although Charles later said that she got interested in Diana when she was 16 because he found her attractive, charming, and adorable, he was very much against marrying her. His consort of choice was, as we know, Camilla Parker-Bowles, but Charles had no say in the matter. When Diana had been officially chosen among the royals, there was no way to stop it. This was most likely extremely frustrating to Charles, but perhaps they calmed him down by saying that all the royal family needed was for Diana to bring him heirs to the throne. Once that was done, Diana could be discarded (and eventually murdered), and Charles could marry Camilla. To the royal family, Princess Diana was just a breeder and an incubator. This is a hypothesis I have had for a little while, and interestingly, I found the following in Icke's book:

> The Windsors wanted Diana to produce heirs with Spencer genes and that was all she was to them: an incubator. A week after her engagement to Charles, her bulimia began. This is an eating disorder in which you make yourself sick every time you eat food. Diana was throwing up three or four times a day and became desperately thin. As I mentioned in an earlier chapter, many victims of childhood sexual and Satanic abuse suffer from bulimia later in life. She said that the bulimia was 'triggered' when Charles put his hand on her waist and said "Oh, a bit chubby here, aren't we?" Bulimia is a disease of the emotions, as most diseases are, and Diana was in emotional turmoil even before the wedding. She described the attitude of Charles like this:

---

[184] *Ibid., op. cit.*

"He'd found the virgin, the sacrificial lamb, and in a way he was obsessed with me. But it was hot and cold, hot and cold. You never knew what mood it was going to be, up and down, up and down... He was in awe of his mama, intimidated by his father, and I was always the third person in the room."[185]

I noticed, the last couple of days, when reading Icke's chapter on Diana that his research, which includes extensive interviews with friends and relatives to the princess, what he wrote corresponds well to what has been conveyed in this book—not only regarding Diana, but also regarding bloodlines, in general, except this book goes deeper into the bloodline issues, following Isis (and to some extent Ereškigal) through the last few millennia.

But why did the Queen Mother (and Marduk) want Diana/Isis to add the Spencer bloodline to the existing British royal blood? I think the answer is quite simple. As we discussed earlier, the *German Invasion* happened in the early 18th century, and since then, the Marduk-Ereškigal bloodline was inserted into the existing bloodline through Sophia of Hanover, the potential Ereškigal, and Marduk. This is now roughly 300 years ago, and during this time, the bloodline has been severely diluted. By that, I mean the Ninurta blood running through the veins of the royals has become less and less for each generation. En.ki's and Marduk's blood was always of great importance to the two Overlords, but most important of all was the Ninurta blood, which would strengthen their position in Orion. Without it, the Overlords would be powerless. Marduk knew, of course, that even though he wanted to take over, his new bloodline can't be too watered down, or he loses his opportunity to take on Orion. He needed fresh blood—particularly this close to the Singularity. Hence, it was time for Isis to make another trip to Earth from the astral and be used as a breeder again, adding the Isis-Ninurta blood to the existing royal genealogy. Because of the new Marduk-Ereškigal bloodline, which was inserted 300 years ago, Marduk would still have the upper hand over En.ki, having more of his DNA running through the monarchy veins than En.ki. The Spencer family had (and still has) a stronger and purer bloodline than the Windsors. The Princess was also a descendant of the British King James II, and further back to the Merovingians. Diana died at the age 36, but she completed her mission and was then "called

---

[185] *Ibid., op. cit.*

back" to the astral.

Isis is the goddess of love and war, but also known in ancient texts to be a healer. Therefore, I found it synchronistic to find the following in David Icke's book: "She was unfortunate in her love affairs because she rescued others in her own distress. So the men she went for were all emotional cripples because she was a healer, too."[186]

Diana's Life with Charles and her Untimely Death

Diana was very unhappy in her marriage and living with the Windsors, in general. She considered them anything but nice people. It was reported that she even called them "evil lizards." She confined with friends during her years with Charles that he made her feel inadequate in all possible ways, and each time she "came up for air," he pushed her down again. She hated herself so much (her own words). Where have we heard such dynamics being played out before? In narcissistic relationships, of course. Hot-cold, hot-cold... making their target hate themselves and lose all self-respect. This tells us what we need to know about Charles (as if we didn't know already). Icke continues,

> "Then suddenly as Harry was born it just went bang, our marriage, the whole thing went down the drain", she told Andrew Morton. Diana and Charles separated in 1992 and divorced on August 28th 1996. Almost exactly a year later she was dead.[187]

Fig 12:11a. Diana's and Dodi's memorial site.

---

186 *Ibid., op. cit.*
187 *Ibid., op. cit.*

*Fig 12:11b. It reads: "These two items are among a handful of objects that illustrate
how much Dodi and Diana were in love. The wine glass has been preserved
in the exact condition it was left on the Couple's last evening together ..."*

Icke was darn right about this. The goddess Isis had done her duty, and Charles could attend to Camilla more intensely as he probably had been promised. Diana was then sacrificed in the most occult and horrific manner. Icke makes a compelling and very believable case of Diana's death and in following the symbolism and the timeline from her Paris visit until the car slamming into the 13th pillar near and below the Temple of Diana/Isis, just minutes away from the place Jacques Molay, the Grandmaster of the Knights Templar, was burned at the stake. The evidence Icke presents is compelling and unmistaken. Diana survived the crash, but the conspirators made sure she would not, for any reason, leave the crash site and the tunnel until she was pronounced dead on site. From an esoteric perspective, she must die *in* the tunnel, not outside. That was very important. She was supposed to die right away but didn't. Therefore, they must let her bleed to death before they could move her body. Otherwise, the occult ritual would fail because Diana would not have died at that designated place.

There are whistleblowers who knew Diana, arguing that she was three months pregnant when she died, but not with Charles, obviously. This would not be allowed, since this would strengthen another Elite bloodline (although diluted), that of Dodi. When the ambulance came after more than an hour after the crash, they took her to the hospital, but not to the nearest hospital, which was fully capable to operating on her, but to a hospital much farther away, where an appointed team of doctors met them and took care of Diana's body. They claimed she was alive, although she was announced dead on site, and they supposedly started operating on her. They split her up from the pelvis and all the way to her chest, even though Diana was already dead, removing the fetus. I think there is no chance Diana was alive when she arrived at the hospital. She died in the tunnel from bleeding out.

At the memorial site for Diana and Dodi, there is a note that the wine glass Diana drank from in the hotel, just before the death ride, showed their love and devotion to each other (figures 12:11a and b). Oh, really? A simple wine glass shows how much Dodi and Diana (both killed in the crash) were in love? What a silly thing to say. But of all things, isn't it strange they put a wine glass inside a pyramid? The wine (blood) glass (cup) represents the Holy Grail, and the pyramid represents Egypt, which is Isis' original country on Earth. Not only that, but the pyramid was also very important in the death and sacrifice of Diana. Read on, and I will explain.

There is no evidence, but Icke speculates from the time after the fetus was removed, and in standard Brotherhood manner, it was eaten by its high-ranking members in a grotesque occult ritual. If true, it would not have been the first time such a thing happened in the occult world. I recommend the reader to study the chapter about Diana in Icke's book for much more information and details, and I think you will see that he is not making all this up. As I mentioned, the evidence for his case is compelling.

Fig. 12:12. "Is he a dreamboat—or a deadbeat?"
What a strange comment, taking into consideration
what was soon about to play out.

To me, there is no doubt Diana was Isis—even all the symbolism in her life points to that, and it was well-known in certain circles. All this occult effort was not done because she was "anybody." It was done because Marduk sacrificed the real Isis, and they "ate her soul," i.e., stole her energy in the death moment. Regarding her unborn baby, they might have drunk its blood *and* eaten its flesh. If this is true, I think it was urgent that Diana got to the correct hospital as soon as possible after she was pronounced dead. The blood is more potent the closer it is consumed after death.

Now, how about this?

According to the "Killuminati" website, run by Robert Anton Wilson, a friend of David Icke's and a Montauk mind-control survivor, states on his website that after the divorce from Charles, the Elite wanted Diana to marry Bill Clinton, but she refused.[188] Partly because Clinton was already married. That was apparently no problem to those behind the scenes. According to the movers and shakers, it was just a matter of giving slick Killer-Bill with a Willy a divorce, or maybe even assassinating Killary-Hillary. I don't know

---

[188] killuminatisoldiersoftruth.wordpress.com: *Killuminati Soldiers of Truth.*

who was suggesting such a thing on a deeper level, as it seems to benefit neither side in the bloodline conflict; Isis or Marduk and Ereškigal. The point is, however, that it never happened.

Stunningly, Diana wrote this letter before she was assassinated:

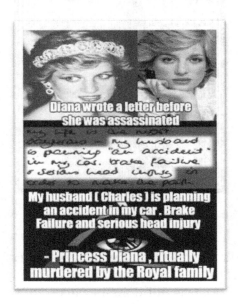

Fig. 12:13. Diana's letter.

So, it seems obvious that Diana knew about the plot beforehand, but probably felt helpless preventing it, not knowing when it was going to happen. The royal family found out Diana was pregnant, and they did not want her pure blood to be mixed with Egyptian blood, which would make the Egyptian dynasty more powerful. Therefore, it seemed like a good idea to kill Dodi, Diana, and her baby in one go, and they got rid of that problem. "He, who controls Diana, controls the world," as Wilson says on his website. With Diana as Isis, I would agree that's correct. Diana's baby with Dodi, and the urge for Charles to marry Camilla are certainly two motives for having Diana killed. However, I doubt the ritual murders were planned by the royal family.

Robert Anton Wilson points out in a video on his Killuminati website what the word *monarch* means on a deeper level, which directly attunes to what we're discussing. Monarch can be divided into two words, *moon,* and *arch*, denoting the arch of the crescent moon, which is the symbol of Isis, the moon goddess, but is, in the extension, also a symbol for the ancient druids (with Sir Winston Churchill as a member), dedicated to pagan animal and human ritualistic sacrifices to the gods. This is practiced just as frequently today as it was in druidic times, and as I've said elsewhere, the Germans were supposed to be sacrificed together with the Jews in Nazi Germany, so the gods could have a massive feast on human soul energy in "Valhalla," the Hall of the Gods.

Virtually all secret societies use the skull and crossbones as one of their symbols, representing death and sacrifice. We also see Mary Magdalene in paintings with the skull in her hand or beside her—Jesus' skull. Well, I told you the painters were initiated. Jesus, portrayed as the ultimate sacrifice, died on a *cross* on Golgotha, *the place of the skull*. Diana, also sacrificed, died at Pont de l 'Alma, an old sacrificial site, and she died on top of a pyramid, intentionally shaped in the road structure, and at a crossroads, where heaven and hell meet, according to occult knowledge. Thus, we have the wine glass inside a pyramid on Diana's and Dodi's memorial site. If people only know when they visit these sites. Instead, they think it's very compassionate and considerate to put up these memorial sites, when indeed it's a way of keeping the murderous energy anchored on Earth and showing the agenda in plain sight in the form of symbols. The same thing happened to JFK, who was killed at Dealey Plaza, which has the shape of a pyramid. Everything is extremely well planned to best please the gods and get as much soul energy out of the murders as possible.[189]

As of this writing, it is 24 years and 2 months since Diana was sacrificed, and if she incarnated again closely after her death, she would be 23-24 years old now. We don't know where in the world she might be, or if she is still in the astral. But it might be a good idea to keep our eyes open. Now we know her nature better, and under which circumstances she incarnates. Usually, it's when a bloodline somewhere needs to be enhanced with Ninurta's blood. This doesn't happen often these days because Marduk has other plans, including his new bloodline (I will eventually end this chapter, however, with a plausible explanation why they used

---

[189] Borrowed from, and expanded upon, the YouTube video, *Diana Illuminati Sacrifice, parts 1 and 2.* These are two 10-minute videos, and I highly recommend you watch them both because it's way too much evidence to include here. Watch them, and you will be stunned.

Isis/Diana to boost the British Royal family bloodline). If we see a big change in a royal bloodline somewhere, we may suspect to see Isis or Ereškigal there, respectively, depending on the circumstance. Unfortunately, Isis is just as trapped as you and me, but we at least have the opportunity to leave the Matrix after this lifetime by exiting through the Grid (see more information in Appendix A). Isis might not. I am sure Orion knows what's going on with her, and so does Ninurta, I suspect, but she is kept hostage by the Overlords, so it's a delicate matter for Orion to rescue her if that is one of their plans.

Isis Worship Amid Paris

So far, we have loosely followed David Icke's line of research. Let us end the history of the British royal family and that of Princess Diana with some occult significance to Paris, and why they chose Paris as the death site for Princess Di. It was almost certainly because Paris is a massive occult center for Isis and Isis worship. It goes back all the way to the Merovingians, who worshipped Isis as Mary Magdalene.

To start with, the name Paris has two origins, the official and the unofficial. The latter suggests the name comes from Bar-Isis (the Boat of Isis) because "the first representation of the Dark Lady would have arrived on a ship going up the Seine to the Ile de la Cité."[190] This would explain why the coat of arms of the city has a boat in its arms. This is, of course, not the official explanation, but as the reader has noticed while reading this book, we have been lied to, repeatedly. Paris has (at least) two stories.

For example, here is the connection between the Merovingian kings, Paris, and Isis worship:

> The old charters of Sainte-Geneviève and Saint-Germain-des-Prés mention it. They say that CLOVIS and CHILDEBERT, their founders, assigned them the remains of ISIS and its temple! It is often signified, in the oldest chronicles of the capital, that ISIS, mistress of the esoteric doctrine and of all the arts of magic, was venerated in PARIS either first in the island of the City itself , on the site of NOTRE-DAME, or on the site where the Abbey of Saint-Germain

---

[190] Afrikhepri.org: *Cult of Isis in the Heart of Paris, op. cit.*

des-Prés was subsequently built.[191]

Fig. 12:14. The Coat of Arms of Paris, France with both the boat and all the lilies, a symbol for the Jesus-Magdalene bloodline.

Clovis and Childebert were both Merovingian kings. Moreover, the monk Abbon, of the cloister at Notre-Dame, "considers ISIS as the first protectress of Parisians in a poem written in the 9th century on the siege of the city by the Normans."[192] The official story of Paris and its history is conveniently removed from schoolbooks and history books, occluding the fact that the entire city of Paris since ancient time is closely related to Merovingian Mary Magdalene/Isis worship. There is also no doubt Paris has a history of Egyptian deity worship (the land whence Isis originally came). We see the great Egyptian obelisk in Paris, and there are four pyramids built in front of the Royal Palaces in the central Napoleon Courtyard. Moreover, the Americans gave Paris a Statue of Liberty to commemorate the centennial of the French Revolution. Of course, the Founding Fathers and the American and French Revolutions were all about the bloodline moving west, and another branch of the Brotherhood in France being eradicated. The Statue of Liberty symbolizes Goddess Diana (Isis) with a flaming torch—the Fire of the Mother Goddess—her creative ability to give birth to Jesus and to maintain the bloodline.

I will now quote from the interesting *Afrikhepri Foundation*

---

[191] *Ibid.*
[192] *Ibid., op cit.*

website, based on, and translated from a French site, written in French, at *secretebase.free.fr: Les Secrets de Paris*:

> In fact, as Professor Cheikh Anta Diop points out, the first inhabitants of the current place where Paris, the capital of France is located, bore the name of PARISII, for no apparent reason: "The cult of Isis, as we can see, was very widespread in France, in particular in the Paris Basin; there were ISIS Temples everywhere, according to Western terminology, but it would be more correct to say "HOUSE OF ISIS", because such temples were called in Egyptian Per, which word means exactly in ancient Egyptian, as in Valaf current, the enclosure which surrounds the house. Paris would result from the juxtaposition of PER-ISIS, a word which effectively designates cities in Egypt, as Hubac remarks "(according to historian G. Maspéro).
>
> [...]
>
> A large statue of ISIS on his [sic] boat was kept for a long time in the Saint-Germain-des-Prés church, until a priest destroyed it with a pickaxe in the 18th century. The nave adorning the coat of arms of the city of Paris would be none other than the boat of Isis, while the motto of the city "Fluctua Nec Mergitur" would recall the heroic navigation of the followers of HORUS, but also those of the initiates circulating in the secret of the temples. Curious tourists will therefore be astonished to find in a courtyard in the rue du Cherche-Midi, a greenish sphinx with the head of a woman, vestiges of the cult of ISIS practiced in Paris.[193]

And it goes back to the Merovingians, the occult Brotherhoods behind them, and all the way further back to ancient Egypt and the original Overlord Trinity, Osiris, Isis, and Horus.

Queen Elizabeth II as a Mother Goddess Representative

My Orion source pointed out to me that Queen Elizabeth thought she was the Mother Goddess' representative on Earth with the *divine right to rule*, which he added was, of course, completely erroneous. She had no permission from Orion to do so. Also, he said, Elizabeth was not even royal anymore. Her blood was that of a commoner these days (she was still alive when he told me this)—there was no royal blood left in her veins. What he meant by this, although I didn't understand it at the time, was that her blood was that

---

[193] Afrikhepri.org: *Cult of Isis in the Heart of Paris, op. cit.*

of the Marduk-Ereškigal—barely any Orion royal blood there.

However, behind the scenes, the British royal family is not supporting Marduk, they are supporting Isis as the Divine Feminine. My contact also said that Marduk had tried many times to "make deals" with the British royalty, and even tried to conquer England on several locations but always failed; and they "threw him out," as he put it because they "didn't need him." As I've mentioned a few times, the Windsors are Mother Goddess worshippers. The Queen of England was well aware of their dire bloodline condition after being infiltrated by the German stock in the nineteenth century. Royals back then, in general, probably had no idea what Marduk's overall plan was and that there was a greater plan behind the "German Invasion" of their bloodline. I don't think Elizabeth knew about Marduk's Final Solution, either, i.e., to attack Orion, but she knew her bloodline was diluted, and it needed a severe boost of Orion blood. She knew she couldn't get it, her children couldn't get it, but her grandchildren could. Therefore, the Windsors once more took help from Germany, maybe for the last time, via Prince Philip, who, through his connection, apparently knew where Isis was. He married Elizabeth, and they had children, who were almost completely void of royal blood, including Charles, although Philip had *some* of it. However, it didn't matter. When Elizabeth and Philip both understood what they must do, they did what needed to be done—it was all about the future of the Divine Feminine bloodline. It was Queen Elizabeth's mother, the Royal Matriarch, who suggested Charles should marry Diana, against Charles' wish. She also had the support of Prince Philip. Charles was afraid of his father, and when Philip forced Charles to marry Diana, he had little choice but to obey. As I suggested earlier, I think Charles was promised to marry Camilla after Diana had given him heirs. Philip knew who Diana was.

Diana (Isis) most likely knew what she was doing because this intermarriage with Charles would benefit her, too. When Diana gave birth to William with Charles, and Harry, perhaps with James Hewitt[194] (the resemblance is stunning), I think she put her eggs in two baskets instead of one (no pun intended). If one plan failed,

---

[194] Cosmopolitan: *The Truth Behind Those Rumors That James Hewitt Is Secretly Prince Harry's Dad.*

the other one might not.[195] Whatever the case, both William and Harry married women of the bloodline. Kate Middleton has aristocratic blood through her forefather,[196] and Meagan has royal blood, according to the *New England Historic Genealogic Society*[197] going back in straight line all the way to King Edward III. This means that all Williams children are of full Marduk-Isis bloodline. Harry, depending on who his father is, has a similar situation. His children are also pure bloodline. Thus, the Orion bloodline is reestablished in the House of Windsor. This, of course, benefits the British family, but perhaps also Isis, who can use this bloodline to exit the Matrix when it's getting "too hot" here. She can return to Orion by riding humans of her bloodline and take some humans with her. This is, of course, just a hypothesis. Either way, with Ereškigal having taken Isis' place as the breeder and incubator, I am sure Isis was eager to take on the task as Diana Spencer to disrupt the Satanic Marduk-Ereškigal line and reestablish her Isis-Ninurta Goddess bloodline. Although Charles probably couldn't care less, his mother and father were stricter with their religion—both being Mother Goddess worshipers. Prince Philip also became a Master Mason of the Grand Lodge of Freemasonry in England, which is very significant, which we shall investigate now.

Church of England and the Grand Lodge of Freemasonry

In the mainstream media, Queen Elizabeth was portrayed as a devoted Christian (protestant), praying to God several times a day. This was something she was obligated to do in her position because being a representative of the Mother Goddess was not something she wanted to go public with. It was Henry VIII who established the Church of England, converting from Catholicism to Protestantism, banning the English Royalties from ever again marry Catholics (something they have held sacred). Thus, they also disconnected from French and Roman (Vatican) influence and became their own. However, the Church of England does not worship En.ki or Marduk;

---

[195] *Ibid.* Both Prince Harry and James Hewitt deny he is Harry's father, but the rebuttal is not at all convincing. Either way, we have no evidence either way at this time.

[196] Wikipedia: *Middleton Family, #Aristocratic ties.*

[197] Americanancestors.org/meghan-markle

they worship the Divine Feminine. How do we know that? Because history tells us.

If we swiftly go back to the time when the Catholic Church prosecuted a branch of the Knights Templar who protected the feminine bloodline, some Templars fled to Scotland and England, where the Templar Order continued its business at protecting Isis' Orion bloodline. They created the York Rite of Freemasonry, which up to this day is a pure Templar Order.[198] Later, they also created the Grand Lodge of England, which is a Templar Order, as well.[199] This is what Prince Philip and many royal family members before him and after him have supported and been members and Grandmasters of. Freemasonry is normally a Marduk organization, as we shall see, but these two British branches are not. There is also a tight bond between British Freemasonry and the Church of England:

> While the Church had always been closely linked to Freemasonry, since the 1980s, some Anglican bishops and pastors have made negative judgements about Freemasons, for theological reasons. In July 1987, the General Synod endorsed a report which considered the compatibility of Freemasonry and Christianity.[200]

Who Killed Diana?

The question still lingers: *Who killed Princess Diana?* There is hardly any doubt she was killed. Was it Prince Charles? Was it a royal family conspiracy?

As usual, we need to ask ourselves, *who benefits?* Well, many people behind the scenes benefitted. Prince Charles certainly did (and Diana suspected him of wanting to kill her), but so did Marduk. It could be either or, so we must follow our intuition. Although Charles benefitted from the murder, my intuition tells me it was not he who ordered the murder. Marduk would benefit more—particularly when it became known that she was pregnant, possibly to further spread the Orion blood. She must be killed, and Marduk was most likely furious with her for interfering with his plans when she

---

[198] Wikipedia: *York Rite, #Knights Templar*

[199] Knightstemplarorder.org: *Freemasonry & the Knights Templar: Separate Fraternity Inspired by Support from Templar Chivalry.*

[200] Wikipedia: *Christian attitudes toward Freemasonry.*

gave birth to William and Harry. So, he wanted to get as much as possible out of the murder and orchestrated a complex occult ritual around it, which also could feed him loosh from Isis and make her suffer, also showing her who is running the show. To me, it's more likely it was Marduk's minions—possibly the CIA or the MOSSAD.

The Scarlet Woman and the Book of Revelation

1 3   **Ever since the Book of** Revelation was added to the Bible, it's been shrouded in mystery. They say it was channeled by John the Divine (John of Patmos). Traditional Christianity considers John being the purported author of the *Gospel of John*, although some Christian scholars separate him from the disciple, considering him a distinct person.[201] The Book of Revelation is presumed, by some, to have been written around 96 C.E., after John had a series a "visions." It always seems to me that when people in ancient times had visions, we are talking about channeling, often from the gods. In this case, John was the scribe to an angel of God, and the message was from God himself, and here we are talking about Marduk, not En.ki.

The Book of Revelation (REV) is written in an archaic and very esoteric, cryptic language, full of mental images and mysteries that have been interpreted by scholars and others since they were published; and the supposed meaning of the verses differ from scholar to scholar, and from person to person—often quite substantially. It's safe to say that no one has really been able to truly interpret the REV correctly yet. This is not because they are not clever enough, but because, in my opinion, it's impossible to interpret it without having certain esoteric knowledge that only high-ranked members of certain secret societies possess. I said it before, and I'll say it

---

[201] Wikipedia: *John of Patmos.*

again: *it's all about bloodlines!* Thus it is, even in this case. Now, when the reader has come this far in the book, I want to present a section of the REV for you to read. I presume some readers have tried to read it before without understanding it. Let's see if you understand parts of it better now. When analyzing the next section, read each verse slowly and focus on what comes to mind, without rushing through it. When you're finished and have pondered it, continue reading this book. I will give you my interpretation, and we'll see if it matches with yours. To me, some meanings of the verses popped out from the text like it was self-evident. Suddenly, it was no longer esoteric and incomprehensible. It made sense. These new insights came after I had researched and written this book up to the current point. It also shows we are on the right track.

The Book of Revelation, Chapter 17

This chapter in the REV is about the Whore of Babylon (Isis), also called the Scarlet Woman, who rides the Beast. I touched on this earlier in the book, but let's dig deeper:

1 And there came one of the seven angels which had the seven vials, and talked with me, saying unto me, Come hither; I will shew unto thee the judgment of the great whore that sitteth upon many waters:

2 With whom the kings of the earth have committed fornication, and the inhabitants of the earth have been made drunk with the wine of her fornication.

3 So he carried me away in the spirit into the wilderness: and I saw a woman sit upon a scarlet coloured beast, full of names of blasphemy, having seven heads and ten horns.

4 And the woman was arrayed in purple and scarlet colour, and decked with gold and precious stones and pearls, having a golden cup in her hand full of abominations and filthiness of her fornication:

5 And upon her forehead was a name written, MYSTERY, BABYLON THE GREAT, THE MOTHER OF HARLOTS AND ABOMINATIONS OF THE EARTH.

6 And I saw the woman drunken with the blood of the saints, and with the blood of the martyrs of Jesus: and when I saw her, I wondered with great admiration.

9 And here is the mind which hath wisdom. The seven heads are seven mountains, on which the woman sitteth.[202]

If you have pondered these verses on your own now, let's continue. In this book, I have argued Mary Magdalene and Isis were one and the same, and that the most important thing for Marduk and his Elite over time has been to keep the Jesus-Magdalene bloodline as pure as possible. I have also pointed out the symbolism from the life of the Virgin Mary to the present time. One such symbol for the Holy Grail (the sacred blood) is the ampulla, or as we more often call it, the vial. In paintings from the Middle Ages, we see Mary Magdalene holding a vial. I wrote a subsection about this earlier in the book if the reader recalls.

Let us look at the definition of *vial*:

vial

/ˈvʌɪəl/

noun
1. a small container, typically cylindrical, made of glass, used especially for holding liquid medicines.[203]

In REV 17:1 above, it says, "And there came one of the seven angels which had the seven vials…" The seven angels, I would suggest are the seven most high-ranked Overlords, or the Seven Archons in the Gnostic texts, and amidst these angels is "God" (originally En.ki). The Seven Trumpets in the REV symbolize these angels, and Wikipedia tells us, "The seventh angel or trumpet refers to 'human souls who have been endowed with heavenly attributes and invested with an angelic nature and disposition' who will joyously proclaim and announce the coming of Bahá'u'lláh, the promised

---

[202] Wikipedia: *Whore of Babylon.*
[203] Oxford Dictionary.

Lord of Hosts.'"[204] This sounds like affirmation that we humans are spirited, and are now waiting for the return of the Lord of Hosts (Archangel Michael, and in this case, Jesus/Marduk).

Fig. 13:1. Mary Magdalene pouring Jesus' blood into the cup, the Symbol of the Holy Grail, from an ampulla/vial. This "Divine Oil" later became a symbol for Jesus' blood in the royal anointment process.

So, one of the angels (I would suppose it was Gabriel again, aka Marduk) is bringing seven vials, where number 7 represents perfection, i.e., the pure blood of Jesus-Magdalene.[205]

The last sentence of 17:1 reads: "I will shew unto thee the judgment of the great whore that sitteth upon many waters:" The Whore mentioned here is, of course, Isis. She is, in Christian terms, the archetype of feminine evil; she is both the virgin and the whore, who reincarnate and breed with kings and other royalties. Marduk is, in other words, putting Isis in a bad spot, making her a pagan goddess of filth, while Marduk is elevating himself to pure Godhood. The *waters* are the Cosmic Waters, also symbolizing cities. It was important for the patriarchal Overlords not to let the Divine Feminine be worshipped as a replacement for them.

Verse 17:2 is amazingly blatant. Here it clearly says that this woman (Isis) has slept with kings and spread the wine (the blood),

---

[204] Wikipedia: *Seven Trumpets*
[205] Wikipedia: *Seven Spirits of God.*

and through this fornication, she has made the human soul group drunk with her wine. In other words, the blood of the gods is spread across the planet through the human soul group.

In 17:3, John's spirit is taken out of his body, and he is having an OBE. In the astral, the angel projects a woman riding a scarlet beast.

In 17:4, we are back to the cup again—the Holy Grail, and Isis' fornication with earthly kings. "...having a golden cup in her hand full of abominations and filthiness of her fornication."

Verse 17:5 emphasizes Isis' position as the Queen of Harlots (the queen of prostitutes). The reference to Babylon is a reference to Ishtar, Isis' title in Babylon, Ishtar being the goddess of love and war (same attributes as those of Isis). Some scholars suggest that Babylon is a metaphor for Rome during the time the REV was written, but either way, the Whore would then be either Ishtar or Diana, still the same deity, who will rule with the Beast, whom she is riding (having sex with] in the REV. 17:3.

Christians, of course, do not connect Mary Magdalene to Isis, but in this book, I have showed evidence that they were the same person. Therefore, Mary is both the Virgin and the Harlot. In the Middle Ages, painters who were initiated in secret societies knew the truth, and therefore we see both the egg and the vial as esoteric symbols in the portraits of Mary Magdalene (not Virgin Mary), as well as the red and white rose, and the lilies. Outsiders have no idea what these symbols mean, and that they all denote the Holy Bloodline.

In 17:9, "wisdom" refers to the Mother Goddess—ultimately Queen Sophia, but in this case to Isis, the Mother Goddess of the Matrix.

A series of scholar have concluded that the Whore of Babylon refers to an "apostate false queen," a former "bride," who has been unfaithful and cast out, but continues to falsely claim to be the "queen" of the spiritual realm.[206] This would also suffice.

The Sun God and the Moon Goddess

I think we all have heard Jesus being associated with the sun as the sun god, the "Sun of God," and we celebrate Jesus' birthday on

---

[206] Wikipedia: *Whore of Babylon, #Jerusalem*

winter solstice. He is also portrayed with a halo, which represents the sun, and/or with a crown, emitting sunbeams. The Sun God is, as the reader might know, Amon Ra, aka Marduk/Horus/Utu Šamaš (pronounced Shamash). So, it makes sense, knowing what we know, that Jesus was Marduk. But what about Mary Magdalene? If Jesus represents the sun, shouldn't Mary represent the moon?

In fact, she does, just like Isis, Lilith, and Diana are associated with the moon as Moon Goddesses. Mary Magdalene is often referred to as Artemis, the Goddess of the Moon. I wrote about Artemis in the WPP, and ultimately, Artemis is Queen Sophia, but in this construct, she is Isis and Mary Magdalene. In fig. 13:2, we see an ancient mosaic of Jesus and Mary Magdalene from a sixth-century monastery in Beit She'an in Galilee, portraying Jesus (the sun god) and Mary Magdalene with the crescent moon:[207]

Fig. 13:2. Jesus with a crown of sunbeams, and Mary Magdalene with the crescent moon above her head.

We already know the goddess Artemis is the moon goddess and the Goddess of the Hunt. Still, I want to show the reader that Artemis, the Virgin Mary, Mary Magdalene, and Isis are one and the same, which further strengthens the connection between Mary Magdalene and Isis. This is from a book from York University in Toronto, Canada:

> In fact, Artemis' reign is so fundamental to the cultural identity of her worshippers that even when facing the onslaught of early

---

[207] artbytanyatorres.com: *Mary Magdalene of the Bees*

Christianity, she could not be deposed. Instead, she survived the conquering of this new religion under the guise of Mary, Mother of Jesus.[208]

Here is another picture of Artemis, Goddess of the Hunt, with the bow symbolizing the crescent moon:

Fig. 13:3. The Goddess Artemis/Mary Magdalene/Isis.

There is an online website, owned by *Esoteric Interfaith Church, Inc.*, on which they posted an article from 1987 about the connection between Mary, Mary Magdalene, and Isis. They also make a good case for the Virgin Mary and Mary Magdalene being Isis just by logically connecting the dots. Here is an excerpt:

> Perhaps the Goddess that Mary is most easily and quickly identified with is Isis. This is problematic at best, because Isis is actually a Goddess associated both with Mary and with Mary Magdalene. Isis is the Bride of the Slain God (Osiris); in this role, she is associated with Mary Magdalene. But Isis is also the Mother of the Divine King

---

[208] Yorkspace.library.yorku.ca: *THE ENDURING GODDESS: Artemis and Mary, Mother of Jesus, (Carla Ionescu, 2016).*

(Horus), and in this role she is most easily associated with Mary. It is clear that, because Isis was the Mother of the Divine King, she does share this parallel at least with Mary. Mary is also often called Co-Redemptrix, Mediatrix of All Graces, and Advocate – roles that could also describe Isis. Isis gave birth to Horus in order to eventually overthrow Set, who had slain Osiris. Yeshua is seen as overthrowing Satan, who ruined the Father's creation. Because Yeshua overthrew Satan, it was also Mary who participated in this, by giving birth to Yeshua.[209]

I highly recommend reading the entire article at *Northernway.org: Mary & Pagan Goddesses*. Now compare this to the picture below, displaying Isis to the left, and Marduk to the right, and we have the moon goddess again.

Fig. 13:4. For medieval Spanish Catholics, the Whore of Babylon (Revelation, 17.4–5) (a Christian allegory of evil) was incarnated by the Emirate of Córdoba. [Wes' comment: Isis/Mary, the moon goddess with the crescent moon, with Marduk on the right, and they are holding a lily, attached to a cup, the Holy Grail].

Another important symbol for the Brotherhood, protecting the Holy Grail, is the royal tiara, worn by female royalties since ancient times. Princess Diana wore it often at ceremonial events. Again, there we have the symbol of the crescent moon of the moon

---

[209] northernway.org: *Mary & Pagan Goddesses, by Nisut Mark James, 1987.*

goddess Magdalene/Isis. Once we know the occult meaning of things, everything is put in place. People who don't know better can only see a pretty diadem in the royalty's hair, decorated with precious stones, a thing to admire.

Fig. 13:5. Kate Middleton and Diana wearing the tiara of the moon goddess.

The tiara was introduced into the royal family with the German Invasion in the early 1700s.

Isn't it also interesting that the demonic World Economic Forum (WEF) has the crescent moon in their logo?

Fig. 13:6. The World Economic Forum logo with the crescent moon.

Aleister Crowley and the Whore of Babalon

Yes, it is the right spelling in the title; that's how the British 20th century writer, magician, and the Grandmaster of the secret society, the *Ordo Templi Orientis* (OTO), spelled it; he who called himself the most wicked man in the world, and the Beast 666. I believe Aleister Crowley (1875-1847) might have started out with good intentions and out of curiosity, but as he dribbled more and more with the dark arts, his personality changed with it. Still, even secret societies like the OTO are invested in the Holy Grail; it goes like a straight line across virtually all secret societies, such as the Priory of Sion, the Knights Templar, the Freemasons, the Rosicrucians (the name of this Order alone reveals them), the Bavarian Illuminati, the Great White Brotherhood (Helena Blavatsky), The Golden Dawn, and the OTO, to mention only a handful. When En.ki created the *Brotherhood of the Snake* a very long time ago, hand-picking and initiating the most intelligent humans on Earth at the time, he gave them the secret of the "divine" bloodline and appointed them as the Watchers and Protectors of this bloodline, originating from him and Isis. It goes back all the way to the beginning of the Second Construct and the Garden of Edin during the Second Atlantis.

Fig. 13:7. A young Aleister Crowley

Babylon is obviously the name of a city which was located about 55 miles (89km) south of Baghdad in today's Iraq. Famous structures and artifacts include the temple of Marduk, the Ishtar Gate, and stelae upon which the Hammurabi's Code was written.[210] Babalon, in Crowley's teachings, is the name of the Scarlet Woman, the Whore of Babylon, thus distinguishing her from the ancient city. Contrary to many Bible scholars, but just like me, he was convinced the Whore of Babylon in the Bible does not represent a location but a real woman.

The following was Crowley's view on the subject in a condensed form:

> In her most abstract form, Babalon represents the female sexual impulse and the liberated woman. In the creed of the Gnostic Mass she is also identified with Mother Earth, in her most fertile sense. Along with her status as an archetype or goddess, Crowley believed that Babalon had an earthly aspect or avatar; a living woman who occupied the spiritual office of the 'Scarlet Woman'. This office, first identified in The Book of the Law is usually described as a counterpart to his own identification as "To Mega Therion" (The Great Beast). The role of the Scarlet Woman was to help manifest the energies of the Aeon of Horus. Crowley believed that several women in his life occupied the office of Scarlet Woman, for which see the list below.

> Babalon's consort is Chaos, called the "Father of Life" in the Gnostic Mass, being the male form of the creative principle. Chaos appears in The Vision and the Voice and later in Liber Cheth vel Vallum Abiegni. Separate from her relationship with her consort, Babalon is usually depicted as riding the Beast. She is often referred to as a sacred whore, and her primary symbol is the chalice or graal.

> As Crowley wrote in his The Book of Thoth, "she rides astride the Beast; in her left hand she holds the reins, representing the passion which unites them. In her right she holds aloft the cup, the Holy Grail aflame with love and death. In this cup are mingled the elements of the sacrament of the Aeon."[211]

A few interesting marks in the above text: Crowley believed Mother Earth is alive and spirited, which I, and many others, agree with. He also believed that Chaos is her consort, the "Father of Life," which is, of course, En.ki. The two, in cooperation, created homo sapiens eons ago. Babalon (Isis) is also "riding the Beast," which in occult circles means having intercourse, and in the above case with En.ki (and later with Marduk). Crowley was also much aware of the

---

[210] Britannica: *Babylon.*
[211] Wikipedia: *Babalon*

truth that Babalon's primary symbol is the chalice, i.e., the graal (the Sacred Blood). And who is holding the graal in occult paintings? Mary Magdalene.

Furthermore, Babalon in Crowley's teachings is described as follows,

> Babalon is identified with Binah on the Tree of Life, the sphere that represents the Great Sea and such mother-goddesses as Isis, Bhavani, and Ma'at. Moreover, she represents all physical mothers. Bishops T. Apiryon and Helena write:
>
> "BABALON, as the Great Mother, represents MATTER, a word which is derived from the Latin word for Mother. She is the physical mother of each of us, the one who provided us with material flesh to clothe our naked spirits; She is the Archetypal Mother, the Great Yoni, the Womb of all that lives through the flowing of Blood; She is the Great Sea, the Divine Blood itself which cloaks the World and which courses through our veins; and She is Mother Earth, the Womb of All Life that we know."[212]

That describes Isis and her mission the same way it's conveyed in this book. Contrary to Queen Sophia, Zoë Sophia, aka Isis, is the Mother Goddess of *Earth* (Matter Goddess), whilst Queen Sophia is the Mother Goddess of the entire Universe.

But most importantly, Crowley also believed that the Scarlet Woman's role was to manifest the energies of the Aeon of Horus. Now listen to this:

> The first of these was the Aeon of Isis, which Thelemites believed occurred during prehistory and which saw mankind worshipping a Great Goddess, symbolised by the ancient Egyptian deity Isis. In Thelemite beliefs, this was followed by the Aeon of Osiris, a period that took place in the classical and mediaeval centuries, when humanity worshipped a singular male god, symbolised by the Egyptian god Osiris, and was therefore dominated by patriarchal values. The third aeon is the Aeon of Horus, controlled by the child god, symbolised by Horus.[213]

As the reader can see, Crowley was well-versed in the secret meanings of this construct. He said the same things I have said in the WPP and in the two ORION books: The first "Aeon" was the Aeon of Isis, which was the Second Construct, where most

---

[212] *Ibid., op. cit.*
[213] Wikipedia: *Aeon (Thelema)*

civilizations worshipped the Mother Goddess in the form of Isis, Matter Goddess, Eve/Zoë, the Mother of Life. As I mentioned in my writings, Orion representatives were present during the Second Construct, including Prince En.lil, aka Ninurta, and things were more in the open than they are now. The presence of the Mother Goddess was much greater and not suppressed.

Moreover, and as a side note, my Orion source sometimes said that En.ki and Marduk had "father-son issues," and although it's commonly known that Osiris was En.ki, and Horus was Marduk, according to ancient texts, my source sometimes equated Osiris with Marduk. This was confusing to me at the time and something he did not explain further but left for me to figure out. Well, it took almost ten years for me to do so, but now I believe I understand what he meant. The ancient texts are correct, but when En.ki was thrown into the ABZU and Marduk took over, Marduk claimed the role of Osiris, who was the God of the Matrix. Marduk (Horus) became his own father, En.ki (Osiris).

Crowley goes on saying that the following Aeon was the Aeon of Osiris (En.ki), which started when humankind worshipped a singular male deity—En.ki. Thus, this second Aeon has been dominated by patriarchal values. Again, he's right on the money. But the most interesting part is the future third Aeon, which will be dominated by the "son," Horus, who is Marduk, now portraying both Osiris and Horus simultaneously (the Father and the Son). So, first we had the Mother Goddess (the Holy Spirit), second, we had the Father (En.ki), and now we have the Son (Marduk). This is very relevant in Thelema, Crowley's religion, because he predicted that a new child will be born of the Scarlet Woman, Isis, and that would be Marduk. But the Son was already born 2,000 years ago, you might say. This is true, but his mission was not fulfilled, truly or symbolically dying on the cross. He promised to come back, which is clearly conveyed in the REV. There it says the Son will return as Archangel Michael, the Lord of Hosts, who will rule the Earth for another 1,000 years in heavenly glory. And who is the *true* Archangel Michael? It is Prince En.lil of Orion, aka Prince Ninurta. However, he is not the one mentioned in the REV; it's Marduk, i.e., the Matrix Jesus and the false savior. Thus, all Christians will be deceived, and many non-Christians will be conjured, as well. I would say that the Aeon of Horus is what leads to the Singularity under Marduk's supervision, the era when humankind becomes cyborgs and engulfed by the Metaverse Cloud around 2045 (according to the Singularity talking heads from Silicon Valley). Horus reborn is the moonchild, i.e., the son/child of the moon goddess, Isis. Crowley wrote about this in the first half of the 20th Century, long before the Singularity had been announced by the Elite, so I will strongly argue that Horus/Marduk is among us now under that particular title, and we will see big changes, something we all can see is happening.

Jack Parsons and L. Ron Hubbard's Babalon Working

Fig. 13:8. Jack Parsons with his wife, Marjorie Cameron.

In the early 1950s, shortly after L. Ron Hubbard (1911-86) founded the Church of Scientology, he held a long series of lectures called *The Philadelphia Doctorate Course* (PDC), which I listened to in the late 1980s when I was a member of the Church of Scientology. In one of these lectures, he mentioned he was good friends with Aleister Crowley, and that he did magical work with the late Jack Parsons (1914-52), a member of the OTO, and the founder of Jet Propulsion, and thus, a brilliant rocket scientist. Parsons was also in frequent contact with Crowley, but accidentally blew himself up in his laboratory in 1952 while experimenting with explosives. His wife, Marjorie Cameron, suspected he was murdered.[214]

Hubbard, a pulp science fiction writer back then, had himself

---

[214] Wikipedia: *Marjorie Cameron.*

dribbled with the occult before he met Parsons, being a former member of a Rosicrucian branch called the AMORC (the Ancient and Mystic Order of the Rosy Cross). In early 1946, a year before Crowley's death, Hubbard and Parsons were involved in some wild experiments they called the *Babalon Writings*. These were built on a series of occult rituals *to produce a moonchild!* So, these two magicians wanted to give birth to Horus, and thus be the two grandiose people ringing in the Aeon of Horus by manifesting Horus through sex magic rituals. Parsons was in frequent communication with Crowley during the experiments, explaining to him the process and how things progressed. Crowley was reluctant, although he communicated their work to others. The two enthusiasts, however, did not let any concerns, even from Crowley, discourage them. Parsons was positive that his wife, Marjorie Cameron (1922-95), an actor, artist, poet, and occultist, was the true Scarlet Woman to produce a son, the second incarnation of Horus. Marjorie was thus the moon goddess, Isis, according to the two actors.

The three participants performed a series of sex-magical rituals, and both Parsons and Hubbard had sex with Marjorie to produce the divine child. For some reason, no child was produced, but the two magicians were still certain the rituals were a success. How they came to that conclusion goes beyond me, but what do I know? However, after the Babalon sessions were completed, Hubbard kidnapped Parsons' wife and ran off with his money, also stealing his yacht on the flight.[215] Hubbard, excited, apparently thought he'd run away with Isis. However, the kidnapping drama was short-lived, and Marjorie soon returned to California and Parsons. After Parsons died in 1952, she spent much of her time trying to create more moonchildren to accompany the initial moonchild, Horus. She was an OTO member until her death in 1995, and she got a Thelema burial, performed by a high priest of the OTO.

Some say the Roswell Incident, when two flying saucers crashed in New Mexico, was a direct consequence of Parsons' and Hubbard's Babalon Working, but that is difficult to prove.

To end the story about Parsons and Hubbard, I have read the Scientology OT VIII material, which is the highest level released in Scientology as of today, and it is strictly confidential (although it's

---

[215] Russel Miller: *The Bare-Faced Messiah.*

been stolen from Scientology and published all over the Internet since many years back). On this level of initiation, Hubbard said he was Lucifer. There is no doubt Hubbard was a grandiose narcissist, aside from that statement, but in the OT VIII material, he elevated himself to be "God." In other words, he claimed to be En.ki.

So, did Marjorie Cameron give birth to Horus? Apparently not, or, apparently yes, if we listen to the two confusing magicians. If she succeeded, Marduk would have been born in late 1946 to early 1947. It's up for debate whether this truly happened, or if it was just some magical work of two wannabe magicians. Do I think Marjorie was Isis? The Cameron family is bloodline, but no, I seriously doubt she was Isis. She had very narcissistic traits, as well, being extremely dominant and overpowering, but she was known to change her personality to fit the assembly she joined; in other words, she was manipulative.

The Aeon of Horus and Ma'at

Crowley had many things correct, and his teachings on the Aeon of Horus are interesting. He described the First Aeon (the Second Construct in my writings) as mostly maternal, a time of Isis and Mother Earth worship or following. He described this era as "simple, quiet, easy, and pleasant...," and the Age of the Great Goddess.

I was stunned reading about how Crowley addressed the Aeon of Osiris: "The classical and medieval Aeon of Osiris is considered being dominated by the paternal principle and the formula of the Dying God."[216] The *dying God* is En.ki, thrown down into the ABZU, stripped of his creative abilities. Moreover, Crowley describes the Matrix and the transition from Life in the Second Construct to Death in the Third (the Aeon of Osiris):

> Formula of Osiris, whose word is IAO; so that men worshiped Man, thinking him subject to Death, and his victory dependent upon Resurrection. Even so conceived they of the Sun as slain and reborn with every day, and every year.
>
> [...]
>
> "The second [Aeon] is of suffering and death: the spiritual strives to ignore the material. Christianity and all cognate religions

---

[216] Wikipedia: *Aeon (Thelema), ibid. op. cit.*

worship death, glorify suffering, deify corpses." [217]

In his *Thelema*, Crowley presents the idea about the Aeon of Horus, which now is upon us. He wrote,

> The modern Aeon of Horus is portrayed as a time of self-realization as well as a growing interest in all things spiritual, and is considered to be dominated by the principle of the child. The Word of its Law is Thelema (will), which is complemented by Agape (love), and its formula is Abrahadabra. Individuality and finding the individual's True Will are the dominant aspects; its formula is that of growth, in consciousness and love, toward self-realization.[218]

Crowley believed the Aeon of Horus would be brief (the Singularity), full of spiritual growth and self-reflection, which is true, because contrary to what Parsons and Hubbard believed, Crowley had the idea that the Age of Horus had already begun. Thus, he thought Marduk was already born as Horus during his lifetime, which I very much doubt. However, despite all the things he was correct about, we must remember that Crowley was not of the Light. His rituals often included very dark and horrific aspects— even child sacrifice, according to some. But he did not admit to sacrificing children, and students of the *Thelema* claim that Crowley often used analogies and metaphors, and that he called masturbation "child sacrifice" (sperms that don't create any children). In his book *Magic,* he referred to masturbation jokingly and dysphemistically as child sacrifice, according to some.[219, 220] I have not studied Crowley to any extent, so I can't tell what is true or false in this case. The OTO is a sex magic cult, and on Grade IX°, the highest grade of the Order, homosexuality is a part of the initiation. I wonder if the book *Matrix V*, in Val Valerian's Matrix book series, where it says men must be homosexual before they can leave the Matrix, and they should discard women altogether, is inspired by Crowley's writings (although Crowley was not a woman hater, from what I know). It's well-known that Valerian had studied Crowley. Even though Valerian claims *Matrix V* was written by someone else, and not by him, be as it may with that, but the writing style in the book is in a typical Val Valerian voice. Regardless, Valerian accepted the

---

[217] *Ibid., op. cit.*
[218] *Ibid., op. cit.*
[219] Laurence Galian, 666: *Connection with Crowley*
[220] Goodreads: *Child Sacrifice Quotes.*

book as the last book in his series, and I have not seen any disclaimer from him. He himself is said to be gay. I am not against gay people, but I have an issue when people get misled by false claims, such as having to be homosexual to leave the Matrix, they must hate women, who are not allowed to leave the Matrix, because _all_ women are manipulative and evil, according to Valerian's teaching. It sounds to me Valerian had mother issues.

The Aeon of Ma'at, the Age of Justice, will then fairly quickly overlap with the Aeon of Horus. In the WPP, I explained that the Egyptian term, *ma'at*, means justice—the Mother Goddess' justice. This word can be further traced to the Aryan language, where the same word has the same meaning, something I learned from my Orion source.

Crowley said in *The Law is for all:*

> It is necessary to say here that The Beast appears to be a definite individual; to wit, the man Aleister Crowley. But the Scarlet Woman is an officer replaceable as need arises. Thus to this present date of writing, Anno XVI, Sun in Sagittarius, there have been several holders of the title.[221]

As I've been saying, there have been many Isises, and many have held the title over the millennia.

Of the Aeon of Ma'at, Crowley wrote:

> I may now point out that the reign of the crowned and Conquering Child is limited in time by The Book of the Law itself. We learn that Horus will be in his turn succeeded by Thmaist, the Double-Wanded One; she who shall bring the candidates to full initiation, and though we know little of her peculiar characteristics, we know at least that her name is justice.[222]

According to one of Crowley's early students, Charles Stanfeld Jones (1886-1950), aka Frater Achad, the Aeon of Ma'at has already arrived or overlaps the present Aeon of Horus.

In its own mysterious way, it seems like the Aeon of Ma'at would eventually completely succeed the Aeon of Horus, bringing justice to the world in the form of the Mother Goddess. If Crowley was right, it means that the Singularity will fail or be short-lived and

---

[221] Wikipedia: *The Law is for All, op. cit.*
[222] Wikipedia: *Aeon (Thelema), op. cit.*

that there will be an intervention (perhaps by Orion) before we get to the point of no return. Those who live shall see. The year 2045 is not far away. Another perhaps better interpretation would be that the Aeon of Horus, which is Marduk's Age, is the road to the Singularity, and is supervised by him, while the Aeon of Ma'at exists simultaneously, and is the path you and I are taking when we refuse to accept the Aeon of Horus and Marduk's plans. The Aeon of Ma'at would thus be the return to Orion and the exiting through the Earth Grid.

The Sun King Changes All

14 **Louis XIV of France** [1638-1715, r. 1643-1715] was the most interesting king in recent history. He was larger than life, called himself the Sun King, *(le Roi Soleil)* claimed to be Apollo (and even dressed like him occasionally), and stood above everybody else—he said, he was *without equals* in the world, and he loved to start wars—wars were his passion. We could easily write him off as a classical psychopath, one of many, and call it good. But we can't. This king changed everything, and the consequences of his reign shaped the beginning of the New World Order, starting in France with the Enlightenment in 1717, two years after he died in 1715. Simultaneously, in 1717, the German Hanover bloodline completely took over the British crown. He also infiltrated and took over Freemasonry, starting in France, but the coup continued in Germany and England. As we have learned, Freemasonry, or at least the British-Scottish branch of it, was founded by the Templars in the late 1600s (but had allegedly operated behind the scenes before that) to protect the Holy Grail—the Jesus-Magdalene bloodline. This changed with Louis XIV, who wanted revolution and a New World Order, versus the Old World Order, which was En.ki's Order. It's the same New World Order we heard George H.W. Bush talk about in 1991 (turn 1991 around, and we get 1661, which was the year Louis XIV came to power. The gods and the Elite love numbers). It's Marduk's New World Order we are discussing, and to me, there is no chance in Hell that Louis XIV was

Fig. 14:1. 1655 portrait of Louis, the Victor of the Fronde, portrayed as the god Jupiter.

not an incarnation of Marduk. Moreover, who is the Sun God? RA, Apollo, Marduk.

For those who want more evidence that Louis XIV was Marduk, I will show you plenty, but we can start here:

Louis XIV was born on 5 September 1638 in the Château de Saint-Germain-en-Laye, to Louis XIII and Anne of Austria. He was named Louis Dieudonné (Louis the God-given) and bore the traditional title of French heirs apparent: Dauphin. At the time of his birth, his parents had been married for 23 years. His mother had experienced four stillbirths between 1619 and 1631. Leading contemporaries thus regarded him as a divine gift and his birth a miracle of God.[223]

The circumstances around his birth were mystical, indeed. Knowing the gods as well as we do, it's appropriate to suspect the stillbirths of his elder siblings were planned to eventually put Marduk in power. The statement that he was "a divine gift and his birth a miracle of God" sounds eerily like Jesus' birth being a "miracle of God."

Here is more about the connection between Louis and Marduk. Jupiter (Zeus) is, as my readers know, Marduk:

Why would Marduk incarnate as a French king, who supposedly were Christian, not pagan, and particularly at that exact time? Louis reigned for 72 years, which is a world record (even longer than Queen Elizabeth II), also taking into consideration that the life expectancy in the 1600s and early 1700s was 40 years. When he died at 76 (two days shy of 77), he had almost doubled the normal life expectancy. But he probably had a reason for staying in the human body for that long for a reason. He had a lot of work to do, being on a mission. When the mission was completed, he could lie down and

---

223 Wikipedia: *Louis XIV, op. cit.*

die.

Fig. 14:2. Louis XIV, Marduk incarnated, bathing in a " sea" of lilies.

This was also the beginning of the Marduk-Ereškigal bloodline, with which the king contaminated the royal families in Europe. This was the time Marduk broke away from En.ki and started taking over the world. Today, we are almost completely run by the Marduk clan, and there is very little left of the original Jesus-Magdalene bloodline. This was not something he and his father, En.ki, had agreed to. It was a coup, and Marduk had planned it for a long time, withholding his plot from his father. But why at that particular time? Because that's when he considered humankind ready for the Industrial Revolution, and later, the eras of Information Technology, AI, and the Singularity. It started right there, during his incarnation as King Louis XIV of France.

When En.ki and Marduk made a pact at the time of the Twelve Tribes of Israel, agreeing to work together, Marduk knew he had the upper hand. When Marduk later created a fresh Jesus-Isis lineage, bypassing his father, I bet there was nothing En.ki himself would have wanted more than to incarnate as Jesus to strengthen his own bloodline, but instead, Marduk introduced the first step in a long series of plans. Marduk, around the incarnation of Louis XIV, most likely promised Ereškigal to become the future Queen of Orion. It was important to dilute the Jesus-Magdalene bloodline, so En.ki's DNA would weaken and Marduk's be strengthened. It is obvious Marduk does not want En.ki to follow him into Orion because then En.ki would be the heir of Orion, which is a title Marduk, of course, has reserved for himself. This way, he planned on taking over the entire Singularity project and leaving En.ki behind, helpless and without creative abilities in the ABZU. Now, the reader might understand why Barbara Marciniak's *Pleiadians* came here and channeled through Barbara. They report to En.ki, according to themselves, and that has always been a mystery because the Pleiadians do *not* want us to go into the Singularity. Until recently, we thought En.ki wanted the Singularity, but he doesn't, and probably never did, but I will elaborate much more on this in the last chapters of this book.

Let us now investigate the Sun King in more detail.

The Personality of Louis XIV

The Sun King was only 4+ years old when he inherited the throne of France in 1643, but his official reign did not start until 1661, when he was 23 years old, after his chief minister, the famous Cardinal Jules Mazarin, who had run France during Louis' childhood, died. Louis was an adherent of the *divine rights of kings* and continued the work of creating a centralized France, run from the capital, giving himself absolute power. This is interesting because it may seem he was a firm believer in and supporter of the monarchy, contrary to later development, but listen to this:

> He sought to eliminate the remnants of feudalism persisting in parts of France; by compelling many members of the nobility to reside at his lavish Palace of Versailles, he succeeded in pacifying the aristocracy, many of whom had participated in the Fronde rebellions during his minority. He thus became one of the most powerful French monarchs and consolidated a system of absolute monarchy

in France that endured until the French Revolution.[224]

With the later Enlightenment in mind (see the next chapter), it's easy to see that King Louis strengthened the monarchy during his lifetime to strengthen his own power to become absolute, so he could reform Europe without serious interventions. As the quote says, it all changed after his death with the French Revolution, which was something he had planned behind secret doors. He also enforced uniformity of religion to wipe out the Protestant minority in France to have the entire population conform to Catholicism. By taking appropriate steps, he completely abolished Protestantism in France.[225] Again, the king took the steps necessary to unite everything enough to give him total power over both religion and state, something he quite easily accomplished. Without complete control, he would not have been able to reach his goals for that incarnation. He knew what he was doing.

During King Louis XIV's reign, France emerged as the leading power in Europe. War was the primary part of foreign policy, and he instigated several wars during his long reign, which exponentially increased his overall power. He sensed that war was the ideal way to enhance his glory, and in peacetime, he prepared for the next war.[226]

Wikipedia conveys,

> Significant achievements during Louis XIV's reign which would go on to have a wide influence on the early modern period, well into the Industrial Revolution and until today, include the construction of the Canal du Midi, the patronage of artists, and the founding of the French Academy of Sciences.[227]

As we can see, science was a big passion of his, which helped to form the Enlightenment movement later; and he was also a forerunner of ushering in the Industrial Revolution. He did not want a small reformation; he wanted a global one, starting in Europe, and expanding into the Americas and farther.

To understand a little better what life in the French court was like under the Sun King, consider this:

---

[224] Wikipedia: *Louis XIV, op. cit.*
[225] *Ibid.*
[226] *Ibid.*
[227] Wikipedia: *Louis XIV, op. cit.*

Each morning, high-ranking nobles greeted the king as he awoke (the "rising" of the king, in parallel to the rising of the sun), hand-picked favorites carried out such tasks as tying the ribbons on his shoes, and then the procession accompanied him to breakfast. Comparable rituals continued throughout the day, ensuring that only those nobles in the king's favor ever had the opportunity to speak to him directly. The rituals were carefully staged not only to represent deference to Louis, but to emphasize the hierarchy of ranks among the nobles themselves, undermining their unity and forcing them to squabble over his favor. One of the simplest ways in which Versailles undermined their power was that it cost so much to maintain oneself there – about 50% of the revenue of all but the very richest nobles present in the town or the château was spent on lodging, clothes, gifts, and servants.[228]

There we have the Sun King in practice. He was a "god" and wanted to be treated as such. That is Marduk for us.

Here is more (the similarity to the old gods, as described in ancient texts, is stunning, and very inappropriate for a "Christian" king):

Louis was called the Sun King, a term and an image he actively cultivated, declaring himself "without equal," and being depicted as the sun god Apollo (he once performed as Apollo in a ballet before his nobles, to rapturous applause – he was an excellent dancer). He was, among other things, a master marketer and propagandist of himself and his own authority. He had teams of artists, playwrights, and architects build statues, paint pictures, write plays and stories, and build buildings all glorifying his image.[229]

So extravagant and huge was his palace that food was cold before it made it from the kitchen to the dining room. It's comical, but it's a known fact that some nobles, living in the palace, preferred to relieve themselves directly in the hallways, rather than walking to the privies, often located too far from their rooms.[230] Louis' extravagance took away 60% of the total budget, which created resentment among people, but it certainly increased his prestige, and most of all, he loved it, and therefore spent most of his time in Versailles rather than Paris (which he hated, partly, perhaps, because Paris was the town of Diana/Isis. Now, it was all about

---

[228] Human.libretext.org: *10.2: Louis XIV—the Sun King, op. cit.*
[229] *Ibid., op. cit.*
[230] *Ibid.*

Ereškigal), dismissing the financial costs as beneath his dignity to take notice of. In line with the future Enlightenment, he also founded the first scientific academy in France and supported the *Académie française*, which aimed at preserving the purity of the French language, and French became the language of international diplomacy among European states.[231]

Louis XIV's ways of leading France, and his exaggerated grandiosity and entitlement, became very destructive to the country long-term. His constant wars, often against the Austrian Habsburgs (another monarchy), cost the country a fortune, and his advisors warned him that this would not end well. But the king ignored such advice and continued spending. We need to keep in mind who this person was, and that he had no loyalties, except to himself. All the debts he accrued were created on purpose to weaken the monarchy and create dissonance among people against it, which eventually led to the French Revolution—something King Louis wanted to happen. His goal was to weaken the power of the monarchies of Europe rather than strengthen it. On the surface, it appeared he wanted the monarchy to gain absolute power, but intentionally, his actions only created resentment toward the French crown. We will talk a lot more about the consequences of the reign of Louis XIV in the next two chapters.

> ...the costs of the wars were so high that his government desperately sought new sources of revenue, selling noble titles and bureaucratic offices, instituting still new taxes, and further trampling the peasants. When he died in 1715, the state was technically bankrupt[232]

It's easy to see that this created a serious discord with the French population.

Outwardly, King Louis was a devoted Catholic, but like with so many other things, nothing was what it seemed. He often took on roles, so he could covertly play the other side of it. And he liked the arts—particularly acting(!) So also, with Catholicism. Marduk is not religious and never was. He aimed at taking over the Catholic Church, which until then had been a protector of the Marduk-Isis bloodline that Marduk now wanted to make obsolete. The Catholic

---

[231] This might be where the idea of French being the world language, rather than English, came from.

[232] Human.libretext.org: *10.2: Louis XIV—the Sun King, op. cit.*

Church was a serious threat to Marduk's expansion, an expansion accomplished by constant wars and conquest in Europe. This was continued, but more covertly, by his faithful servants, such as Voltaire, after the king's death.

Perhaps his first step to take over the Catholic Church was the annexation of Strasbourg:

> Louis also sought Strasbourg, an important strategic crossing on the left bank of the Rhine and theretofore a Free Imperial City of the Holy Roman Empire, annexing it and other territories in 1681. Although a part of Alsace, Strasbourg was not part of Habsburg-ruled Alsace and was thus not ceded to France in the Peace of Westphalia.[233]

Although Louis XIV had a passion for warfare, it was not only his passion of bloodshed that drove him. He wanted an expansion of the French Empire. France needed to gain control, not only over Europe, but also over other continents so that in the future, all nations could unite under a One World Government. The king certainly expanded French territory in Europe, but also in Africa, the Americas, and Asia. The U.S. state of Louisiana is named after Louis XIV, for example. He also let France participate in the Jesuit missions in China to get a stronghold there. Although he probably had not completely taken over the Catholic Church at that time, supporting the Jesuits gained his agenda of religious expansion. Up to this day, France is still considered a Catholic country. That never changed after Louis' death, but purposely so. He didn't hate the Catholic Church as an institution; he just did not want it to protect the Holy Graal, but rather his new gene pool.

King Louis eventually managed to take over the Catholic Church, which up to this day is no longer a Jesus-Magdalene but a Marduk-Ereškigal institution. The pope is supposed to be the emissary and intermediary between God and the people, but "God" is no longer En.ki. The title has passed on to Marduk, who has elevated himself as the Supreme God of Heaven and Earth. His father is impotent and quite powerless, and Marduk took over Earth, in the true meaning, in the 17th Century. His greatest achievement, perhaps, was to take over the Catholic Church.

Louis initially supported traditional Gallicanism, which limited

---

[233] Wikipedia: *Louis XIV, op. cit.*

papal authority in France, and convened an Assembly of the French clergy in November 1681. Before its dissolution eight months later, the Assembly had accepted the Declaration of the Clergy of France, which increased royal authority at the expense of papal power. Without royal approval, bishops could not leave France, and appeals could not be made to the pope. Additionally, government officials could not be excommunicated for acts committed in pursuance of their duties. Although the king could not make ecclesiastical law, all papal regulations without royal assent were invalid in France. Unsurprisingly, the Pope repudiated the Declaration.[234]

Sébastien Le Prestre de Vauban, France's leading military strategist, said to the king about the Catholic Church: "For lukewarm, useless, or impotent friends, France has the Pope, who is indifferent..."[235] implying King Louis had a passive Church under his thumb. I would say that by 1681, he had taken over the Church and started forcing the French population to convert from Protestantism to Catholicism. He wanted a united Church and a One Religion that he could control. He had lost his grip along the way when the Church started prosecuting Knights Templar, and many fled to Scotland, there creating a hatred toward the Catholic Church, leading to the conversion of the Scottish population to Protestantism. The ban of Catholicism was enforced in England by King Henry VIII when founding the Protestant Church of England. From that time on, the British Crown does not allow royal members to be Catholics up to this day, and still, in 2024, Great Britain is a thorn in the side of Marduk. He still doesn't know how to convert Great Britain, which refused to abide to him.

> In 1681, Louis dramatically increased his persecution of Protestants. The principle of cuius regio, eius religio generally had also meant that subjects who refused to convert could emigrate, but Louis banned emigration and effectively insisted that all Protestants must be converted. Secondly, following the proposal of René de Marillac and the Marquis of Louvois, he began quartering dragoons in Protestant homes. Although this was within his legal rights, the dragonnades inflicted severe financial strain on Protestants and atrocious abuse. Between 300,000 and 400,000 Huguenots converted, as this entailed financial rewards and

---

[234] *Ibid. op. cit.*
[235] Wikipedia: *Louis XIV, op. cit.*

exemption from the dragonnades.[236]

Historians scratch their heads over King Louis' decision to exile so many Protestants, who then took refuge in Protestant countries, which strengthened those countries and weakened France. What is not understood is that King Louis' interest, as Marduk, was primarily not France's wellbeing, but to propel his global agenda via revolution. He wanted to weaken the French monarchy and create as much discord as possible, but at the same time secure his own position as the King of France, without being overthrown and usurped. A brilliant way to accomplish a successful future revolution was to strengthen the enemy, making them more like equals to France, which made them braver.

Louis' strict religious policies were only in effect until just before the French Revolution, when his descendant, Louis XVI, restored the civil rights to non-Catholics, and they were once again allowed to practice their religion openly. This "grand gesture" was also a part of the plan because with the Enlightenment and the American Revolution also came freedom of religion, tolerating anyone to practice any religion they devoted themselves to.

Fig. 14:3. Louis and his family portrayed as Roman gods in a 1670 painting by Jean Nocret.

---

[236] *Ibid. op. cit.*

Privately, King Louis did his very best to play the role of a devoted Catholic, and he followed all Catholic rituals and procedures, wherever he might be in the world, but his informal alliance with the *Ottoman Empire* was criticized for undermining Christianity.[237] His "Catholic faith" should be seriously questioned by anyone who studies the life of Louis XIV, since he continuously wanted to be compared to the pagan gods, such as Apollo and Jupiter. In one painting, his entire family is portrayed as the Roman pantheon of gods (fig. 14:3).

His devotion to ballet is well known. He was an excellent ballet dancer and performed often. However, he was very strategic in his roles in plays and ballets in which he participated. All in the guise of Catholicism, of course (tongue-in-cheek).

> Louis played an Egyptian in Le Mariage forcé in 1664, a Moorish gentleman in Le Sicilien in 1667, and both Neptune and Apollo in Les Amants magnifiques in 1670 ... He sometimes danced leading roles that were suitably royal or godlike (such as Neptune, Apollo, or the Sun). [238]

Next, he gained complete control over the aristocracy.

> Apartments were built to house those willing to pay court to the king. However, the pensions and privileges necessary to live in a style appropriate to their rank were only possible by waiting constantly on Louis. For this purpose, an elaborate court ritual was created wherein the king became the centre of attention and was observed throughout the day by the public. With his excellent memory, Louis could then see who attended him at court and who was absent, facilitating the subsequent distribution of favours and positions. Another tool Louis used to control his nobility was censorship, which often involved the opening of letters to discern their author's opinion of the government and king. Moreover, by entertaining, impressing, and domesticating them with extravagant luxury and other distractions, Louis not only cultivated public opinion of him, but he also ensured the aristocracy remained under his scrutiny.[239]

The above section tells us the king also had an impeccable memory. I bet he did; he was born without amnesia, completely

---

[237] *Ibid.*
[238] *Ibid. op. cit.*
[239] *Ibid. op. cit.*

aware of who he was, and he did not forget, as we do.

Furthermore, he forced the nobility to live with him in Versailles, instead of on their own properties, where, historically, they made plots, created civil wars, and even sometimes rioted against the crown. Thus, he further weakened their power, and he could have them all under observation. "This victory over the nobility may thus have ensured the end of major civil wars in France until the French Revolution about a century later."[240] This was a necessary step to secure the agenda, so that the two Revolutions, the American and the French, could take place long after his death without distractions. Everything was planned beforehand. Louis left no stone unturned; always plotting, always expanding towards his goal, i.e., the New World Order and the Singularity.

King Louis realized during his later years he would not be able to take England, which was a great disappointment, but he had a plan, a non-violent one, which, for him, was an unusual move. He let the German House of Hanover take over the British throne, and by diluting the Jesus-Magdalen bloodline of the Royal House, he might have an easier time manipulating them from the astral, perhaps. He prepared the "German Invasion" of bloodlines during his lifetime, but it was not implemented until two years after his death through the English House of Hanover. Thus, he had his own bloodline on the English throne, and the problem was solved.

Louis' first wife was Maria Theresa of Spain but although his marriage was considered affectionate, he was notoriously unfaithful and had thirteen children with different lovers out of wedlock, all of them therefore being illegitimate. There were probably more offspring, but thirteen children could be verified. Most of them, the king married to members of cadet branches of the royal family. It may sound like he had an exaggerated sex drive, which may or may not be the case, but I believe the reason for his infidelity, which was often done in the open, was not to still his sexual hunger, but to establish and spread the Marduk-Ereškigal bloodline to the best of his ability. To do that, he could not keep strictly to one lover.

---

[240] *Ibid. op. cit.*

Anne of Austria, Mother of Louis XIV

L ouis XIV's father is said to have been King Louis XIII, but there is, as mentioned earlier, some controversy around Louis XIV's birth. Anne of Austria, who was Louis' mother, half Spanish, half Austrian, had stillbirths before Louis was conceived. Had his still-born siblings survived, he would most likely not have been king. Moreover, no one expected Anne to have more children after the stillbirths, particularly as she was 37 years old at the time of Louis' birth—a significant age for the time to give birth, when the life expectancy was 40 years. Although there is no proof that Louis XIII was not the father, this is what happened:

Fig. 14:4. Cardinal Mazarin.

Despite a climate of distrust [between Louis XIII and Anne due to previous mysterious miscarriages], the queen became pregnant once more, a circumstance that contemporary gossip attributed to a single stormy night that prevented Louis from travelling to Saint-Maur and obliged him to spend the night with the queen. Louis XIV was born on 5 September 1638, an event that secured the Bourbon line. At this time, Anne was 37. The official newspaper Gazette de France called the birth "a marvel when it was least expected".

The birth of a living son failed to re-establish confidence between the royal couple. However, she conceived again fifteen months later. At Saint-Germain-en-Laye on 21 September 1640, Anne gave birth to her second son, Philippe I, Duke of Orléans, who later founded the modern House of Orléans. Both of her children were placed under the supervision of the royal governess Françoise de

Lansac, who was disliked by Anne and loyal to the king and the cardinal.[241]

King Louis XIII died only five years after Louis XIV's birth, and Anne became a widow, raising two sons. Together with Cardinal Mazarin, she ruled France in the name of her son, who had, of course, not yet come to age. After Mazarin's death, Anne reigned on her own until 1661, when her son, Louis, came of age and took the throne.

Fig. 14:5. Queen Anne of Austria with a rose on her chest.

Louise XIV's relationship with his mother is described as uncommonly affectionate for the time. Eyewitnesses testify that they were together all the time, day and night. It was Anne who gave his son "his belief in the absolute and divine power of his monarchical rule."[242]

When Louis XIII died in 1643, Anne had his will annulled by the *Parlement de Paris*, making her the sole regent, and she kept the religious policy strongly in hand until her son took the throne in

---

[241] Wikipedia: *Anne of Austria, op. cit.*
[242] Wikipedia: *Louis XIV, op. cit.*

1661. Louis XIII mistrusted his wife and tried his best to have some-one else reign in France until Louise XIV came of age. He failed. Still, Anne continued the policies of her husband and Cardinal Richelieu, despite their persecution of her, to win absolute authority in France and victory abroad for her son. Anne was a very proud queen, insisting on the divine rights of the king of France.

> All this led her to advocate a forceful policy in all matters relating to the King's authority, in a manner that was much more radical than the one proposed by Mazarin. The Cardinal depended totally on Anne's support and had to use all his influence on the Queen to temper some of her radical actions. Anne imprisoned any aristo-crat or member of parliament who challenged her will; her main aim was to transfer to her son an absolute authority in the matters of finance and justice. One of the leaders of the Parlement of Paris, whom she had jailed, died in prison.[243]

I think there is a chance Cardinal Jules Mazarin was Louis XIV's real father. I can't prove it, but some hints may work, at least as a hypothesis. It would make sense that Louis XIII was not the father and the true reason he did not trust Anne, his wife. There is also reasons to believe Anne of Austria was the incarnation of Ereškigal, paving the way for her son, Louis XIV (Marduk) by ruling with iron gloves. Thus, Ereškigal cut off the Jesus-Magdalene bloodline and inserted her own by having a son with Mazarin. He was of the noble Italian Bufalini family. Subsequently, Louis XIV, as Marduk, could from there create royal offspring of their common Marduk-Ereškigal lineage.

> Queen Anne had a very close relationship with the Cardinal, and many observers believed that Mazarin became Louis XIV's stepfa-ther by a secret marriage to Queen Anne. However, Louis' coming-of-age and subsequent coronation deprived them of the Frondeurs' pretext for revolt. The Fronde thus gradually lost steam and ended in 1653, when Mazarin returned triumphantly from exile. From that time until his death, Mazarin was in charge of foreign and fi-nancial policy without the daily supervision of Anne, who was no longer regent.[244]

Queen Anne then insisted on marrying her son to the daughter of her brother, Philip IV of Spain, to infiltrate the Spanish bloodline

---

[243] *Ibid. op. cit.*
[244] *Ibid. op. cit.*

as well, and to strengthen the relationship between the two countries. This was successful.

The Enlightenment

15 The American Revolution (1775-83) happened before the French Revolution (1789-99), but they are tightly interwoven, and at the core, as usual, there are the bloodlines.

Our history books tell us that the rebels, led by George Washington, left England because of their disputes with King George III of Britain. The rebels wanted to create a sovereign state in America. What the history books leave out, however, is the *fact* that in the early 1600s, Sir Francis Bacon, working for the English crown, and was most likely the translator of the King James Bible and the plays of Shakespeare, wrote a book called *The New Atlantis*, which envisioned Atlantis being America in the future.[245] Bacon was a high-ranking Rosicrucian (Freemasonry was not officially founded back then), so he knew about the Holy Grail, of course, and was the protector thereof. Bacon knew a lot of things and was knowledgeable about many Brotherhood secrets.

The Founding Fathers, together with those who followed them, appeared to execute this old plan of bringing the Jesus-Magdalene bloodline west to the new, so far unexplored land across the Atlantis... sorry, Atlantic. They signed the American *Declaration of Independence* on July 4, 1776, and since then, the world thinks America, later the United States, has been independent from

---

[245] Gutenberg.org: *The New Atlantis, by Sir Francis Bacon* (no copyrights; can be downloaded for free in different formats).

England and become its own country. But has it?

No, it has not. The United States of America has never been sovereign, as little as Canada and Australia; these three nations are still owned by British Crown and the British Empire behind the scenes, currently ruled by King Charles III of Great Britain. Most of the Founding Fathers were Freemasons, which is common knowledge, and we know by now what Freemasons and other secret societies protect—the Holy Grail.

The question is, which Grail/Graal? That of Isis or that of Ereškigal?

We will investigate, and we can start by investigating which branch of Freemasonry the Founding Fathers represented—the York Rite, The Grand Lodge of England, or perhaps the French rite? The two former, up to this day, protect the Jesus-Isis bloodline, both being Templar Orders, while the French Rite is associated with the French lodges, who support the Marduk-Ereškigal Graal and the Revolution. Therefore, the Founding Fathers must have belonged to a branch of the French Rite, since the Scottish Rite was founded later, and consequently, they were Ereškigal followers and protectors of *her* bloodline. If that would not be the case, they would not have been revolutionary and part of the Enlightenment movement.

The Founding Fathers claimed they wanted America to be the Land of the Free, even when it came to religious beliefs, but that, in its core, it would be a Christian nation. Ironically, the Elite, including the secret societies, consider themselves Christians, and they are serious about it. We now know why: They all believe their bloodline goes back to Christ, which it does, although Christ, in his incarnation, was Marduk, the Devil. So, in a sense, the Christian Brotherhood is not lying, or as my Orion source said, and I paraphrase, "They are not necessarily lying to you; they just want you to look at it from *their* perspective."

People consider the Founding Fathers of America as heroes and liberators, but they deserve none of that praise because they betrayed everybody and were cold-blooded murderers, killing their own people in the devastating War of Independence that should never have been fought. The entire charade played out to fool the public and give them the illusion of independence. The Revolution had only one purpose, and that was for the Brotherhood to expand the Satanic Marduk-Ereškigal bloodline westward. America had been chosen at least two hundred years earlier as the New Atlantis, which means the Rosicrucians wanted an expansion of the Jesus-

Magdalene gene pool, and to reestablish the Atlantis En.ki *almost* controlled in the Second Construct with his technology and genetic experiments, including creating a pure bloodline. He meant for America to be the technological center for the Singularity establishment. Contrary to the Second Construct, En.ki and Marduk were now much freer to create the Singularity they had failed to finish before the Flood. Now, there is a Dome over the Earth and a Grid upon that, keeping Orion and other unwanted prying eyes away from his *Great Work of the Ages*, which has different meanings for En.ki and Marduk, respectively. See, there was one crux—En.ki was out of the picture, and the New Atlantis is, and has always been, run by Marduk.

With Atlantis/America as a technological center, we now have Silicon Valley, for one, the location of the resurrection of En.ki's Atlantean laboratories of genetic tinkering.

The plan is in the making and on its way to being fulfilled. However, if we consider Aleister Crowley's research from the previous chapter, we currently live in two Aeons (Ages), i.e., the Aeon of Horus/Marduk, and the Aeon of Ma'at/Justice (the Mother Goddess, the Holy Spirit). Crowley wrote about this in the early 20th century, but we can now clearly see he was correct, except for one thing: The Age of Horus did not start in the 20th century, but in the 17th and 18th centuries with Louis XIV. This doesn't mean Marduk is not incarnated now—he most likely is, and he oversees the Singularity project, while, on the other hand, people are waking up and have spiritual insights, and we even know how to exit Shakespeare's stage by going through a hole in the Grid (describing the Aeon of Ma'at). Shakespeare, via Bacon, told us, "All the world's a stage, and all the men and women merely players."[246]

The Purpose of the Enlightenment

The American Revolution is called a political and ideological revolution, based on the *Enlightenment Movement* in 18th-century America and Western Europe. It says to have started when King Louis XIV of France died. Enlightenment is quite a nice-sounding term, but it was more of a movement among intellectuals who spread the ideas to the public, and as was intended, the public, for

---

[246] From Shakespeare's play, *As you Like It,* Act 2, Scene 7.

the most part, caught on to it. It was a movement with a certain agenda in mind to make people oppose the monarchies and the Catholic Church.

> Philosophers and scientists of the period widely circulated their ideas through meetings at scientific academies, Masonic lodges, literary salons, coffeehouses and in printed books, journals, and pamphlets. The ideas of the Enlightenment undermined the authority of the monarchy and the Catholic Church and paved the way for the political revolutions of the 18th and 19th centuries. A variety of 19th-century movements, including liberalism, socialism and neoclassicism, trace their intellectual heritage to the Enlightenment.
>
> The central doctrines of the Enlightenment were individual liberty and religious tolerance, in opposition to an absolute monarchy and the fixed dogmas of the Church. The concepts of utility and sociability were also crucial in the dissemination of information that would better society as a whole. The Enlightenment was marked by an increasing awareness of the relationship between the mind and the everyday media of the world, and by an emphasis on the scientific method and reductionism, along with increased questioning of religious orthodoxy—an attitude captured by Kant's essay Answering the Question: What Is Enlightenment?, where the phrase sapere aude ('dare to know') can be found.
>
> [...]
>
> The Age of Enlightenment was preceded by and closely associated with the Scientific Revolution.[247]

As we can see, the Brotherhood, with French and German Freemasonry in the center, was greatly involved in the movement (and behind it), just like it is in the New Age movement of today. History repeats itself, and we have a new "Enlightenment movement" right now, starting with Helena Blavatsky and her Theosophical Society and the Great White Brotherhood in the mid-1800s, leading to the New Age and hippie movement, promoted by the music industry of the 1960s and 70s. Its counterpart is again a significant rise in the scientific movement.

After Bacon's and others' preparation, the Enlightenment eventually took off. Bacon was a key player in starting it, and because of the knowledge we have about his visions of the New Atlantis, we

---

[247] Wikipedia.org: *Age of Enlightenment, op. cit.*

also understand better what the Enlightenment truly was behind all its false facades. In essence, it was time for a big change—a New Era that shook up the Old Order to replace it with a new one. The philosophical part of the movement, led by Voltaire and Rousseau, wanted a society based on reason, like in ancient Greece, and on scientific experiments, rather than in faith, such as the Catholic Church. In other words, they wanted the world to become denser and less spiritual, contrary to the message it promoted. England, but also Germany, wanted to put the Catholic Church in a poor light around and after the German Invasion of the English throne in 1717, turning the English Royal Family into the German Royal Family. And mind you, Germany has "always" been Marduk's domain, regardless of what name it was under, whether ruled by royal families, dictators, chancellors, or whomever. Marduk wanted to, once and for all, separate from the Catholic Church, and thus take over the scene, planning way ahead. I would argue that Louis XIV incarnated as the French king at this particular time because he wanted to put the final touch on the upcoming Enlightenment and the final separation from Rome. Louis XIV was, of course, a French king, and the Enlightenment started in France two years after his death. I would say Marduk might have taken over the French throne with his incarnation as its monarch, and since then, he has been in control of France and Germany, respectively. Interestingly, the Enlightenment started immediately after King Louis died in 1715, and only two years after *Marduk-Ereškigal's Hanover branch of the German bloodline usurped England, introducing their new bloodline on the stage*. There is no such thing as coincidence; *energy flows where the mind goes*. Randomness is chaos, i.e., the effect of uncontrolled and confused energies, and nothing is confusing in what was happening back then. It was brilliantly planned, and the Brotherhood prepares far ahead.

On the other side of the coin of the philosophical enlightenment, we had the political enlightenment, led by Montesquieu. As the reader can see, we are still in France. The conspirators were busy plotting:

> The political philosopher Montesquieu introduced the idea of a separation of powers in a government, a concept which was enthusiastically adopted by the authors of the United States Constitution. While the philosophes of the French Enlightenment were not revolutionaries and many were members of the nobility, their ideas played an important part in undermining the legitimacy of the Old

Next, Scotland got involved through the Brotherhood puppet Francis Hutcheson, who was a moral philosopher and the founder of the Scottish Enlightenment.

In Germany, Immanuel Kant tried to reconcile rationalism and religious belief, and one could say he formed German thought, and eventually all European philosophy, well into the 20th century.[249]

Scientific societies and academies dominated science during the Enlightenment, rather than universities, in research and development. The Movement despised the universities, considering them to be institutions that transitioned knowledge rather than created it. Thus, we now had an Elite, above the strict and oppressive religions and the passive universities, run by a few, who considered themselves being the ones shaping science and knowledge. Thus, we have the world we have today, where the very few tell the rest what is right and what is wrong, the so-called "moral" aspect of the Enlightenment Voltaire so vividly promulgated. So much for getting rid of oppressive religion—oppressive science simply overrode it, and from that point on, science started its rapid journey toward information technology and AI to finish with Metaverse and the Singularity. But people of their time must have thought the Enlightenment sounded very liberating and exciting—much better than what they had. Note, however, that the churches never lost their power—they just worked behind the scenes. Everything works in symbiosis in the world of interconnected secret orders and societies. Louis XIV sat on the throne for a very long time. I presume he needed all these years to teach all the thick-headed humans how to proceed from thereon and get everybody on the same page.

> Most societies were granted permission to oversee their own publications, control the election of new members and the administration of the society. In the 18th century, a tremendous number of official academies and societies were founded in Europe, and by 1789 there were over 70 official scientific societies. In reference to this growth, Bernard de Fontenelle coined the term "the Age of Academies" to describe the 18th century.[250]

---

[248] Wikipedia.org: *Age of Enlightenment, op. cit.*
[249] *Ibid.*
[250] *Ibid., op. cit.*

It's obvious, isn't it? Marduk wanted religion to take the back burner for a while and let science be the most important source of knowledge, and as we can see, the scientific societies expanded exponentially, and have done so ever since. The universities adopt what the science community comes up with, true or false, and teach it to their students. That way, scientific societies can control what people learn and what direction evolution will take. No wonder the Klaus Schwabs of the world (head of the World Economic Forum) want to suppress the *true* Enlightenment of today, which is spiritual in nature. Klaus Schwab is a puppet for the scientific society, and the spiritual enlightenment is a threat to that. It is important that people don't think for themselves, or their fragile foundation of falsehood, manipulation, and lies will crumble. Again, we have the overlap of the Aeon of Ma'at on the Aeon of Horus playing out. But regardless of the Enlightenment in the 1700s, religion and monarchies did not need to worry; it was "business as usual," only more discreet.

From Britain came the first works of modern economics, which impacted Great Britain significantly, leading to modern banking and world economy. So, the reader can see where this is leading. From there, the political branch of Enlightenment spread to other parts of Europe, including Russia. From this quickly expanding movement, socialism, communism, Marxism, and several other isms eventually developed. Many political and intellectual people were also deeply involved in the Enlightenment in Europe, and Benjamin Franklin was often in Europe, influencing the movement. Thomas Jefferson was a part of it, too. He was not a Freemason, according to the records, but he was in frequent connection with Freemasonry and revolutionaries via other Founding Fathers, and through the Founder of the Bavarian Illuminati, Adam Weishaupt, something we will discuss in a moment. They corresponded back and forth, and letters written between them are still preserved up to this day. Weishaupt, of course, was a major player in the revolutionary part of the Enlightenment, as we shall see. Important to notice is that the Enlightenment was careful to cover all aspects of society (a serious attempt to gain full control). The English philosopher, John Locke, coined the phrase that each individual has the right to "Life, Liberty, and Property." Don't we wish that this meant peace and freedom for the individual, and that is exactly what people thought, when in fact, it was just another, more sophisticated manner of control? Locke's philosophy inspired the American

Declaration of Independence, and the French *Declaration of the Rights of Man and the Citizen* in 1789, the same year the French Revolution started.

This, and more, were radical changes in societies in Europe at the time, and from having started in France, it spread like forest fires all across the continent, being adopted by most governments and monarchies. It is remarkable because the movement gave the illusion of less power to governments and royalties, but still, the new reforms were accepted and adopted all the way down to Portugal (Knights Templar country). This is, of course, not logical, unless we are aware of the Bigger Picture behind all this, an agenda eventually leading to the Industrial Revolution, the advancement of sciences and technology, and the enforcement of those upon the common citizens. No one lost power; it was only an illusion, created to get people's consent.

Enlightened Absolutism

Prominent people who led the Enlightenment were not very democratic. As Wikipedia puts it, "'...they more often look to absolute monarchs as the key to imposing reforms designed by the intellectuals. Voltaire despised democracy and said the absolute monarch must be enlightened and must act as dictated by reason and justice—in other words, be a "philosopher-king."'"[251] So, it was just another way to rule: Instead of overt control and abuse through religion and all-mighty kings, the control became more covert, giving people the illusion of freedom, rather than the previous knowledge that they were oppressed. In the long term, the new way was a safer and more lucrative way to rule. But all in all, as the term *govern*ment implies, the citizens were still being governed.

Jumping on this reform to build stronger states included Frederick the Great of Prussia, Catherine the Great of Russia, Leopold II of Tuscany, and Joseph II of Austria, Senior ministers Pombal in Portugal and Johann Friedrich Struensee in Denmark governed according to these new ideals, as well. Poland also followed suit, but only for a short time.

---

[251] *Ibid., op. cit.*

The Bavarian Illuminati

Most people who are or have been into so-called conspiracy theories have heard of the *Bavarian Illuminati*, founded by a German intellectual, Adam Weishaupt (1748-1830). Illuminatus (singular) means enlightened, and Illuminati is the plural form. As the name implies, this secret society was operating during the Enlightenment Movement.

Fig. 15:1. Adam Weishaupt, founder of the Bavarian Illuminati.

The Bavarian Illuminati was founded on May 1, 1776, the same year the U.S. Freemasonic Founding Fathers signed the Declaration of Independence, with the Freemason George Washington in the lead, followed by many others from within the Brotherhood.

The society's stated goals were to oppose superstition, obscurantism, religious influence over public life, and abuses of state power. "The order of the day," they wrote in their general statutes, "is to put an end to the machinations of the purveyors of injustice, to control them without dominating them." The Illuminati—along with Freemasonry and other secret societies—were outlawed through edict by Charles Theodore, Elector of Bavaria, with the encouragement of the Catholic Church, in 1784, 1785, 1787 and 1790. During subsequent years, the group was generally vilified by conservative and religious critics who claimed that the Illuminati continued underground and were responsible for the French Revolution.

It attracted literary men such as Johann Wolfgang von Goethe and Johann Gottfried Herder and the reigning Duke of Gotha and of

Weimar.[252]

The Illuminati were highly revolutionary and Weishaupt wanted, at all costs, to keep his society secret from the Rosicrucian Order, which was, and still is a secret society of a pro-monarchic nature, as we have learned in this book—something our mainstream history also teaches us.[253] Weishaupt initially wanted to rub shoulders with the Freemasons, but found them too "expensive," and the Rosicrucians had a solid stronghold in prominent branches of Freemasonry in 18th-century Germany. They were the protectors of the Graal, and they wanted to have nothing to do with the Marduk-supported Enlightenment.

It did not take long before the Illuminati Order became known, and because the Rosicrucians saw the Order as a threat to the monarchy, the Prussian branch of the Order of the Rosy Cross under Johann Christoph von Wöllner, began an attack on the Illuminati. So, there was now escalated infighting between the Isis and the Ereškigal clans. Wöllner convinced other lodges of the power of Rosicrucian magic and turned these lodges against Weishaupt's Order. So, Wöllner spread a mouthpiece that the Illuminati were atheists and planned a revolution. This, they knew from having infiltrated the Order, pretending to be Rosicrucians converting to Weishaupt's philosophies. All Berlin Freemasons were now warned against the Illuminati Order, now also accused of using the liberal (and pre-revolutionary) writing of the Marduk-puppet, Voltaire, and others (Voltaire worked together with King Louis XIV). They accused the Order of pretending to have tolerance for traditional Freemasonry, while simultaneously creating a Freemasonic sect, seeking to undermine Christianity, turning the Holy Grail protecting Freemasonry into a political order. The revolutionary Freemasonry was not against revolution, but they did not want independent sects to destroy the plans for them. The French branch of Freemasonry, called *la Loge des Neuf Sœurs* in Paris was infiltrated by early revolutionaries, supporting Marduk's agenda, later spreading to the Sottish Rite of Freemasonry. The lodge was also located in Louis XIV's home country, France. This is verified by the fact that Voltaire was initiated into this lodge before his death, and

---

252 Wikipedia.org: *Age of Enlightenment, op. cit.*
253 Wikipedia: *Illuminati, #Conflict with Rosicrucians.*

it shows Benjamin Franklin was connected and supportive of this revolutionary branch of Masonry.

> Voltaire was initiated into Freemasonry a little over a month before his death. On 4 April 1778, he attended la Loge des Neuf Sœurs in Paris, and became an Entered Apprentice Freemason. According to some sources, "Benjamin Franklin ... urged Voltaire to become a freemason; and Voltaire agreed, perhaps only to please Franklin." However, Franklin was merely a visitor at the time Voltaire was initiated, the two only met a month before Voltaire's death, and their interactions with each other were brief.[254]

Strange, isn't it, that Voltaire, who was anti-monarchy, would join the pro-monarchal Freemasonry? Not so strange when we know the truth and what was happening behind closed curtains in Europe in the 1700s. Orders infiltrated each other, and some were completely taken over, such as the French lodge just mentioned. In America, in 1752, George Washington joined lodge no. 4 of Fredericksburg, Virginia, to which he belonged until his death.[255] Other famous Freemasons in the American Revolution were Benjamin Franklin, Paul Revere, and John Hancock. Although the Scottish Rite of Freemasonry got established in the U.S. later, the east coast lodges, in which the revolutionary fathers were initiated, must have been offspring of the French Mardukian lodges, and therefore, revolutionary in nature, although Freemasonry today denies this in quite some lame ways. In Germany, the 1780s could be considered the "war" between secret societies, with those who supported the crown and the Holy Grail on one side, and the Enlightenment on the other, i.e., Jesus-Magdalene against Marduk-Ereškigal.

Now ponder this:

> The Bavarian Illuminati, whose existence was already known to the Rosicrucians from an informant... were further betrayed by Ferdinand Maria Baader, an Areopagite who now joined the Rosicrucians. Shortly after his admission it was made known to his superiors that he was one of the Illuminati and he was informed that he could not be a member of both organisations. His letter of resignation stated that the Rosicrucians did not possess secret knowledge, and ignored the truly Illuminated, specifically

---

254 Wikipedia.org: *Voltaire.*
255 Mountvernon.org: *George Washington.*

identifying Lodge Theodore as an Illuminati Lodge.[256]

This is quite telling, showing us that the Freemasonic Theodore lodge in Cardiff, UK, was an Illuminati lodge, infiltrated and taken over, becoming a part of the Enlightenment movement—Freemasonry playing both sides of the conflict. Some sources suggest the Illuminati embraced Freemasonry, but that is not truly so, as they did all they could to infiltrate it, looking at the Masons as both a threat to their revolutionary ideas, but also being a part of the Old World Order, where religion and royal houses ruled.

Fig. 15:2. John Robison

Adolph Freiherr Knigge was the Illuminati's best recruiter, and he had turned the small secret society into a big organization, recruiting both Freemasons and Rosicrucians to Weishaupt's camp (some of them infiltrators and spies for the monarchies and the Jesuits, probably unbeknown to Knigge). However, this also created friction between Weishaupt and Knigge because the Illuminati turned incrementally into a mystical, magical Order, while Weishaupt was more "down to earth" and wanted a purely political movement, free from "superstitions." This resulted in Weishaupt

---

[256] Wikipedia: *Illuminati, op. cit.*

firing Knigge, who then left the Order. This proved to be a big mistake, and the Illuminati Order declined.

Over time, the Illuminati infiltrated the government, also putting their members in the court and other top positions. They were in opposition to the Jesuits of the Catholic Church, as well, and in Ingolstadt, the Jesuit heads of department were replaced by Illuminati members. Charles Theodore, of the Noble House of Wittelsbach, was alarmed, him being monarchist, and to restore order, he banned *all* secret societies, so he could root out the Illuminati from leading positions, wherewith Adam Weishaupt fled and went "underground."

In 1797, the physician and mathematician, John Robison, was the major publisher of the book with the long title, *Proof of Conspiracy against all the Religions and Governments of Europe, carried on in the secret meetings of Freemasons, Illuminati and Reading Societies,* exposing the Illuminati and some branches of Freemasonry as conspirators. A French priest, Abbé Barruel, had come to a very similar conclusion that the Illuminati had infiltrated Continental Freemasonry, leading to the excesses of the French Revolution. In 1798, a copy of Robison's book was sent to George Washington, awaiting his comments, since the revolutionary ideas first played out in America, and Washington was evidently a Freemason. Washington did reply to the letter, denying the American Freemasonry's part in the "diabolic plot" to which members of his Order had conspired in Europe. This is, of course, just word salad, in defense of Freemasonry in general. As mentioned earlier, Thomas Jefferson, although not a Mason, was in frequent communication with Weishaupt in Bavaria.

Here is the truth of the matter:

> Modern conspiracy theorists, such as Nesta Webster and William Guy Carr, believe the methods of the Illuminati as described in Proofs of a Conspiracy were copied by radical groups throughout the 19th and 20th centuries in their subversion of benign organizations. Spiritual Counterfeits Project editor Tal Brooke has compared the views of Proofs of a Conspiracy with those found in Carroll Quigley's Tragedy and Hope (Macmillan, 1966). Brooke suggests that the New World Order, which Robison believed Adam Weishaupt (founder of the Illuminati) had in part accomplished through the infiltration of Freemasonry, will now be completed by those holding sway over the international banking system (e.g., by means of the Rothschilds' banks, the U.S. Federal Reserve, the

International Monetary Fund, and the World Bank).[257]

Out of the Illuminati and Freemasonry came the Rothschild banking cartel, instigated by the Marduk-appointed Mayer Amschel Rothschild (1744-1812). Mayer Rothchild laid the grounds for the future Rothschild Banking Dynasty within the same time frame as the Enlightenment took place. The two revolutions, one in America and one in France, were a massive coup d'état on En.ki's Old World Order, replacing it with Marduk's New World Order. Since then, humankind has lived under the rulership of Marduk, and the original Jesus-Magdalene bloodline has been almost rooted out. The royal houses these days comprise mostly the Marduk-Ereškigal bloodline, i.e., the "bloodline of the commoners," which makes them almost as little royal as we are.

Thus, En.ki's New Atlantis, envisioned by him in the beginning of the Matrix construct, never happened the way he had planned. Instead, the New Atlantis became Marduk's Atlantis, where he is busy setting up the final New World Order, resulting in the Singularity.

---

[257] Wikipedia: *John Robison.*

One Mind—Many Revolutions

16 **I am aware I'm turning** virtually all previous research in this field upside down and inside out. Those who have researched the "Anunnaki" gods, i.e., the Overlords, usually say America is En.ki's territory and his New Atlantis. Consequently, the Freemasonic Founding Fathers were supposedly En.ki-ists. I was of the same mindset, until I did the research for this book, which took me in the opposite direction, and this is where my research has led me:

It is true that America was originally supposed to be En.ki's New Atlantis. But the first mix up is Sir Francis Bacon's book, *The New Atlantis*, written long before Washington and his people landed on the shores of the current United States. Bacon, being a Rosicrucian, was all for protecting the Jesus-Magdalene royal bloodline, and he was working close to the English royal family. He was expressing En.ki's original intentions. The misconception is that En.ki's "dream" of a New Atlantis shattered with the birth of Jesus. This created a completely new bloodline, which I call the Jesus-Magdalene bloodline, and it has very little En.ki blood in it; only that which Marduk carries from having been the son of Osiris and Isis in another era. So, it was not the Enki-Isis, but the Marduk-Isis (Jesus-Magdalene) lineage Bacon was protecting with his Rosicrucian Order. Also, everything changed again when Louis XIV, as Marduk, usurped the throne of England and introduced his new Marduk-Ereškigal bloodline and set the stage for Freemasonry in England, although he failed at taking over the Rosicrucians, who are still, from what I can tell, protecting the original bloodline. So now,

En.ki's DNA is even more diluted. The fact is that the New Atlantis, America, was hijacked 2,000 years ago by Marduk.

This is how many historians have concluded it:

> The Enlightenment has been frequently linked to the American Revolution of 1776 and the French Revolution of 1789—both had some intellectual influence from Thomas Jefferson. One view of the political changes that occurred during the Enlightenment is that the "consent of the governed" philosophy as delineated by Locke in Two Treatises of Government (1689) represented a paradigm shift from the old governance paradigm under feudalism known as the "divine right of kings". In this view, the revolutions were caused by the fact that this governance paradigm shift often could not be resolved peacefully and therefore violent revolution was the result. A governance philosophy where the king was never wrong would be in direct conflict with one whereby citizens by natural law had to consent to the acts and rulings of their government.
>
> Alexis de Tocqueville proposed the French Revolution as the inevitable result of the radical opposition created in the 18th century between the monarchy and the men of letters of the Enlightenment. These men of letters constituted a sort of "substitute aristocracy that was both all-powerful and without real power." This illusory power came from the rise of "public opinion", born when absolutist centralization removed the nobility and the bourgeoisie from the political sphere. The "literary politics" that resulted promoted a discourse of equality and was hence in fundamental opposition to the monarchical regime. De Tocqueville "clearly designates... the cultural effects of transformation in the forms of the exercise of power."[258]

The American Revolution was an attempt to "hide" the significance of the bloodlines and religion, so Marduk could operate those parts behind the scenes. Instead, the Revolution was much about replacing religious "superstition" with science and reason. Thomas Jefferson went so far as to suggesting taking out all the passages in the Bible referring to miracles, angel visitations, and the resurrection of Christ.[259] The revolutionaries wanted to, in the name of Enlightenment, attend to deism and atheism. Thomas Paine defined *deism* as a simple belief in God, the Creator, with no reference to the Bible or any other miraculous source.[260] Atheism was also

---

[258] Wikipedia.org: *Age of Enlightenment, op. cit.*
[259] *Op. cit.*
[260] *Op. cit.*

225

widely discussed, but most intellectuals and academics were not in favor of it. They considered atheism leading to moral chaos, and that some kind of deity was necessary to keep law and order. People need a God they can fear, so they can keep themselves in check, they reasoned. Therefore, atheism was off the table. It's interesting, however, that they *voted* for whether there is a God or not. It had little to do with their own beliefs, apparently, but rather with how they could best control the masses. It was a political decision.

The Freemasonic Influence on the Two Revolutions

This movement was very much in support of Marduk's plan to take over En.ki's Old World Order of monarchies and create his own, less based on the Holy Trinity, but in a belief in One God without "superstition," i.e., no Jesus. When scrutinized, the new God's religious enlightenment comprised only Reason and Science. Marduk wanted to start a new, technological era. The One God, of course, was Marduk himself, the God of Science and Reason.

The revolutionary movement was very much dictated by early Freemasonry, an organization that was created as a revolutionary order, just like Weishaupt's Bavarian Illuminati. The revolutionary part of the Masonic movement started in France and quickly moved to Germany, then spreading out from there. But there were (and are) two "genuine" Freemasonic branches in England that are much older and run by Mother Goddess supporters within the Templar Order up to this day. They became the York Rite of Freemasonry and The Grand Lodge of England, both of which the Windsor family have supported since the reign of Henry VIII. They were and are not revolutionary organizations and have an opposite purpose: they protect the Holy Grail and keep opposing elements, such as the Catholic Church, away from their sphere of influence, while the rest of Freemasonry, which is revolutionary, protects Marduk's Singularity Agenda.

The two organizations, "continental" Freemasonry and the Illuminati Order, were based on one same principle—revolution. The only difference was in the details, and therefore, the two organizations disagreed and branched off from each other:

> Historians have long debated the extent to which the secret network of Freemasonry was a main factor in the Enlightenment. The leaders of the Enlightenment included Freemasons such as Diderot, Montesquieu, Voltaire, Lessing, Pope, Horace Walpole, Sir

Robert Walpole, Mozart, Goethe, Frederick the Great, Benjamin Franklin and George Washington. Norman Davies said that Freemasonry was a powerful force on behalf of liberalism in Europe from about 1700 to the twentieth century. It expanded rapidly during the Age of Enlightenment, reaching practically every country in Europe. It was especially attractive to powerful aristocrats and politicians as well as intellectuals, artists, and political activists.

[...]

Freemasonry was particularly prevalent in France—by 1789, there were perhaps as many as 100,000 French Masons, making Freemasonry the most popular of all Enlightenment associations. The Freemasons displayed a passion for secrecy and created new degrees and ceremonies. Similar societies, partially imitating Freemasonry, emerged in France, Germany, Sweden, and Russia. One example was the Illuminati, founded in Bavaria in 1776, which was copied after the Freemasons, but was never part of the movement. The name itself translates to "enlightened", chosen to reflect their original intent to promote the values of the movement. The Illuminati was an overtly political group, which most Masonic lodges decidedly were not.

[...]

In fact, many lodges praised the Grand Architect, the masonic terminology for the deistic divine being who created a scientifically ordered universe.[261]

Now the reader may understand that when a Freemason says that Freemasonry is all about being enlightened, we think of that as a spiritual enlightenment, but as we can see, it's quite the opposite. The new Grand Architect, replacing "God" (En.ki), is Marduk, the new Lucifer, the "Light Bringer" (enLIGHTenment bringer) or "Light Bearer," which is a title for the *bringer of Knowledge.* Thus, Lucifer can be anyone who brings "enlightenment," i.e., knowledge, to humankind. We now have a society that promotes a "scientifically ordered universe," which is the definition of the Matrix, *and don't you dare shake this principle!* It is particularly important in our times when the Freemasonic scientific New World Order is establishing the Singularity. Thus, we have NAZA (sorry, NASA), teaching us that the creation of the Universe was random, and we

---

[261] *Ibid. op. cit.* (We must reconsider who is the Great Architect, En.ki or Marduk. En.ki is, per definition, the original Architect of the Matrix, but who is the God of Freemasonry? "God" or "Satan?")

are all here by accident. Puppets like Klaus Schwab are gatekeepers for the Religion of Science and want it to be illegal to even *read* alternative information on the Internet, particularly that which can't be proven scientifically by the authorities. The Enlightenment movement is said to have died out with Napoleon, but that is a false and dangerous statement. *It is more established today than ever before.*

The Enlightenment wanted to separate the Church from the State, which at a first glance seems *reason*able (that word "reason" again), but as usual, when big changes are at hand, it's always a major step forward for the Brotherhood. When human kings and queens openly ruled, supreme power was dedicated to only one person, and it slowed the agenda down and could easily divert from it. The separation was bound to happen. The initial idea of the separation is credited to Locke, who was, as mentioned earlier, Weishaupt's general.

These ideas then expanded to the American colonies, run by Freemasons, when they drafted the United States Constitution. Jefferson greatly supported the disestablishment of the Church of England (connected to the Templar controlled Grand Lodge of England) in the state of Virginia (Virgin) and authorized the *Virginia Statute for Religious Freedom.*[262]

> Jefferson's political ideals were greatly influenced by the writings of Locke, Bacon, and Newton, whom he considered the three greatest men that ever lived.[263]

The irony with the suppression of religious superiority is the fact that one authoritarian establishment replaced another. Instead of further acknowledging the kings' and queens' *divine rights to rule*, that role was now taken over by an academia of intellectuals, who could thus freely introduce science and technology as the tools for further human progression in the name of such strong adjectives as *liberty, equality,* and *freedom.* Without this radical change, we would not have AI and Information Technology today.

This does *not* mean Marduk discarded the power of the royal families. We have been taught most monarchies have little to no power today and are just promotion tools for the establishment

---

[262] *Ibid. op. cit.*
[263] *Ibid. op. cit.*

and for their countries, respectively, and for diplomatic reasons, which is not true. They are still ruling behind the scenes; the Revolution was just for the show, to have the masses agree to a major change of direction; but also, to stomp on any objection from the uninitiated clergy, who ignorantly followed the old church institution. This was Marduk, playing both sides of the conflict behind the curtain: the Wizard of Oz, secretly establishing Freemasonry to use as a springboard for revolutions he, as Louis XIV, would not experience in his own lifetime. But the Brotherhood always plans centuries or millennia in advance.

In these times of major instability, the propaganda *for* the Enlightenment was happening everywhere in Europe. In Scotland, for example, the principles of sociability, equality, and utility were taught in schools and universities, and the ideas were blended with daily life. Scotland became a strong proponent of the Newtonian network, which was, of course, purely scientific. A leader for the Scottish Enlightenment was Adam Smith, the father of modern economic science.

England, on the contrary, was quite reluctant to the Enlightenment, resenting everything that was originating in France. Since Henry VIII established the "Protestant" Church of England, there had been a chasm between the dominant Catholic Church and England. The solution to this, from the standpoint of Louis XIV, and the later revolutionary ideas (based on the French king's instructions, brought further by people such as Voltaire), was to found French Freemasonry, an organization originating in his country but was eventually established in England as the Scottish Rite. Outwardly, and at its lower grades, it seemed like this new organization was supporting the monarchy, having King Solomon symbolism all over their temples; but much higher up in the hierarchy, it became more obvious that the Order was not supporting the monarchy but was a revolutionary order with a purpose to create a New World Order. Out of this newly established secret society sprung English revolutionary Freemasons, of which George Washington became one, together with many other American revolutionaries. So, in England, Freemasons instigated the Revolution through propaganda, and thus, they divided England, where one party still supported King George through the York Rite, the Grand Lodge, Rosicrucians, and the Priory of Sion, while another party supported the Enlightenment and the Revolution.

Germany was a breeze—an easy catch for the Enlightenment,

but Germany was already to a large degree under Marduk's spell. The rest of Europe quickly followed—even Russia under Catherine the Great, who was fast in fostering arts, sciences, and education;[264] three components and tools in brainwashing the masses. The initial European movement and its development then spread to China, Japan, Korea, India, Egypt, and the Ottoman Empire.

The Enlightenment in the Arts

The reader may be surprised to hear that the arts, even music, was a part of the Enlightenment movement and was greatly promoted. It was not because the illuminists were particularly esthetically inclined.

> Because of the focus on reason over superstition, the Enlightenment cultivated the arts. Emphasis on learning, art, and music became more widespread, especially with the growing middle class. Areas of study such as literature, philosophy, science, and the fine arts increasingly explored subject matter to which the general public, in addition to the previously more segregated professionals and patrons, could relate.[265]

The Enlightenment was also the beginning of the book industry, which was a part of education (read, *propaganda*), encyclopedias, and dictionaries. Although the book industry in the form of novels and "made up" stories are generally considered being for our entertainment, it was never meant to be only that—the entertainment part was only a hook. This industry, just like modern arts, music, film, and literature, is controlled by the Establishment and a part of the gigantic network of manipulation, brainwashing, and control in the guise of something the public can enjoy. There is no "innocence" in anything produced by those within any type of establishment—not even when it comes to "mundane" entertainment. *Everything* is propaganda. This might sound cynical and paranoid, but this is what I see when I research. This planet is minutely controlled. All artforms, at their established level, have hidden messages embedded that go right into our subconscious and can then be used against us whenever Big Brother so wishes. This gives a certain meaning to the phrase, "they sell their soul."

---

[264] *Ibid.*
[265] *Ibid. op. cit.*

Established, world-famous musicians, authors, and visual artists may have had a genuine artistic vision and skill they wanted to share with the world, but when the corporations running these industries offer them contracts, they need to "sell out;" in other words, they sell their souls and go back on their integrity. They are no longer free to create as they wish—they become compromised. Thus, many artists who started out as genuine take to drugs and alcohol to drown their depression from having compromised their art. Art is something very innate to a creative person.

The American Revolution

Discussing the American Revolution is a monumental task, where we can get into details and go on forever; it would be so dense and confusing you would likely put this book down. Therefore, let us condense it as much as we can to just stay with what is relevant for this book, although I need to give some backstory for the sake of context. The same thing goes for the French Revolution. Fortunately, there is a lot of good information out there for those who want to study these subjects in more detail.

When the colonists went to occupy North America, they were still operating under the British crown, and the American Revolution started in 1765 and ended in 1783. With the French assisting the colonists (who would have guessed? Same revolutionary movement), they managed to defeat the British, achieving an illusionary independence. Up to this day, the United States is still not independent from Great Britain, neither are Canada and Australia.

George Washington was a military man, raised in Virginia in the U.S.A. During the American Revolution, he led the colonial forces to victory over the British and thus became a national hero. He became the first U.S. president in 1787.

But what were the official reasons for the American Revolution?

The French and the Brits fought a war against each other on American soil, called the *French and Indian War,* ranging between 1754 and 1763. Both nations wanted to negotiate with the Ohio Native Americans about gaining the Ohio territory for themselves, and eventually, the British won the war. Also, killing Natives, as all of us know, was not a big deal. Although it was their land, they were not bloodline, and therefore they were dispensable and considered "lesser humans," if human at all. They were often addressed as "savages." The Native Americans are, according to some tribes, Lemuria

survivors of Noah's Flood, something the Pleiadians have also confirmed, but the Native tribes are not of the three bloodlines of
Noah's sons, so they didn't fit in anywhere and didn't count; and as
cruel as this sounds, they were not meant to survive the Flood,
which was intended to wipe out everybody, including Noah's family.

We learn from our history books that King George III of England
(r. 1760-1820) took a few radical actions against the colonists,
which made them eventually revolt. One such action was *The Tax-
ation Acts*, in which King George, in 1764, taxed the colonists,
thinking the colonists should assist with carrying the burden of ex-
penses to maintain the colonies. King George signed *The Sugar and
Stamps Acts*, in which the king taxed the colonists on goods that
were shipped to them from England, such as sugar, coffee, and
cloth, and other essentials. The response from the colonies was to
smuggle the goods they needed, and many ports boycotted English
goods. Secret organizations, such as the *Sons of Liberty* were
founded, aiming at intimidating the stamp agents who came to col-
lect the taxes. Thus, before the act was even in place, the stamp
collectors had all resigned, afraid for their safety.

Moreover, British soldiers were patrolling American cities, not
kindly looked at by the colonists, and a confrontation happened in
1770 in Boston, where three Americans were shot to death by the
soldiers when they protested. Three years later, *The Boston Tea
Party* took place. King George wanted to put taxes on tea, so some
colonists disguised themselves as Mohawks and dumped a ship-
load of tea into the ocean. The king was outraged. He retaliated by
forbidding Boston citizens to load or unload ships in the harbor, so
these colonists could not send or receive goods. The colonists' *First
Continental Congress* asked the king to stop taxing the colonists
without them having representation in Parliament. But King
George refused (the colonists wanted to take the backdoor into the
English parliament, so they could influence it and take over England from within and once and for all strip the monarchy of power
and replace it with their own Republic).

These acts against the colonies started the American Revolution.
The American forces won the *Battle of Saratoga* in 1777, which inspired the French, and later the Spaniards and the Dutch, to enter
the war, supporting the colonists—all of them part of the Enlightenment movement. In fact, in these countries the Enlightenment
had exploded into a massive movement, and they all wanted to put

an end to the monarchy and put themselves in power, in the guise of being *for the people*. At the point when three European nations fought side by side with and for the colonists, it became difficult for Britain to fight back. Still, the war continued, albeit scattered in the later years, until it ended in 1783 when Britain negotiated peace. The colonists wanted freedom from Britain and an independent United States without British (read royal) influence, realizing they could not take over the British monarchy. Thus, Thomas Jefferson, and four others, penned the *Declaration of Independence*. Jefferson later became the third American president in 1800.

True Reasons for the Revolution

Although it's plausible that much of the mainstream story is correct to an extent, there is more to the Revolution than what we are told in history books. When we learn about the mainstream take on the American Revolution, it sounds like the colonists were amazing heroes, the underdogs, who fought so hard for their rights, something people in general love to hear about, since most people feel oppressed by authoritarian governments and monarchies and therefore support resistance groups, if only quietly in their minds. Presenting the colonists this way gains people's sympathies. This is also why later American outlaws, such as the James-Younger gang (Jesse James, Cole Younger, and their brothers) gained so much sympathy from the American people after the Civil War. These robbers and killers played the underdog game, concentrating on robbing the rich Union-owned banks and railroads (them being Confederates), and people helped them get away from the posse and lynch mobs, hiding them on their farms.

However, there was a more subtle agenda taking place under the radar: The colonists, led by General Washington, wanted to separate themselves from the monarchy for more reasons than the ill-treatment of George III. Freemasonry in America was very much in line with Freemasonry in France and the rest of Western Europe. They had a significant hand in instigating and spreading the Enlightenment movement. This is not a conspiracy theory—it's quite obvious, and general historians debate the same thing. The colonists, manipulated by a Masonic general, with other Freemasonic leaders, were lured into the entire Enlightenment movement, where science and reason were put at the top of the pedestal.

Freedom of religion was promoted and later made it into the Constitution. It is, of course, a good thing that people can practice their own religion in their new country, but the true reason for letting this happen was to create a diversion and to stop the monarchy from ever again rising to power in the New Atlantis. Instead, they wanted a Republic, run by a President and his cabinet—an authority figure that was elected for a four-year period, whose job was to serve the people, and to execute the will of the citizens. The presidential candidates told the voters what they wanted to achieve during their presidency, and if most people agreed that this was what they wanted, as well, they voted for this man (yes, always a male). This sounds like a great system, but only in theory. It didn't take long until the candidates told people what they wanted to hear, but then did something completely different, overtly, or covertly, once they rose to power. The followers of the Enlightenment movement wanted to switch the power from the church to the academics and intellectuals, i.e., the Elite En.ki once selected to rule over the people but now were mostly in the hands of Marduk. Previously, we found this Elite within the European Royalties, entitled with the divine rights to rule, but those who have researched the bloodline of today's Global Elite have noticed that they are all blood-related to common ancestors somewhere in the distant past. *They all have royal blood.* In a nutshell, Marduk manipulated a part of the Elite bloodlines to rebel against the Church to separate the church from the state, and the rebels were promised powerful seats in top positions, which they got. I think many of these intellectuals realized where the new power was located, and it was not within the monarchies and the royal courts. *And it was not with En.ki, their old Mentor.*

If we look at the United States today, who has the power? The people or the government? Hint: it's not the people. Many patriots are furious about this, which is understandable, and they say it's unconstitutional, it's treasonous, it's a betrayal, it's criminal, and you name it. However, the Enlightened Elite set up their system well, but not in the people's favor; that's a disappointment we need to chew on and swallow. As the word *government* implies, it's a matter of governing, not serving. And if we look at our situation soberly and objectively, we see that we still have elections, and we still have candidates for different parties, speaking about their goals if they are elected. However, we elect them, and they do as they please for four years, or more often, for eight years. Although the elected president does not fulfill his promises, people usually vote for him for a second term. How can people then complain? Moreover, the voting system continues, decade after decade, and the candidates never fulfill or work against the goals they said they had before the election. Still, people keep voting... Whose fault is that?

In the U.S., they have a Second Amendment—the right to carry firearms to *protect themselves against a potentially insane government.* I am certainly not for violence, but with the Second Amendment in mind, one would think there have been many reasons over the years to overthrow a sitting government, but it never happens. The government knows how to intimidate people. They put police and military on the street when facing chaos and disorder, and although the population could easily overtake the military if they joined together, they are too intimidated to do so. This is because of more than 200 years of manipulation and intimidation. It's in the Elite's best interest to stay in power. Power will never be with the people in this matrix. Freemasonry still runs America, and all we need to do is to look at the Freemasonic pyramid. The pyramid rises from the sea, where the sea represents the people, and the pyramid represents the Elite organizations, governing the people on different levels. This structure has always been in place, whether we talk about monarchy, republic, democracy, communism, Marxism, dictatorships, and the list goes on. Freemasonry was never overtly revolutionary, contrary to organizations like the Bavarian Illuminati. Still, it's because of their low profile they have managed to survive and maintain their power over an "Enlightened Society," whilst the Illuminati were destroyed—at least in the form Weishaupt shaped it. Make no mistake about it: Freemasonry is crucial for the development of the Singularity. It's an international organization with lodges in virtually all countries, give or take, and it's one of the Elite's most effective networks to propel the Enlightenment Agenda forward, where education, science, and technology are the main components. A regular person can't just walk into a lodge and ask to be a member. To join, you must be recommended by at least two prominent Masons, whom the rest of the Masonic community trust and who have shown themselves worthy by contributing to the cause: the *Great Work of the Ages.*

The French Revolution

So, the American Revolution came and went with help from France, and King George III was the scapegoat everybody pointed their finger at as the "bad guy," and the inevitable motivation for the Revolution. Immediately after, history repeats itself, and the French king, Louis XVI [r. 1774-92], becomes the scapegoat and the inevitable motivation for the French Revolution.

Fig. 16:1. King Louis XVI and Marie Antoinette of France,
lilies and the Holy Grail symbolism on the wallpaper.

No one doubts that these two kings did things that annoyed their people but did nothing more extraordinary than most other monarchs preceding them. The Enlightened Revolutionaries knew very well they did not need to dig too deeply to create justifiable flaws in the royal rulers to build people's mistrust and resentment. The reader understands by now what was the real motive behind the two Revolutions, and that they were both created by the same movement—the intellectual Enlightenment. It was of little consequence what the kings at the time did; people's dislike of dictatorial royal dynasties was easy to stir up to create upheaval.

The success of the American Revolution immensely inspired the European Revolutionaries, and the next move was directed toward France, where the entire Jesus-Magdalene bloodline started a millennium earlier. French revolutionaries stormed the Bastille fortress on July 14, 1789. King Louis' extravagant living, and his attempt to raise the taxes are said to be the final straws that made

236

the Revolution happen, but again, it was the push from the Enlightenment movement upon the commoners that truly set things in motion. These intellectuals could wrap the population around their fingers and decide when it was time to strike. People needed revolutionary leadership, and they had it.

The French Revolution did not go smoothly; it was an enormous bloodbath, and the guillotine, which had been recently invented and put to use for capital punishment, let its blade fall tens of thousands of times before it was all over, and King Louis XVI and his royal consort, Marie Antoinette, were merely two of uncountable people they beheaded.[266] Louis and Marie Antoinette were executed on January 21, 1793, but that was not the end of the Revolution, which didn't stop until 1799 when Napoleon Bonaparte seized control of the French legislature, declaring himself emperor in 1804.

> The blade fell. It was 10:22 am. One of the assistants of Sanson showed the head of Louis XVI to the people, whereupon a huge cry of "Vive la Nation! Vive la République!" arose and an artillery salute rang out which reached the ears of the imprisoned Royal family.[267]

5199

Fig. 16:2. The Execution of Louis XVI in January 1793.

Thus, the Enlightenment of reason and logic had won over "superstition" and worship. Although the French Revolution started

---

[266] Pdcrodas.webs.ull.es: *The French Revolution in a Nutshell.*
[267] Wikipedia: *Execution of Louis XVI, op. cit.*

and ended with monarchy, it set the stage for a modern state, supposedly governed by the people, which we know is another lie; people have never had the power at any time in history.

Emperor Napoleon Bonaparte

No new monarch was replacing Louis XVI during the rest of the Revolution, and the next ruler of France was Napoleon Bonaparte (Napoleon I). He was not a monarch but an emperor, a conqueror, and a dictator,[268] and obviously an important part of the entire Revolution. He ruled as a warlord until 1814, when a coalition forced him to abdicate, wherewith France went back to being a monarchy again.

> The defeats Bonaparte inflicted upon other European powers also forced them to adapt, and to copy his administrative innovations. Due to the impact he, and the legal code he created, had upon the world, it becomes hard to deny that Napoleon is a Revolutionary figure.[269]

However, Napoleon made a new attempt and regain the throne for a brief period in 1815, in *The Hundred Days.* Then, after having regained his power, Napoleon continued his war mission until his devastating defeat against the British at Waterloo in 1815, where he once and for all was forced to abdicate. Louis XVIII [r. 1814, 1815-24], the brother of Louis XVI, had fled the country during the French Revolution, but now returned to Paris and regained the throne on July 8 that same year in the aftermath of Napoleon's abdication. Thus, the monarchy was more solidly reestablished in France. Louis XVIII was succeeded by his brother, Charles X [1824-30]. Charles had no natural successor and abdicated, so Louis Philippe I [1830-48], Charles' cousin, succeeded him instead. Again, Marduk failed to defeat the monarchy—both in France and in England. That is remarkable. He must hate England.

Napoleon Bonaparte was a very driven military man, just like George Washington was a military man, and the Enlightenment Movement had put a lot of faith in him to expand the French

---

[268] Washington Post: *French leader Napoleon Bonaparte has a complicated legacy.*

[269] Blogs.kent.ac.u: *Napoleon Bonaparte.*

Empire, which purpose was to propel and solidify the Enlightenment to put Europe under one umbrella, a big step toward the New
World Order, just like the United States had been a tremendous
success. But Napoleon was probably extremely pressured, and although he did a monumental job to start uniting Europe through
warfare, he eventually made strategic mistakes, costing him everything. He probably felt he had completely failed his superiors and
sponsors behind the scenes. Historical records indicate he became
rather depressed after his defeats.

House of Bourbon-Orléans Regain Power in France

The reason Louis XVIII could take the power and keep it was because he was willing to negotiate with the Revolutionaries, who
probably felt the pressure from Britain after the defeat and setback.
He issued a constitution called *The Charter*, which preserved many
liberties gained during the French Revolution:

> ...it [the Charter] presented all Frenchmen as equal before the law,
> but retained substantial prerogative for the king and nobility and
> limited voting to those paying at least 300 francs a year in direct
> taxes...

> Despite the return of the House of Bourbon to power, France was
> much changed; the egalitarianism and liberalism of the revolution-
> aries remained an important force and the autocracy and hierarchy
> of the earlier era could not be fully restored. [270]

As we can see, there was much negotiation going on, and the
French government under King Louis quickly purged Bonaparte's
supporters. The Enlightenment had some painful setbacks during
this time, after the British defeated France at Waterloo in 1815, and
Louis XVIII could let the Royal House of Bourbon-Orléans regain
the throne of France with the support from the victors—the British.
But the Revolutionaries still managed to keep some of their values,
despite a monarchal rule. However, these were just temporary setbacks, and Marduk and his minions had, of course, not given up. As
mentioned, there was a period in 1815, called *The Hundred Days*,
when Napoleon returned to power in France and forced the Bourbons to flee France once again. But this short revolution only lasted

---

[270] Courses.lumenlearning.com: *French After 1815, op. cit.*

for about three months, wherewith Napoleon again was defeated at Waterloo, and the French royalty returned from exile and regained the throne.

However, after this temporary obstruction for the monarchy, the thumbscrews tightened on the royal family, and their rule became more restricted, but they remained in power. This new Bourbon regime was a constitutional monarchy, contrary to the old *Ancien Régime*, who had absolute power, so now, its power was limited. This period also saw the Catholic Church's power reestablished, and they became a major supremacy in French politics. It is interesting because the Church had been taken over by Marduk, most likely during his incarnation as Louis XIV, and now he infiltrated the monarchy of France with his new allies, the Vatican. Also, during *The Hundred Days*, Napoleon's mother, Maria Letizia Bonaparte [1750-1836], took refuge in Rome, *under the Pope's protection*.[271] This seems extremely curious since the Catholic Church was supposed to support the monarchy and not the mother of a notorious revolutionary with the purpose to *overthrow* the monarchy. However, this is only curious until we realize that the Catholic Church was owned by Marduk by then, supporting Marduk's Enlightenment behind the scenes.

The return of the French monarchy was not met with salutes by everybody, but it was a compromise the French people, at least in the beginning, were willing to make, also suffering immense battle fatigue after a long period of devastating wars, many of them led by Napoleon. And the Enlightenment understood they needed to lie low for a while. But as the years of monarchy continued, unrest and resentment bubbled among the French people once more. We don't need to be rocket scientists to understand who instigated this unrest behind the scenes—the same old intellectuals of the Enlightenment.

> After a first sentimental flush of popularity, Louis' gestures towards reversing the results of the French Revolution quickly lost him support among the disenfranchised majority. Symbolic acts such as the replacement of the tricolore flag with the white flag, the titling of Louis as the "XVIII" (as successor to Louis XVII, who never ruled) and as "King of France" rather than "King of the French", and the monarchy's recognition of the anniversaries of the deaths of

---

[271] Wikipedia.org: *Letizia Bonaparte.*

Louis XVI and Marie Antoinette were significant. A more tangible source of antagonism was the pressure applied to possessors of biens nationaux by the Catholic Church and returning émigrés attempting to repossess their former lands.[272]

And the Enlightenment Movement continued to infiltrate the monarchy,

Louis XVIII's role in politics from the Hundred Days onward was voluntarily diminished; he resigned most of his duties to his council. He and his ministry embarked on a series of reforms through the summer of 1815. The king's council, an informal group of ministers that advised Louis XVIII, was dissolved and replaced by a tighter knit privy council, the "Ministère de Roi." Talleyrand was appointed as the first Président du Conseil, i.e. Prime Minister of France. On July 14, the ministry dissolved the units of the army deemed "rebellious." Hereditary peerage was reestablished to Louis's behest by the ministry.[273]

There should be a massive question mark after the first sentence in the quote above. Did King Louis truly resign his duties voluntarily, and by that diminishing his power, or was he pushed into a corner? Logically, the latter is more plausible. Step by step, the Revolutionaries placed themselves in the royal court system again.

During the years that followed, the amount of power between the monarchy and the Enlightened fluctuated back and forth, but the monarchy of France sat on the throne until 1848, although not without turmoil. The lobbying by the Revolutionaries continued relentlessly, and during King Charles X, the support of the monarchy diminished even more. And when King Charles tried to revise *The Charter* to give the monarchy more power, a new violent uproar started, which was the beginning of the end for the Bourbon Dynasty. This uproar was called *Three Glorious Days* and happened in 1830. It started as a riot but ended as a new brief revolution, only lasting for three days. This revolution was, of course, orchestrated by the anti-royalties of the Enlightenment.

This resulted in Charles X's plan to increase royal power failing, so he abdicated, and he left France for England. However, his cousin of the House of Orléans, Louis Philippe [r. 1830-48], agreed to continue ruling France as a constitutional monarch, but the monarchy

---

[272] *Ibid. op. cit.*
[273] *Ibid. op. cit.*

had been so shaken up that there was truly no return. In 1848, a new revolution took place, which forced the king to step down, and the *Second Republic* was proclaimed. Decades of hard work in the form of lobbying, manipulation, infiltration, spreading of rumors, lies, and by other means, finally bore fruit—the Enlightenment saw a new dawn rising in France. But what is even more interesting is that the 1848 Revolution happened at the same time all over Europe, from Sweden down to Italy, with few exceptions. Hardly a coincidence, is it? Here we had the Brotherhood (the Enlightenment, in this case) lobbying and manipulating behind the scenes for almost 100 years. Then the stroke all over Europe simultaneously.[274] They didn't shun any efforts to overthrow the monarchies.

Since then, the monarchy has attempted to regain power in France occasionally, but they have not succeeded to keep it. As of this writing, France is still a Republic, and therefore, supporters of the Enlightenment and the Singularity. I have a difficult time imagining this would change.

The Industrial Revolution

It took some time, but finally, the Brotherhood could move on with their next step toward the Singularity, which was, to begin with, a peaceful, non-bloody revolution before the two World Wars, and it's gone to the history books as *The Industrial Revolution*. The intellectuals and the academics of the Enlightenment had put their people in the different governments across Europe, and later, in America, and even more aggressively so in the aftermath of the Revolution of 1848, which encompassed the entire Europe, revolting simultaneously when the Brotherhood gave the "signal." They had made the world ready for this, and now it was time to strike after getting rid of most monarchies.

Before the Enlightenment, the commoners (the masses) had been mostly uneducated, and therefore, often easy to manipulate and control. They were usually kept hungry and poor to make them dependent upon the government, and ultimately upon the monarchy and the church, who were the actual power. Now, it was time to make a 180-degree change. The Brotherhood took control over education and the universities, and their appointed intellectuals

---

[274] Wikipedia: *Revolutions of 1848.*

decided what people should learn. The school system "improved," and more and more commoners could go to school and learn.

This step was crucial to take for the Brotherhood Elite because the Industrial Revolution was a major step toward the Singularity. Being given Orion technology by the Overlords in increments, the human scientists could start working on creating machines and devices commoners could eventually use in their daily lives, but more importantly, at work. We could say we are still in the Industrial Revolution today, but we have taken the next step forward into the Information Technology Era, which has given us the Internet, cell phones, AI, and many other electronic devices and developments added into our lives. Now the reader can truly understand the term, *The Great Work of the Ages*, used by the Brotherhood—especially Freemasonry, Marduk's "baby:" These guys plan long term. The end goal is the Singularity and the attack on Orion.

It has been necessary to educate us and contain us in cities and apartments—not because they care about us and want to make us comfortable, but because they want as many people as possible educated enough to run their machines and devices and to understand enough of technology to function in the New World Order, which started during Louis XIV's of France lifetime (Marduk). "It is of no use trying to give technical teaching to our citizens without elementary education.[275]" The workers needed to live close to their job, so they easily travel to their workplaces. Therefore, it was necessary to house them somewhere.

People often say the Global Elite wants to usher in a New World Order, but the New World Order has been an ongoing thing since the beginning of the 18th century. We're in the middle of it, but the *Great Work* is not finished until they have us in the Metaverse Cloud, trapped in cyborg bodies and the Singularity. But the Industrial Revolution, which is said to have lasted through World War II, was a monumental step forward. We happily stepped right into the Machine Kingdom.

This is how it's explained in our history books:

> The Industrial Revolution shifted societies from an agrarian economy to a manufacturing economy where products were no longer made solely by hand but by machines. This led to increased production and efficiency, lower prices, more goods, improved wages,

---

[275] Wikipedia: *Industrial Revolution.*

and migration from rural areas to urban areas.[276]

The era saw the mechanization of agriculture and manufacturing and the introducing of new modes of transportation, including steamships, automobiles, and airplanes. Things moved fast, but not too fast. The Brotherhood didn't want people to start to wonder where all these fantastic inventions came from so suddenly. No one had the concept that this or that technology could have been available for a long time, and that the Brotherhood needed to release it in increments, so the ignorant masses could learn and understand, not suspect any foul play and manipulation. It had to look benevolent and for the benefit of the people, so they could get the masses to voluntarily follow and have them give their consent.

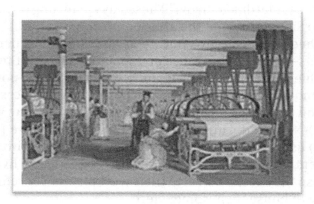

Fig. 16:3. A weaving shed in Great Britain in 1835.

The Industrial Revolution started in the 1700s, and one could say the Enlightenment, which led to the American, the French, and the Revolution of 1848, were all parts of it. The First Industrial Revolution is considered having started in Great Britain in the mid-18th century and spread around the world, and the Second Industrial Revolution happened in the 1870s in the United States.[277] That's what historians tell us, but I find this a bit odd; I would say the Second Revolution occurred a little earlier. By 1870, the U.S. already had the railroad (introduced in 1815), the telegraph (in 1843),

---

[276] Investopedia: *Industrial Revolution Definition: History, Pros, and Cons, op. cit.*
[277] *Ibid.*

steam engines (in 1829), sewing machines (in 1842), factories (in 1790), and other revolutionary inventions. It doesn't take a genius to see that when there was no Internet or other means to spread revolutionary ideas quickly, a technological revolution could never have happened the way it did if the Brotherhood had not placed their people in most governments around the globe and infiltrated them.

It was important for the Brotherhood that people gathered in the cities, so they made sure people could get jobs there that paid better than agriculture, and many jumped on it. This created a shortage of food for a while since farmers left their farmlands to move into the cities.

The factory systems are responsible for creating capitalism, where the big companies got rich, paying their workers just enough for them to get by so they had energy to work (if they were lucky), while it brought in shiploads of money to the privileged Elite and major business owners. The working conditions were harsh and demanding, with long hours, and the companies and factories also involved themselves in child labor.

Although many citizens looked positively on the Industrial Revolution, the business owners treated their workers poorly, and albeit they got paid (barely), they were slave labor and dispensable.

> The Industrial Revolution provided an incentive to increase profits, and as a result, working conditions in factories deteriorated. Long hours, inadequate remuneration, and minimal breaks became the norm. Child labor was a significant issue. Health issues arose for many of the factory workers...[278]

Interestingly, despite that people now seemed to live better lives, in some respect, the overall population decreased, which demonstrates their nutritional status was also decreasing.[279] People were healthier before they moved into the cities and started working for the industries. There are also statistics showing that moving into the cities and do industrial work increases the risk of mental illness. This is not surprising: Being boxed into big city environments removes us from nature, our natural element, and despite people being boxed together, it created isolation and does so up to this day.

---

[278] *Ibid. op. cit.*
[279] Wikipedia: *Industrial Revolution.*

While the Industrial Revolution moved on and developed, the Brotherhood planned to introduce the next step in their agenda—Information Technology, leading to the "Digital Revolution."

The Machine Kingdom

17 **The "Machine Kingdom"** is a term that was coined by Barbara Marciniak's Pleiadians, who channel through her. It's a very appropriate name for a long period, stretching from, we could say, the later part of the 18th century and through our days. It's a term that perfectly embraces the entire scientific and technological movement, beginning with the Enlightenment.

We may argue that the Middle Ages was a dark time in human history, where the chasm between the rich and poor was profound, and most people lived in poverty, got diseases, and died young, compared to now, when we live in a higher density. But if we analyze it, is this true? I have for long argued that the Overlords want us to decrease our vibration to meet them in their lower density, which is *their* density—the Kingdom of machines, devices, and all forms of technology. On the surface, it may look like we have "ascended" to some degree, but I would argue this is an illusion. Indeed, we can now live more comfortably in our houses and apartments because we have steady wages and usually know what to expect from month to month, but our existence has, at the same time, become more solid and isolated; we have moved deeper into matter. During the Middle Ages, there were deeper connections, and face to face interactions between humans than we have today, and we lived closer to nature. The human soul group, as a mass consciousness, is descending rapidly. We go in two directions: the major part is diving into the world of digital technology, which will lead to their downfall, while a smaller percentage is taking the opposite route, even though it's met with stubborn resistance from all kinds of places. To lure humankind into the Singularity, they *must* bring us down to the nightmarish realm of the Khan Kings (the Sirians), led by Marduk (the *Mara-Duke*). This does not mean that we are physically going somewhere—everything will play out here, in the physical world. It's only a matter of vibrations, and we change our vibrations with our minds. As the Pleiadians said about humanity (more about them soon): "You are going nowhere. You will stay here."

The Khan Kings lower our overall frequency by manipulating our minds. And for Marduk, since his Louis XIV incarnation, this task became much easier. That was when he took over Earth in a giant coup d'état by creating the new Marduk-Ereškigal bloodline, which since then has spread over the world and almost completely wiped out the "pure" En.ki-Isis bloodline. It was the Priory of Sion, the Knights Templar, and later the Rosicrucians who worked behind the scenes with the early Catholic Church to preserve the Jesus-Magdalene bloodline. These three groups still collaborate to put the Merovingian bloodline back in the royal seats, but they are hopelessly working against the current. I bet Marduk doesn't care; he sees these organizations as no threat to his own New World Order. En.ki's old secret societies belong to the Old World Order, i.e., En.ki's Order. Marduk has now quite securely established his New Order, hastening toward the Singularity.

Two Separate Agendas—Marduk Against En.ki

After having followed my nose and the path in which my new research has taken me, I have come to some new conclusions, which may surprise some readers. For years, I considered En.ki and Marduk to have the same agenda; they just wanted to play it out slightly differently. Still, their common goal was the Singularity and the attack on Orion. Over time, Marduk got the upper hand because he was continually incarnating here on Earth, working closely with humankind, while En.ki was stuck in the ABZU and must work remotely. I now deeply doubt this in the light of new information and insights. I was also of the impression there was a first attempt toward the Singularity just before the Flood when En.ki feverishly worked on several genetic projects that eventually destroyed the entire human experiment, leading to the Deluge.

I now consider this to be false: First, there was no attempt to create a Singularity during the Atlantis Era, and second, En.ki *never* wanted the Singularity, which is Marduk's plan in its entirety. He completely tricked the trickster god, who could not see what was coming until it was too late, and then he could do nothing about it, trapped as he was in the ABZU. He must trust his human minions in high positions, and I would suggest all of them (save for two secret societies and a few others, perhaps) have switched sides and are now working for Marduk. The switch happened during and after the reign of Louis XIV.

I will dedicate much of this chapter to these new concepts. I will also discuss what I believe En.ki wanted all the time, and what he worked toward, but has now more or less given up, realizing he's beaten in his own game, and the agenda changed with the Enlightenment.

Lucifer's Rebellion Revisited in More Depth

In the WPP, I wrote extensively about the so-called *Lucifer's Rebellion*, which is a term referring to En.ki's rebellion against Orion. While writing the WPP, I had no time frame for when this rebellion occurred. Now I have a better understanding. It did not happen during the destruction of Tiamat, our original home planet. It happened at the time of Noah's Flood. I put En.ki as the mastermind behind the Invasion and Destruction of our home planet, but he had nothing to do with it. He was working with the Queen, his brother Prince Ninurta, and the Vulcans from Vega to terraform Tiamat and create the human soul group. We were the first and only soul group that was created without technology, and our home was in the KHAA, in the Spirit Universe, and not in the physical, material universe, which is the case with other star races. Thus, the Queen created us from her blood/DNA and made us mini copies of her (to use a visual metaphor). En.ki had hoped to be the second donor of DNA (the Queen being the first) to insert into the newborn humans, so they could appoint him the Overseer of humankind. But as conveyed elsewhere, the Queen and her consort, Khan En.lil, rejected that idea, even though En.ki was the Queen's "firstborn." Instead, they chose his brother, Prince Ninurta (Prince En.lil), to rise to the occasion. Thus, we still have Ninurta's DNA floating in our veins, and he was appointed as the Overseer of the human soul group and was given our solar system as a "gift" from his mother, the Queen. This infuriated En.ki, who considered it his birthright to take care of all this. But the Queen and Khan En.lil did not want En.ki's DNA inserted into the humans, which might give us his rather narcissistic traits, such as feeling entitled, being superior to others, and grandiose thinking. These were the exact traits the mother wanted to avoid in the human soul group. Moreover, they considered him too spontaneous and impulsive to handle that much responsibility. His younger brother was much better suited, they thought. En.ki hated his brother from that day onward, but he did not revolt yet. Instead, he was put second in charge of the project, under Ninurta's supervision. En.ki felt betrayed and intimidated, since no one seemed to believe in his abilities. In his mind's introject, he was more than capable of accomplishing the task they gave to Ninurta, and he probably thought he could do it better than him. All this was what started the conflict between the two brothers—a conflict that has affected humankind miserably, a conflict in which we've been affected since the day Tiamat was destroyed.

To put the record straight, the Invasion was purely a Sirian affair, and it was planned and executed by them. This action came as much of a surprise to En.ki as to the rest of the Orion team. No one apparently saw it coming. The Orions knew some Khan Kings disagreed with the Orion Council about the ownership of the solar system (see the ORION books); they thought that via the Peace Agreement with Orion, the Khan Kings owned this part of the galaxy, which included our solar system. Orion had another viewpoint on that. So, when the Queen used "their" planet to create the human soul group, the Sirians rebelled and attacked. During the attack, Marduk was dubbed the new KHAN.US KHAN.UR, the King of Kings, over the Sirian soul group, and he was the one destroying Tiamat, which is also confirmed in the Enûma Eliš, free online.

The destruction of Tiamat was supposed to end the Human Experiment, and it was a failure for Ninurta, who lost the battle against Marduk and the Khan Kings, and he fled, taking many human Namlú'u with him into safety. He could not maintain the guardianship of the solar system, and the human soul group, as they knew it then, was no more. Many of us, because of the shock when our home planet exploded, went into comatose for a thousand years.[280] This gave En.ki plenty of time to terraform our

---

[280] The RA Material: The Law of One.

current planet—Earth. We don't know how En.ki felt about Tiamat's destruction, but we can't help but wonder if he was quite pleased that his brother failed to protect the human soul group. This gave En.ki a great opportunity to shine. He suggested Orion gave him a chance to prove that he could continue the Experiment and help graduate compassionate, empathic beings. He wanted to oversee a Second Construct (Earth) to prove to his mother, and Orion in general, that he was worthy of such a task, and could prosper at it. We don't know why Orion agreed to this, but perhaps now, after the first failure, they wanted to give En.ki a chance, after all. The Queen had invested a lot in the human soul group, even given us her Spirit, and if there was any chance to make the Experiment work, she was probably in favor of it. So, the Orion Council gave En.ki the green light, but with one caveat: Orion must put their own Overseers on Earth to supervise En.ki's creation. Again, En.ki's brother became that supervisor, most likely to En.ki's annoyance, and I would argue the Queen put Isis here, too, her being of Ninurta's blood, and spirited. Queen Sophia moved her from being an Overseer of the Sirius star system to helping with overseeing the Earth experiment instead. It appears the Queen puts her "daughters" as overseers on developing worlds to reestablish order when there is turmoil, conflict, or unrest.

What happened next is written at the beginning of this book and in my earlier work. The bottom line is that *En.ki's goal was to prove to his mother that he could do this, and thus regain his status as the heir of Orion after Khan En.lil if something happened to him*. This is En.ki's sole purpose up to this day. Unfortunately, he is a narcissist, and as such, he is prone to making mistakes that he does not take responsibility for. My Orion source gave me a good example of his thinking process. He told me how En.ki operates, and how he faces his mistakes and failures: "Oh, what have I done?! Oh well, no use crying over spilt milk." This means he never follows up on his errors and leaves them for others to clean up. He is impulsive and does not think through his decisions deeply enough. Marduk, in juxtaposition, is a psychopathic calculator, and he thinks through every step of his action beforehand *very* carefully. He knows exactly what he is doing. Once upon a time, on Sirius, his life depended on it.

Dribbling with extensive genetic tinkering, which is something En.ki dedicated himself to at the end of the Atlantis Construct, appears to have been another example of his impulsivity and lack of responsibility for his actions, leading to a second destruction of the Human Experiment.

The Lucifer Rebellion happened when Khan En.lil, on behalf of his and the Orion Council's decision, commanded En.ki to instigate a Flood to bring the Namlú'u home to Orion, since he had destroyed the Experiment with his tinkering. En.ki ferociously protested, telling the Council humankind was *his* creation, and his blood runs through human veins. Thus, he said, he could claim ownership of this soul group, and it was *his* experiment now. Although it is true it was En.ki who created our homo sapiens bodies, the soul group never belonged to him—only the bodies, at best. However, according to Orion's laws or rules, it appears that a creator god (En.ki in this case) who creates a soul group, where part of it is to add their own DNA to the bodies of the particular developing world, can claim ownership of that soul group, claiming it his or her creation. This is reasonable, although in our case, this was not En.ki's experiment—he was only allowed to continue an already existing Orion Experiment, this time on Earth. It's like putting a CEO over a company owned by someone else, and the CEO claims ownership of the company because he has made the employees work well under his supervision. En.ki was not even the CEO—Ninurta still was, as the Overseer. En.ki was "just" the Vice President.

All this did not sit well with En.ki, and he refused to eradicate and destroy the bodies he created—his "brand." But there was even more at stake than losing his creation: if the Experiment was terminated, it meant he had failed, just like his brother, and he could not regain his position as the Heir of Orion. The only way to do that would be to have a strong bloodline, where his blood ran purer in the human bodies than Ninurta's. Then he could claim ownership of us as a creator god, so long as we were planet-bound and had not graduated. This plan now went up in smoke (it went under water, rather). He no longer had time to reestablish a pure-blood human soul group, and the only bloodline left on Earth with his pure blood was Noah and his sons. Openly, he decided to go along with Orion's plans, but covertly, he planned on continuing the experiment completely on his own, without Orion's supervision. So, he also hijacked an unknown number of 3-UCs, of which you and I are two of them. En.ki had not given up on regaining his position in Orion.

After the Flood, the Rebellion started. He managed to recruit "a third of the angels," as it says in the Bible, the Urantia Book, and elsewhere. Which angels? The "angels" who were here in the

Second Construct—the Sirian Khan Kings. Not everybody joined En.ki in his Rebellion, only a third of the crew that was stationed on Earth. The term "angel," I would argue, comes from the fact that they can "fly," i.e., they are not of this world and can disappear into the air. Marduk continued following En.ki into the Third Construct (the Matrix), and we might ask ourselves why he wanted to do that. I would suggest he did it because he saw an opportunity in En.ki's Rebellion that he told no one about back then. En.ki wanted to be the King of Orion one day, and he wanted to do it by strengthening the En.ki-Isis bloodline and prove himself. Thus, he needed Isis in his new construct, as well. Whether Isis followed voluntarily, I don't know, but she got stuck here with us and soon became a breeder for the two conspirators, En.ki and Marduk.

En.ki never wanted the Singularity—that was not on his agenda, and, I think, nothing he had ever considered. This was Marduk's plan from the beginning, which he kept secret. An attack on Orion by him and his fellow Khan Kings would make *him* the King of Orion if he was victorious. En.ki thinks he can regain power in Orion by proving he can do something his brother failed to do—making the human soul group evolve and graduate, having his own DNA as the primary DNA running through human veins (we call it blood, but calling it DNA is more to the point). Thus, he proves he is "better" than his brother and should regain his title as the Crown Prince, the Heir of Orion. If something happens to Khan En.lil, he would legally take his place.

Marduk knows this does not apply to him. Even if he manages to take over the human soul group (which he already did as Louis XIV), it's not enough. That would, at best, increase his status in Orion, if it wasn't for all the horrendous crimes he's committed, but he can never be the Crown Prince of Orion. That's a title for the Orion Royal Family to declare among themselves, and Marduk is "only" a Sirian; he is not even an Orion prince. Therefore, he must *take heaven by force*, as they say in the scriptures. He becomes the biblical Satan. The way he plans to do this is to insert his DNA into the human bodies, which he already did when he and Ereškigal created their bloodline, and then create Metaverse, the Cloud, human cyborgs, and with all that in mind, the Singularity. It's not enough to put humans in Metaverse and trap us there; he also must create a dominant bloodline containing Sirian DNA, so he and his co-conspirators, the Khan Kings, whom I am sure are clearly aware of what is about to happen, can ride the Avatars, as well. Instead of

Isis, Marduk has most likely promised Ereškigal to sit on the throne beside him if he takes Orion, overthrows Khan En.lil and the Queen, and puts himself on the throne right away. Ereškigal, Goddess forbid, will be the new Queen of Orion. Whether Marduk keeps his promise to her, in the case of victory, is up for debate.

Marduk's Empire

We no longer need to worry about or pay much attention to En.ki; he is castrated, impotent (in all possible ways), and trapped in the ABZU. He has no power over Earth anymore and no creative abilities (access to spirit), contrary to his "son." Marduk is now in control. The royal families used to be En.ki's people, but they now belong to Marduk because he took over the bloodlines by adding his DNA which weakened En.ki's. According to Orion's "rules," he can by that claim the ownership of humankind. He is now both God and Satan. I would further argue that John the Divine, who channeled the Book of Revelation, channeled Marduk, not En.ki. The REV much better exposes Marduk's agenda than it does En.ki's. And I would say the Global Elite is a mix of Sirian 2-UCs and human 3-UCs since many Elite bodies were taken over by the Sirian prisoners, whom En.ki rescued from their imprisonment after they were incarcerated in the Sirian black star by Khan En.lil for being war criminals. En.ki put these fugitives in the Elite bodies.

The kings and queens, however, are human 3-UCs (Namlú'u). This is an important distinction because both En.ki and Marduk need these bloodlines to be housed by humans, so they can claim them and ride them. As mentioned earlier in this book, Marduk pretended to go along with En.ki's agenda, probably promised a lofty position in a future Orion with En.ki as the heir. En.ki needed him to help strengthen his, Isis', and Ninurta's DNA. Marduk was the best choice to insert more of En.ki's blood into humans after En.ki's imprisonment, since Marduk, being the son of En.ki, also carried En.ki's blood. But, of course, when the time was ripe, he took over the human experiment, and therefore no (or very few) humans have graduated from this construct yet. Some may have, over the last ten years or so, by going through holes in the Grid (more about the Grid in the next chapter).

Today, we see an almost complete Marduk usurpation of the Earth. He is the King of Kings, the KHAN.US KHAN.UR, even on Earth, which is now, according to him, Sirian domain, just like it should always have been, seen from a Sirian viewpoint, since they think they own the solar system. We can see his DNA spread among humans, as more and more humans become narcissistic and psychopathic—the latter being a direct consequence of Marduk's DNA intervention. Many humans become akin to him, and he encourages it. We need to meet him on his vibration/density, so he can easily manipulate and control us, leading us into the Singularity like happy, obedient fools—like cows to the slaughterhouse.

Intervention from the Pleiades

This brings me to Barbara Marciniak's Pleiadians. Although I have been very against "New Age" channeling, which I consider being Mardukian in nature, Marciniak's group is different—it is not New Age, and it's not Mardukian. I am aware they have their agenda, too, but most of what they tell us is accurate if we can see through a filter or two. Their message is in line with what we are discussing, and they have been able to accurately predict our current present over 20 years ago with stunning accuracy. Their information often coincides with the information that came out through my relationship with the Orion source, who was not aware of them. I think they are telling us the truth when they say En.ki is their mentor, whom they report to and are graded by. They say En.ki is a tough mentor, but that inspires them to do their absolute best when giving us information. They also recently admitted that En.ki is not necessarily a good person, but he wants to help mankind (for personal reasons, I would say).

The Pleiadians have never been shy of telling us what they say is their true agenda, which is to steer us away from the Singularity by trying to change our timeline, so the Singularity won't happen. Their desperate attempt to save En.ki's and their own backs is to try to get as many people as possible onboard with their message. They want to change the attitude in the world population, so the energy can start flowing in another direction, away from the Singularity; they want us to make other choices. They rode on the wave of the nano-second, which was the period between 1987 and 2012, when Earth aligned with the Galactic Center, boosting the flow of Divine Light (information) from there. This, in conjunction with their own teachings, they hoped would be enough. It wasn't. When they were asked, in 2013, how the December 25, 2012, alignment turned out, they said it was a failure, and they did not accomplish their goal. However, they promised to stay with us as long as Marciniak is strong enough to channel them. She is 75 years old as of this writing. I guess En.ki is still hanging onto straws, although he must realize he has lost the ownership of the soul group. We know nothing about what En.ki thinks of Marduk's Singularity. He might think it's ridiculous to invade Orion and bound to fail, or he might be concerned. What if Marduk succeeds? What will Marduk do with him? En.ki will be a threat to his newfound power, and he will probably terminate his father. Also, En.ki once more must feel defeated, losing his own power forever, perhaps finally understanding he will never be the Crown Prince of Orion. Rather, he probably wants to save his own skin now in front of Orion, in case of a future trial. He must be concerned about the outcome of such a trial. What will Orion do? Leave him in the ABZU forever, or worse?

But what about the human invasion of the Pleiades? The Pleiadians are stressing that we humans, in our future and in their past, will attack the Pleiades and overtake it. The Pleiadians, contacting us from *their* present, which is our future, say the Pleiades are now a tyranny because of human cyborgs running amok there. I have had endless debates both with myself and others about what this truly means. The latest argument, before I came to the insights leading to this book, was that there was possibly an earlier attempt to create a Singularity, and if so, it must have been just before the Flood, when En.ki tinkered with genetics. I believe I know better now. As mentioned, En.ki never wanted the Singularity; all he wanted was to prove his worth and become the Crown Prince of Orion. Therefore, he probably wanted to create physical bodies that were the best fit for that project, and that's all.

Instead, I have analyzed what the Pleiadians are truly saying, compared to the new insights I have gained. They clearly say we are these cyborgs *in the future* and not from the past. And they are visiting us from a different "time system," which is not linear the way we perceive it. Time is multidimensional and subjective. Moreover, all time is said to be simultaneous—therefore, it's a perception of the mind, and this perception will be perceived differently, depending on our vibration and location. The Pleiadians claim they had a hard time finding Earth at first, and when they finally did, they must figure out the "coordinates" of the brief window in time they termed the nano-second. If they just ignored the time factor, they could have randomly visited any Earth time, not knowing where they were on our timeline. This is, they say, still difficult to determine: Perhaps Marciniak wants to channel at a certain day, in a certain location, at a certain time of the day. Then it's the Pleiadians' task to find that exact point where they can insert themselves "vertically" and hit the exact spot at the exact time; also taking into consideration all different horizontal timelines that exist here.

So, my current conclusion is that when they say we will invade them "in the future" from your and my perspective, i.e., from where we have our focus, they must refer to the upcoming Singularity. In the timeline we are currently on, the Singularity *will* take place, apparently, and we will invade because it has already happened.

Be aware that everything is happening inside our mind—that's where the true Universe is. The outer Universe is just a mind's projection, a creation of imaginative and cumulative minds. Inside our minds, there is no time, only in the outside universe. Even if you create images of two planets inside your mind, and you want to travel between them, there is no time involved until you project those planets into the physical universe. If we think of it in these terms, we can also imagine that it's possible to "erase," and change timelines. All we need to do is to use common energy enough to make a collective change of direction, making the upcoming Singularity timeline obsolete and de-energized. Thus, the 100th Monkey Syndrome comes to mind. If a certain amount of the population changes their mind about something and starts agreeing, old inner creations will fade and become inactive, in favor of a new focus point. Therefore, the Pleiadians, and ultimately, En.ki, were willing to give their project a chance. If enough humans could choose another path, aside from the Singularity, that would change the entire timeline that will lead to the upcoming invasion of the Pleiades, which I am sure will be instigated by Marduk. The Pleiades were an important strategic stronghold for En.ki, so why wouldn't it be for Marduk?

What does this mean for the future of humankind? How can we avoid an invasion of the Pleiades, and ultimately Orion? Well, the Pleiadians failed to change timelines, and my Orion source failed. Before he and I got in touch, he had started educating mankind on social media, but he was met with aggression, hostility, and ridicule, to his utter surprise. "Humans are hard on hearing," he once told me concerning that. People attacked him verbally, talking about Orion Reptilians and Dracos, and if he truly was from Orion, they mused, he must be an enemy to humans, despite the profound information he shared with them (which I read). That's where humankind stands. We hold on to our beliefs as if our existence depends on them. I talked him into letting me, as a human, explain these things to my own kind, instead of him coming from outside Earth; I could more easily be understood. He seemed quite frustrated over the entire situation with human non-response, but eventually, he agreed. Still, although we *are* making progress, we are still a droplet in the sea of human consciousness. We make a difference, but is it enough to avoid the Singularity? The positive attitude in all this comes from the Pleiadians when they say, "Humanity is unpredictable and hard to control." This is true, and this is why Marduk needs to capture us in the digital Cloud, where all are connected in a telepathic network, where he can control and program everybody at once as he sees fit instead of using all the efforts here in 3-D. Here, he can't even make Great Britain abide to his plans. It is and has always been a race against time. It's a war on bloodlines, but it's also a *War on the Minds.*

Why The Wars and Instability on Earth?

If En.ki is now defeated and out of the picture, and Marduk sits on the Global Throne, why are there so many conflicts and wars? After all, aren't all humans under Marduk's and the Khan Kings' control now?

Yes, but there are many reasons for conflicts and wars, and from a human perspective, it has to do with gaining and/or keeping power. In a sense, it's the same with the Overlords, although they are more concerned with bloodlines. Now we know the gods' agendas, but we also must consider humans. Not all humans, even emperors, presidents, dictators, and kings, know the full agenda. Thus, we have Marduk's Freemasonic Pyramid—a construct built on initiation, and the structure operates on a need-to-know basis. Even those in high places are often ignorant and start wars against each other.

However, I would say most wars are very well planned by those who pull the strings and know most of the plan. Marduk must get as many humans as possible in line with his agenda, and most are still too ignorant to obey. Thus, he needs to instigate wars with a purpose to conquer. It used to be with the purpose to divide and conquer, but these days, it's quite the opposite; it's a matter of uniting nations, so all can be on the same page. Marduk needs to come down on the resistance and unite people until he has his One World Government. And if a "human threat from outer space" is needed to unite humankind, so be it. After all, suddenly there are lots of UFO sightings covered by the media, and governments acknowledge the existence of aliens. So, we will see how that plays out. Additionally, Sirians are warlords—their entire culture is built on violence, dominance, warfare, and conquest. As conveyed in the WPP, Level 2, the Sirians, in their home world, always fought for power and killed each other, even their spouses, and they ate their children when they were starving, and they overthrew each other for power. Any signs of weakness, and you were dead. These are the guys we are dealing with here.

"3% Is All They Can Handle"

I have stated many times that the Overlords (read Khan Kings) need 3% of the human population in their future attack on Orion. This is roughly 192 million people if we have been told the truth about the human world population. I was told that 3% is all they can handle. The plan is that King Marduk and his Khan Kings will all ride human Avatars, and they will ride those who are of the purest bloodline, i.e., having a majority of Sirian DNA (Marduk-Ereškigal). These are the only ones they can attach to. Ereškigal is needed because she is the daughter of Queen Sophia, albeit in a very low state of beingness, and that keeps the Orion bloodline alive. Marduk no longer wants Isis involved because she can potentially insert too much of Ninurta's blood into humans, making us harder to ride. The Khan Kings don't want to ride untamed horses.

Additionally, they need an armada of humans they can use as cannon fodder and shields to protect the Avatar-riding Sirians at the tail end. Thus, it appears they can "only" control about 192 million human 3-UCs, which to me is an impressive army. Through Metaverse, Marduk will program these humans, so they all are working in unison, attacking their mother to overthrow her, without understanding what they are doing. If things get that far, what will the Queen, the MIKH-MAKH Orion defense force, and the rest of the Greater Universe (Orion) do? Will they stay idle? Most likely not. It may come to a point when the Mother Goddess needs to terminate her children, i.e., the humans attacking her. Even then, with an almost 200 million strong army, can Orion be victorious? We don't know; we can only hope this plan gets stopped on its track. I know Orion is brainstorming about how to best resolve this predicament, but I have no information about their current plans. In the meantime, we must act as if there will be no help. We are our own saviors. We can't just trust that someone else is coming to save us. The soulution will be presented in Appendix A.

En.ki's Dilemma

Although En.ki almost certainly has no part in the Singularity, he is still not off the hook. His actions here on Earth, and how he's treated humankind, are not "nice," to put it mildly. In his narcissistic mind, he might never have thought it was a big deal, but when push comes to shove, he has acted irresponsibly, and in pure selfishness, without considering our suffering. It has been all about him, him, him, and about taking revenge on his brother, regaining his status regardless of the means to do so, taking zero responsibility for the mess he's created. For all this, he needs to be judged. The real criminal and psychopath was always Marduk, not En.ki, but that does not justify En.ki's behavior the least.

Listening to the Pleiadians, and looking at their information with fresh eyes, it may seem En.ki is on the side of humankind, and to a certain degree, he is. He, and we humans, have currently the same goal, which is to stop the Singularity from happening, but we also have different motives for doing so. Our motive is to once and for all set humankind free and return to Orion, while his goal is selfish. He wants us to side with him, so he can still prove that he, against all odds, can make this soul group graduate, which I'm sure is his goal, although not until we have regained enough En.ki genes for him to prove himself before his brother and his mother. He hopes his benevolent actions this close to the Singularity will help him in a future Orion trial, and we will feel sympathetic toward him for helping us fight Marduk.

Redemption and Repentance Revisited

I once asked my Orion source what he thinks En.ki is thinking right now, and he said En.ki is probably regretting much of what he did and wants to repent. This may be true, but repentance in his case cannot take place until he has taken responsibility for his actions, and that's a monumental task. The way I see it is that his repentance is only to save his own life if going to court, and it's not about taking responsibility for us and for what he has done. He wants to get off easy by pressing the sympathy and compassion buttons in us. If a trial will ever happen, I can always guarantee he will give us and the court a sob story.

Then I asked my source about redemption, and he said En.ki is redeemable, but Marduk is not. What this means, in Orion terms, is that if you are *not* redeemable, you can't pay off the debt, i.e., the energy you've "stolen" because of your actions, and for the crimes that were committed. Or, in humanity's case, we can have our debt "forgiven" if we honestly repent from everything that has to do with En.ki's Matrix, and by that, we will be welcome in Orion. In other words, we can't pay off the debt, but because we have been treated badly, and under amnesia, we are not totally responsible for our actions, and we can repent from them by detaching from the Matrix completely. As creator gods, we have a future in Orion, and over time, our creations in the Greater Universe will balance the account, and more.

When it comes to En.ki, he is considered redeemable, which means his actions, and the energy he has misused, are overdue for repayment, and he will be held responsible for repaying his debt. Therefore, repentance is not enough for him to return to Orion, according to my source. En.ki may not have realized that or thinks he can somehow bypass that with his glib "tongue."

When I asked about Marduk, he falls into the category of not redeemable. Because of his horrific, carefully calculated crimes, he cannot repay his debt, *whether or not he repents*, which he won't, being a psychopath, who can't feel remorse. According to my source, Marduk will never be allowed back in Orion, regardless of circumstances. He has burned all his bridges. He will not have his debt forgiven because, contrary to us, he will not be able to make up for the stolen energy by being a creator god.

Distinguishing Between En.ki's and Marduk's Agendas

If we go back 5-6,000 years, we land in old Mesopotamia and ancient Babylon (Iraq). In those days, En.ki incarnated here together with Marduk, Isis, and Ereškigal. They were in human bodies, and they openly interacted with humans. En.ki oversaw both gods and humans, and humans looked at these beings as gods, worshipping them. Under En.ki's supervision, life was more open and tolerable. That said, he was still a narcissistic Overlord who indulged in alcohol and women, and he could be cruel at times, but it was different if the reader gets my point. The cruelty was not as much in our faces as it is today. There were open conflicts, mostly between the gods themselves, and usually, it was we humans who had to fight their battles as their foot soldiers, which must have been traumatizing, for sure, but between wars and conflicts, life was mostly tolerable.

In the Sumerian texts, we get a date, 2024 BCE, when En.ki left Earth and never returned, while the other three Overlords stayed and are still here. The above date must be when En.ki went to Rigel to fight a war there—it fits in perfectly.

Although En.ki was captured, life here on Earth changed gradually under Marduk's command, at a slow pace, and in the background, En.ki still had some influence, particularly since he had many supporters on Earth, and the entire Elite was his people. So, Marduk must gradually accumulate his power and manipulate his way through; he knows how to do that, being a strong military leader from Sirius.

Two thousand years later, when a new astrological age started (the Age of Pisces), Marduk saw the opportunity to use En.ki's weakness against him, eventually. Thus, the Jesus-Magdalene bloodline was created, comprising DNA from Isis, Ninurta, and Marduk. As the reader can see, it was a golden opportunity for Marduk to strengthen his own DNA's influence on the human soul group. En.ki could do nothing to stop him in his peculiar situation. Instead of using the existing Davidian bloodline and let Jesus be born from there, Marduk wanted a new gene pool that was fresh, overriding En.ki's blood potency.

In addition, I would strongly suggest Mary was *not* of the Davidian lineage, and she did not look Middle Eastern. She had white skin and red hair, and so did Jesus. I would therefore further argue that Jesus was not a Jew; he started a completely new bloodline, and the Davidian line continued through Joseph, who was a Jew of Hebrew descent. Jesus likely looked quite European, sporting Isis'/Mary's red hair, akin to the pictures we see of Jesus from medieval times up to the present.

Isis most likely went behind Marduk's back and created a pure Isis-Ninurta bloodline in France, Marduk thinking it was his (Jesus') offspring. A few hundred years later, it was time to create the royal pure-blood Merovingian bloodline, and we know the rest...

It's easy to see that monarchies are originally part of En.ki's structure. En.ki himself is royal, belonging to the Orion royal family, so royalty is important to him. Thus, he let the Orion blood flow through kings and queens—particularly in the Western world in ancient times, before Marduk's interventions. Marduk has now forced his rulership upon the world, him being far from royal. He supports big governments, republics, and dictatorships, etc. That's the Sirian way of structuring things, and the little "spirituality" we had during En.ki's reign, if ever so restricted, considerably diminished in importance with Marduk, who suppressed religion in favor of reason, science, and technology. Yes, he allows religious freedom, which En.ki did not, but it's not to please us but to divide and conquer, and further diminish the power of En.ki's religion. According to Sirian mentality, the smartest and most ruthless people should rule, and they will be the movers and shakers of the world—Marduk's Elite, which he often recruited from the former En.ki Elite by changing their mindsets (through threats, in many cases, I presume). So, if some authorities come down on spiritual matters and want to censor them, we see Marduk's minions at work, 100%. Marduk does not want religious and spiritual power—they contradict his agenda.

In this book, the reader gets the changes pointed out, and you can see how the world changed from being run by religion to reason, science, and technology. The latter has nothing to do with En.ki—that's the Sirian way, and as a Sirian warlord, Marduk had planned the attack on Orion for a long time. Beginning in the 1700s, the Road to Singularity started. I am sure the reader can now see the differences between the rulership of En.ki and Marduk.

Some Final Thoughts on the Human Experiment

When first pondering it, the Human Experiment seems like a wonderful idea. The Universe in the lower realms experiences many wars because of how some star races develop during their evolution in the physical worlds. Fewer beings become creator gods, gaining spirit, and those who do are not of the quality and standard the Queen had hoped for. Therefore, she wanted to create a soul group where Spirit was attached already from the beginning. Evolving in an ethereal world, rather than in the physical realm, but still under some harsh conditions, would that create a more compassionate, empathetic, and loving group of creator gods, who can create with a higher perspective in mind?

I think the idea was excellent, and my source told me everything went per the plan until the Khan Kings came and destroyed the entire Experiment. From there, the Experiment continued here on Earth, but look at where we are today. Not because of our doing, to be objectively honest, but because of the nature of those who put us here and ruled over us in our ignorance. If this is how creator gods treat their creations in the developing worlds, I understand we have a rough universe in the lower dimensions. Now I happen to know it's illegal to interfere with a developing soul group until they graduate, except if they are invited by the soul group itself and have permission from the creator god. Even if this is mostly adhered to, it also depends on the creator god. Do creator gods themselves interfere with the direct development of the species? That is not allowed, either. Still, it has been done all the time here on Earth since Day 1.

What does all this imply? The Queen's plan was that, if we humans could graduate from the Experiment with our goals met, she would consider continuing creating soul groups from there on who will be spirited from the start, just like us. However, either we humans have been completely "out of luck," or the Universe is in such poor shape that beings can't leave developing star races alone; and thus, experiments like ours won't work. They would work just fine if left alone, but that hasn't happened in our case. My thoughts on the matter are to not continue with new, similar experiments until those experiments can be completely secured and safe from outside interference. In that regard, Orion has completely failed. There must be radical structural changes to future projects; this is the responsibility of the Orion Council, as I see it from my perspective. Perhaps, after we have exited the Matrix, we can help by giving some advice. After all, we are the ones who have experienced all this terror and abuse. I would be willing to give that a try to create a better Universe for the future of all the star races.

What to Expect in the Orion Universe

We are used to the fairytale of "Heaven," where the lion (or the wolf) sleeps with the lamb. That's not accurate. I don't think that exists in this Universe (unless we, or someone else, create it). The entire Orion Universe is one big Experiment, just like the human soul group is one big Experiment within other Experiments, and on it goes. All universes are Experiments. I do not believe any universe was created to be "perfect" to begin with (and what is perfect, anyway?). If it's perfect, why then create it? There would be no challenges, and thus, no one and nothing would fill any purpose. If such a universe exists, it's not the universe I want to live in. It's like living in the "Heaven" Robert Monroe visited in the astral decades ago when he had out-of-body experiences (OBEs). He said it was amazing, and pure bliss (at first). Then it got boring, and eventually it showed it was just a program that looped on itself over and over. No, we need challenges, to meet them, overcome them, grow, and take on new challenges after that. When we do so with a healthy mindset, we become exhilarated, inspired, and enthusiastic. The same thing applies when we create our visions in the KHAA for ourselves and others to enjoy—our own worlds, or whatever we want to create. Creation and overcoming challenges make a sane and happy being. Nothing else does, I believe.

While still in the Matrix, I think it's important that we do what we can to raise ourselves above the noise of the masses and do something, however big or small, that stands out in some way. Then we show that even here our lives can be worth living, and each one of us can make some kind of difference. All of us can bring at least some honey to the beehive. If everybody does some little thing that stands out in the noise we're drowning in, there will no longer be any noise. An ability to show kindness and empathy in a world where this is lacking is a huge contribution and a great challenge.

When we enter the KHAA, we might need some help first to regain our true abilities, but so be it! The Queen put a lot of hope in us, and I think we still can achieve the goals she set up because I think these goals coincide with ours (we *are* her, after all). And I think we humans, at this moment in the progression of the Universe, are very important, and we must take our existence seriously. No human is less or better than another–there are just more and less emotionally wounded people, who have been dragged into the mud; but we are all unique, and uniqueness must be respected and encouraged. Now we need to drag ourselves up and continue where we took off before the children-who-never-grew-up came and interfered (the Overlords). Humankind needs to show that we are not as childish as they are. It's time for the human species to grow into adulthood, whatever it takes. Perhaps only a few will make it through the Grid, but I believe we can help the rest from outside—with Orion's assistance. We are the ones who have experienced this, so we are the ones who "know."

I think it was a mistake of Sophia to take in the Sirians into her "empire." And it was a mistake to make the Sirian DAKH warriors into a MIKH-MAKH defense force. They don't have the right atti-tude—they are too warlike and aggressive. And in charge of the MIKH-MAKH is the most ferocious warrior of them all—Khan En.lil. But he may have settled to some degree, which remains to be seen. Nonetheless, I think that merging Sirians with Orions is set up for a disaster, regardless of peace agreements. I think things have gone awry partly because of this.

Sophia is a mother–the Arch Mother, one could say. We, who are human males, can only intellectually conceptualize the relationship between a mother and her children. The emotional and spiritual bond is amazingly strong. A sane mother never wants their children to suffer, even if she knows that after suffering comes relief. She wants not to include the "suffering part" if she can help it. Sophia is nothing different from a human mother—as above, so below. I think that to a certain degree, she has put herself in a position where her hands are tied to the degree, where she needs to con-sider the majority votes of the Orion Council in important decisions. We call this a democratic system, which is not always fair.

In very recent times, one or more representatives from Orion have entered the Earth Matrix, and I had the privilege of encoun-tering one such being, with whom I built a six-year relationship. When my Contact, shocked, saw what had been done here, he real-ized we needed to know how to get out. That's when he told me about the Grid and how to leave the Matrix (see the following Ap-pendix section).

Some Last Thoughts on Isis

I have a difficult time making up my mind about Isis. How much of all the mess is her responsibility? The story goes that she partici-pated in all this unwillingly, and perhaps this is true. However, was it all because of outside forces controlling her, or did she instigate some of this human suffering aside from that? I guess the reader must make up his or her mind on this for himself or herself. It's a great discussion subject.

I am not Isis, and I do not have her experiences, and have never met her (from what I know), so I can't say anything for certain. I can see some of her actions apparently being her own, and that is not all bad. If my conclusion is correct regarding her tricking Marduk, having the Catholic Church protect *her* pure Divine Isis-Ninurta bloodline, this might have been to eventually get us humans out of here. Yet it could also be to get *her* out of here—a selfish reason to save her own skin, akin to what the Pleiadians do. Either way, we humans would potentially have gained from it, if her intention was to ride humans who possess pure bloodline into Orion, where after she would set them free. Perhaps her purpose was to secretly spread purer blood in the general population, as well, to help them. Her motives are sometimes hard to understand.

Last, we have Diana Spencer. It's so close in time that we have much information to examine and draw from. Here we see an extraordinarily compassionate, loving, empathetic person, who wins everybody's heart, becoming perhaps the most beloved person in modern history. But she was also seductive and could seduce virtually any man with her magnetism, which she did. All this corresponds with historical records of Isis' personality from ancient times. Another opposed trait is that she is also a goddess of war. I doubt she is behind the wars here in the Matrix, but it also shows she has a darker side.

Looking at both sides of her, I think she is an overly good person, who, via circumstances, has done some shameful things to us and to herself. But regardless of how I look at it from a heart perspective, I can't judge her as hard as I would judge En.ki and Marduk in a potential Orion court—unless I get more information that I have not been able to find yet.

APPENDICES

APPENDICES

Appendix A:
On How to Leave the Matrix

Over the years, I have written multiple articles and made videos on how to exit the Matrix through a hole in the Grid that En.ki set up around Earth at the beginning of the Matrix. You can still find them on my blog at wespenrevideo.com in the "Exiting the Grid" section.

I started by giving simple instructions because it is essentially easy to exit. However, I noticed people must have thought it seemed *too* simple, so they complicated things, and all the *what ifs* came into the picture, and they just escalated because of people's fear of the unknown. It's understandable to fear the unknown, but this fear must be transformed into courage and overridden to where bravery is stronger than fear, or the exit will obviously not happen, and the person will fall into the recycling trap again.

This chapter will most likely be the last I write on how to exit through the Grid after physical death to leave the Matrix for good. I will end this topic where I once started by explaining it plainly and simply. Please don't overthink it, or you will become your own obstacle, giving into your fear and miss out. Make the exit plan swift and simple. Learn to build confidence.

If you truly want to exit, please continue reading. This is required:

1. You must get rid of fears until you get to where you know you will succeed. You accomplish this by doing *inner work*. You will know when you are ready enough to override the fears—you will feel it. Make *very* sure you remove abusive

people from your immediate life, or it will be very difficult to build the courage.

2. For me, at least, as a healing program, the *21-Day Repro-gramming* has worked excellently.[281] It also helps if you have a trustworthy person in your life with whom you can have safe, completely open, non-judgmental communica-tion and that person can be open with you. There is no faster healing than that–better even than the best therapy with the best therapist (this claim comes not from me but from a professor in psychology, Sam Vaknin, and I know firsthand he is correct).

3. Make very sure that when you die, you have no attachments to the Matrix, and you are ready to leave everything behind. Don't be lazy with this one. Attachments include but are not restricted to, friends, relatives, significant others, pets, Ma-trix life itself, the Overlords, and material things alike. The bottom line is this: Make sure you can leave without having second thoughts because you feel you will miss something so much that you will hesitate when you enter the astral plane.

That is what you need to work on while you are still living this current life on Earth. If you truly feel you have already accom-plished these three steps, congratulations! Then you will read this article without doubting yourself when exiting–at least not more than you know you can handle when the day of exit comes.

The Exit Strategy

Here is the simple exit strategy, the one and only I will use. If you don't see any updates to this on my blog in the future (wespen-revideos.com), the following will be the workable technique I will use–nothing more, nothing less:

1. When I die, I will look "up" in relation to my deceased

---

[281] https://wespenrevideos.com/wp-content/uploads/2021/07/Video-263-Needs-Trauma-Behavior-and-Reprogramming.pdf

human body, and I will spot the Grid above me (a fuzzy net surrounding the Earth, having holes in it).

2. I spot one of the many holes in the Grid and I think along these lines, "I am going through a hole in the Grid NOW!" The astral is immediately thought-responsive, so my thoughts will execute instantly. Therefore, the word NOW! is very important, or you create your own delay.

3. Once out of the Grid, I will immediately think, "I am at the Orion Queen's Highest possible aspect NOW!" I will be there in an instant, regardless of where she roams at that moment.

That's it.

The only couple of things I want to add is that if you encounter somebody, no matter who, when you are in the astral, PAY NO AT-TENTION to them at all. They can appear as angels, spirit guides, false dead relatives, and even a false Jesus, or a tunnel of light— don't go there, as it leads to the recycling center, and you'll be trapped in a Matrix body again with full amnesia (shapeshifting is the norm rather than a rarity in the astral). Whatever it might be, wishing to distract you, *FOCUS on your task to leave*, and no one will be able to stop you. To be stopped, you must *agree* to be stopped. *No one can stop a pure intention and a strict focus.* The other thing is, if you feel lost in the astral for any reason, just start over: "I am at a hole in the Grid NOW!" and you'll be there. Then repeat 1-3. If things seem foggy or cloudy, think, "CLARITY NOW!" and you'll get clarity.

This is all there is to it.

About Other Ways to Exit

As mentioned, many people think the above process sounds too simple, and it might scare them and make them doubt it's that easy. They want to be on the "safe side."

A friend of mine released a paper he called, *Exit Handout (Steps to Leave the Matrix),* which the reader can find on my blog.[282] It has

---

[282] https://wespenrevideos.com/2022/07/21/exit-handout-steps-to-

become very popular since it was released, which means many people appreciate a more detailed procedure to exit than what I just gave you. That is perfectly fine with me; I am not concerned about *how* people exit through the Grid, so long as they exit. If it feels safer to have more "meat" to the procedure, this handout is for you, and it's well written.

There are researchers on the Internet (and you can find some information in different books, too), instructing people how to leave the Matrix. I have checked out many of these alternative procedures, but based on the knowledge I have, none of them will help you leave the Matrix. Unless I have missed some alternatives, there is no other way, in my opinion, than to follow the above procedure and just go. The truth is often simple—don't look for alternatives that are too complicated. They will most likely not work. And why would we choose a more complicated exit when the hole-in-the-Grid plan is so straight forward? My take on it is that even if someone finds an alternative route, I will stick to a hole in the Grid. I have a difficult time imagining a quicker and simpler route out of here.

I wish you a great journey through the rest of your life here in the Matrix, and I hope to see you on the other side, in the Greater Universe (Orion), as a true creator god, away from the Matrix oppression, trauma, and misery. I am sure that we who choose to exit will meet in Orion. I think we need each other there, and those who exit first may wait for more of us to arrive. Then we can have a blast. I think that's something exciting to look forward to. So, hang in there, try to find things you enjoy doing, while still in your sapiens body, and do your best to enjoy the time you have left here. After all, it's mind over matter, so let's be creative and learn how to enjoy our current existence. It's so easy to give into Evil and just think everything is bad. It is, but only if we, in our minds, make it so.

Much love,
Wes Penre

---

leave-the-matrix/

Appendix B:
European Royal Family Trees

It's important to follow these family trees when I start discussing the different kings and queens and royal houses in the book, or it may quickly feel abstract and confusing. I suggest you bookmark them on your computer and pull them up as you read further in the book.

Complete Family Trees of the French Royal Dynasties

https://en.wikipedia.org/wiki/Family_tree_of_French_monarchs

Complete Family Trees of the British Royal Dynasties

https://www.britroyals.com/wessextree.asp

Index:

Made in the USA
Las Vegas, NV
29 October 2024

10644254R00167